Reinhard G. Hubel

The Book of Carpets

Translated by Katherine Watson

Barrie & Jenkins
London

First published 1971 in Great Britain
by Barrie & Jenkins
2 Clement's Inn, London WC 2

SBN 214 65129 0
Printed in Germany by Gerhard Stalling AG, Oldenburg

The Book of Carpets

Contents

Abbreviations

C. Cotton, K. knot, P. Persian (Sehna) knot, T. Turkish
(Ghiordes) knot, W. wool, dm. decimetre, sq. dm. square
decimetre.

S-spun, S-plied: spun or plied (of spun threads) anti-clock-
wise. Z-spun, Z-plied: spun or plied clockwise.

In the captions to the plates the main colours are written in
italics.

If a multiple weft threads shows no twist or ply, for a length
of about three knots it is described as untwisted.

Quality is described in the order pile, thickness and underside.

Knot count is given according to the scheme on p. 32.

Measurements are given length or height first, then width.

Selvedges: unless otherwise stated 1 cord is round one pair
of warp threads.

Preface

A few important exceptions apart, very little in the existing literature on the subject of carpets has anything new to contribute to the study.

The oriental carpet became highly fashionable in Germany after the Second World War, not least as a prestige symbol in the competitive social atmosphere of returning affluence; a spate of literature on the subject followed in the wake of fashion.

The present book is different. It is the outcome of years of intensive study by a man motivated purely by enthusiasm for the oriental carpet. At first he could only look and admire, later he became a collector and finally was able to devote himself to its study.

Reinhard Hubel has managed, in a manner that is all too rare in these days, to convert his enthusiasm into serious research; this book is the fruit of these labours.

Craftsmanship is something which has always interested Hubel. In his youth he worked as a locksmith, smith and carpenter, and his father understandingly encouraged this inclination by doubling his earnings. All the money, or at least what was left from the purchase of antiques, went on travels in central and southern Europe. Wherever he went he was drawn as if by magic to the workshops of craftsmen. His father's people had for generations run a textile manufactory which in his grandfather's time had fallen victim to the machine age.

Small wonder then that once Hubel took an interest in oriental carpets he very soon devoted himself intensively to a study of the structures underlying each different technique.

R. v. Oettingen and Grothe-Halsenbalg had already repeatedly insisted that a detailed study of the structure of handknotted pieces would produce many new facts, and even some surprise concerning the attributions and dates of oriental carpets.

Hubel paid particular attention in his research to the work of nomads, and equally to all the knotted and woven work of the orient. These are closely related to the true carpet and are produced in the home, providing information which cannot be derived from the carpet alone. All the many kinds of bag, cloth, decorative strip, harness, saddle-cover etc. which are produced with such loving care for family use, and without a thought for the market, are far more valuable evidence of traditions and techniques than the majority of carpets knotted for sale and export.

While one of the most comprehensive German collections in private hands was growing from its small beginnings, Hubel began systematically sifting through all the relevant material in the trade, and hardly missed an auction in the whole of southern Germany.

He undertook several journeys to the East in order to elucidate on the spot the long list of questions which had accumulated during his years of study, and to gain insight into living conditions and methods of work. The author always sees the knotted work of a region in relation to its culture, its history and geography. Who could hold it against Hubel that he profited from these occasions to acquire rare pieces from the nomads in order to round off his collections?

A skilled hand and patient work (in the Museum of Islamic Art in Cairo and the Türk-ve-Islam Museum in Istanbul alone, Hubel spent over three weeks studying the structure of the earliest carpets and fragments) brought to light the interesting and in part new material which is embodied in this book.

It can now be established that the accepted dates in the current literature on Anatolian and Caucasian carpets are untenable.

The work done hitherto on the Fostat finds had certainly not produced satisfactory answers. For one thing there are pieces showing Anatolian methods and structure, for another the Egyptian fragments are not velvet pile-woven loops subsequently cut, but a looped imitation of orthodox knots. Here connoisseurs both professional and amateur are offered food for thought and for further study.

Lastly this book demonstrates that it is still possible today to assemble a serious collection of oriental knotted work without excessive financial outlay. Possession of one such carpet naturally rouses the desire to know more about its origin, and this in turn leads to research and so to collecting.

But serious investigation will never reduce one's pleasure in an individual piece; on the contrary, the pleasure grows as one's knowledge and understanding increases.

H. Jacoby

Oriental carpets and the West

The widespread popularity of oriental carpets is comparatively recent in the West and does not go back much more than a century. Spurred by a demand which had been growing in the past few decades Persia sent a selection of examples to the Vienna World Exhibition of 1873. Europe, then in the full flush of the machine age, with its faith in progress and the future, was for the first time brought face to face with these exquisite carpets, every knot of which had been laboriously tied by hand. Their subtle combinations of colour, deriving from a consummate colour sense far more developed than that of the West, were a revelation. Although these examples had been made centuries after the golden age of the oriental carpet, they created an immediate sensation with the fairy-tale atmosphere lent to their designs by the natural gift of the East for ornamentation. These works of art emanating from an ancient culture released an unconscious memory of something mysterious, apart, incomprehensible to the westerner, though he had perhaps acquired some inkling of it from oriental fairy tales or *A Thousand and One Nights*. The appeal was direct and immediate. Each one of these carpets, individually created through long hours of work, seemed to speak a language all its own, yet one that was common to them all. Of course it was not the same language which had inspired its creator, for the European cannot plumb the depths from which the fantasies of the mythical world of the East arise; but some spirit, the spirit of its creator, had entered through the deft and skilful hand that knotted it, and this spirit seemed to give an answer to the questions that sprang up in the western mind.

How poor the ordinary machine-made carpet seemed in contrast. The machine, constructed by European genius, turned carpets out automatically and without inspiration to perform their function, identical one with another, in huge series, perfect and impersonal. The product of the West remained dumb even to the questions of its own maker.

Now arose the great craze for the oriental carpet. It had not been entirely unknown in Europe before then, but its use — mostly as a coverlet or wall hanging — since the Crusades, and particularly during the ostentation-loving Renaissance, had been mainly confined to the houses of the nobility, a few patricians and artists and certain churches. Now, like an epidemic, practically the whole of the bourgeoisie was possessed with the desire to furnish its rooms with the knotted carpets of the Orient. If they were chosen with taste they fitted in well and both improved the look of a house and enhanced the well-being of its inhabitants.

Paradoxically enough this flood of enthusiasm for the oriental carpet proved to be of extreme danger to its survival. The spontaneity of the passion threatened to suffocate its object. The sudden wave of demand encountered only a limited supply. While heretofore the court manufactories had been able to satisfy the rulers' oriental love of splendour and their requirements for gifts, and the large city manufactories and the smaller domestic ones had easily coped with the not inconsiderable export trade as well as the internal market, now business-like local merchants and European capitalists alike founded factories with an eye to a quick profit. In Isparta (Sparta) and Smyrna (Izmir) especially, where there was an old tradition of knotting, they began to produce as quickly and cheaply as possible, ignoring the traditional methods of dying and their age-long standards of quality.

Even though the wages paid for knotting were unimaginably low, a carpet with its millions of knots was very dear to produce. So they reduced the number of knots and made them looser. Where before the best wool had been carefully chosen for the pile, they now were content with the poorest machine-spun wool, even wool from the hides of dead animals, removed with chalk (*tabachi*). Natural dyes, often laborious to extract and applied by methods guarded as family secrets, which give the oriental carpet its incomparable mellowness of hue, had to make way for garish ready-made aniline dyes which, furthermore, the work-people did not know how to handle to the best advantage. The unsatisfactory general impression of the finished piece was rectified by reckless bleaching of the colours with chlorine and other harsh chemicals. If Persian or Chinese designs were in demand then they were copied in Smyrna. Even the fast-changing colour fashions in Europe and America were followed and background colours changed on request. Granted, these products were hand-knotted, but they were inferior in quality as to durability, colours and structure. Where they have survived at all to the present day they sell at auctions for minimal sums.

It is only fair to note that industrial colours today are at least the equal in quality of natural dyes from the technical point of view; that they are less attractive is purely an aesthetic matter.

In Persia also many manufactories reduced the density of the pile, and so could not render satisfactorily the traditional fine patterns. Aniline dyes accelerated the decline in quality. Before the turn of the century the Shah found it necessary to prohibit completely the use of aniline dyes under threat of serious punishment (loss of the right hand).

To meet all requirements — the quicker the better — many producers were prepared to depart completely from the rules of style proper to oriental carpets and to knot European patterns. It is true that at other periods the influence of European designs had occasionally affected Persian and Caucasian patterns, but these had been episodes limited to a few manufactories. Now this influence was so overwhelming that it brought about a universal deterioration of the oriental carpet, and the jeremiads lamenting its decline were not to be ignored.

Aniline dyes had penetrated even as far as Turkestan, as evidenced by the sad washed-out rags that occasionally appear on the market today as 'antique Samarkand carpets'. In China a similar development took place as a result of the American interest in Chinese carpets aroused at the time of the Boxer rising. The nomad carpet however, apart from some minor exceptions, did not share in this decline.

Thus the West, even if unconsciously, contributed to the crisis of the oriental carpet. But it also provided for its rehabilitation: since about 1870 scholarship had begun increasingly to make oriental knotting a subject of research. Museums and collectors brought any available antique pieces together and preserved them from further destruction. The efforts of responsible European undertakings — and here in the foremost place is found the German Petag (Persische Teppich-Gesellschaft AG) (Persian Carpet Company), before the First World War and in the period between the wars collaborated with oriental craftsmen who were conversant with the true tradition and succeeded in raising the quality by reanimating the old methods of dye production, dyeing and neat knotting. The two world wars and the years following them have by accumulating demand brought about a reduction in quality which has hindered the improvement.

With increasing prosperity the Federal Republic of Germany rose in the 'fifties to be quantitativly the foremost importer of oriental carpets in the world. Qualitatively it has held this place since the turn of the century. Unfortunately the wares offered by pedlars and some merchants are fit only for the frantic search for novelty. Under changing labels, usually the names of small Persian villages, large quantities of carpets, often of poor quality, are extolled to unsuspecting purchasers. Yet it is unfair to say that the sellers are always lacking in good faith. Unlike the professional native carpet dealers with their fundamental knowledge and rich experience, the expertise of many of the new dealers who have established themselves recently in almost every large town does not extend beyond the constantly available mass-produced item. They receive the carpets from importers who are often equally ignorant, and sell them under the label quoted in the invoice, and at the same time, because they know no better, they will sometimes sell off older pieces they have received in part-exchange at ridiculously low rates because they need repairing, while they over-value other carpets which seem to them old but which in fact owe their patina to an 'antiquator'. There is a chance here for the collector with a trained eye (cf. the chapter on collecting).

Reputable dealers have for years been offering new hand-knotted carpets, beautifully made, in good materials, besides the older pieces which come less from imports than from European and American owners. The simplest of these new carpets are not much dearer than the best factory wares.

The universalization of patterns and the increasing standardization of the underweave make it impossible to label many types except by the pattern; the area or country of origin can only be established by closer examination. Thus it is more than ever incumbent on the trade not to leave the purchaser uncertain of the real place of origin, not to offer him a 'Tabriz' but to state clearly that it is a 'Bulgarian carpet with a Tabriz pattern' when it is a Bulgarian imitation. Ultimately what matters is quality, and it is at present improving steadily even though prices are high. The oriental carpet is alive, and alive in the West as well.

The countries where carpets are made, except for Russia, are backward countries now beginning to develop. Their ten- and five-year plans for industrial development will change the relative numbers of the population employed on the land and in industry, and raise the standard of living and incomes. In western Turkestan, which lies within Russia's development area, the change has already taken place. We will discuss it later in more detail, since, political factors apart, the development in Turkey and Iran will follow the same course in the future. Istanbul and Teheran are cities of world status with two million or more inhabitants. Erivan has over 600,000, Tabriz with its famous gardens 400,000, blue Isfahan (so called because of the faience facings of its mosques) 300,000, and romantic Shiraz 200,000. Factories are going up round the edges of the cities and attracting the population, as refineries do in the petroliferous areas.

Good oriental carpets will be expensive in the future. An extreme example is a tent bag (choval, fig. 117) which was not in fact made to be sold and which is exceptionally finely knotted (over 7,000 knots per square dm.). This piece, a little over half a square metre in size, sells at £60-70 in the trade today, but, taking European wages as a basis, it would cost about £250 for the labour alone. The 'Smyrna' models offered in Europe to be finished at home (by pulling through and cutting off only about 120 loops to the square dm., on a ready-prepared under-weave) cost more than £10 a square dm. simply for the materials. Whether oriental carpet production maintains a high quality depends ultimately on the buyer; what he buys is produced and delivered by the trade. Consistent rejection of all inferior knotted wares will force the manufacturers to see quality and not quantity as the chief concern of the craft and encourage those workshops which until now have carried on the old traditions to produce only the best and finest handwork on their looms. Responsible people in the East are always complaining in conversation that their calls for better quality can make no headway with the producers because western importers are always asking for cheap wares. The author approached the director of the largest manufactory in Hamadan and asked him for hard-wearing stair carpets with the lovely old designs; the director was quite astonished. None had been ordered for decades, and he could not believe this was a serious order. He did stress however that he was ready at any time to knot the beautiful Hamadan carpets instead of the 'Kirmans' which stood on the looms at the time. When we congratulated him on the natural dyes and hand-spun wool in his dye-works he could only answer with regret that this was a special order; for economic reasons chemical dyes generally have to be used.

Four historical events, originating alternately in the East and the West have intensified the contacts of eastern and western culture: the conquest of the Iberian peninsula by Islam, the Crusades, the conquest of Byzantium and the Balkans by the Turks — whose defeat before the gates of Vienna left many carpets to fall into the hands of the victors together with the tents of the vanquished — and lastly the advent of technology, which bridges all differences and revolutionizes the conditions of life and the ordering of society.

There are many oriental features fused into the daily life and thought of the West, and integrated to such an extent that we are no longer aware of their origin. Some may have read about the pocket watch which Harun ar-Rashid presented to Charlemagne almost 1,200 years ago. But who remembers that it is to the East that we owe the Christian religion, the foundations of our mathematics and astronomy, many contributions to medicine and other sciences, our numerals, many words in daily use, the knowledge of spices, or the preparation of coffee, to name but a few?

It is different with the oriental carpet. It immediately conjures up before us a picture of the Orient, true or imaginary. No attempt to replace it by a native produce, to combine it with our own designs or to take over its production meets with any lasting success. Despite all crises it has outlived every style since the Crusades and it still remains indispensible to the modern home.

The aim and purpose of this book is to present the character, development, stylistic laws and technique of the oriental carpet. It offers guidance through the bewildering multiplicity of patterns and origins and advice on choice, purchase, laying and upkeep. For those who enjoy fine carpets it provides a link between the carpets in the house and the places of their fabrication.

Practice is equally as important as taste and theory for sharpening eye and judgment. This means looking, looking and looking once again and — touching.

The detailed descriptions of the structure of every piece illustrated will give useful information to the prospective collector and we include a small section of advice to him on how to give intelligent outlet to his respectable passion, a passion which can help to fulfil a cultural task. No work of craft, no cultural treasure, undergoes such hard wear as a carpet in the normal course of treatment if it is put to its proper use. The comparatively rare early examples and fragments that have survived are preserved in a few museums and only accessible to the majority of those interested by means of lengthy journeys. But because of the changes which the East is undergoing, the old carpets of the nineteenth and late eighteenth century, whether made in manufactories or by nomads, have almost reached the status of classics. Fortunately there are still chances of acquiring them, even though they often need repair. The owner and collector will find daily delight in them. By careful use and expert repair he can preserve for future generations these quickly disappearing products of a vanishing epoch of the East.

The peoples of the Orient gaze with fascination at western civilization and technology; it promises them a better life. As long as that has not become a reality we cannot expect them to be concerned with the values of things made by hand. Little time is left, either, for collecting the work of the old traditional crafts of the nomads. The small dyers, who work for the nomads as well, tell us that though they are still masters of the art of natural dyeing, they do not practise it any longer, because they are asked to dye the good handspun wools as cheaply as possible. The collections of the oriental ethnological museums are on the whole poor in examples of knotting by the nomads, and original pieces are only rarely to be found in the bazaars, tents and villages.

Early history and spread of the knotted carpet

The oldest known hand-knotted carpet was discovered in 1949 by the Russian archaeologist Rudenko and others, among the grave goods preserved in the ice in Kurgan V of the Pazyryk valley in the Altai, southern Siberia (pp. 16—17).

Kurgans are mounds which may be 20 metres high and 250 metres in circumference raised over the graves of Scythian chieftains. The graves themselves are dug deep into the ground and supported by wooden structures. Tribes of Scythian horse-riding warriors overran the Middle East as far as the borders of Egypt at the time of their greatest expansion in the seventh century BC. They combined both European and Mongolian racial features. About 600 BC the Medes pressed them back beyond the Caucasus into the plains of southern Russia. From there, their art, now affected by their contact with the high oriental cultures, radiated as far as Lausitz. They had never broken their connections with related tribes on the Siberian plain. The latter on their side maintained relations with the Empire of the Achaemenids which in the sixth century stretched to the Syr Darya, and with the Parthians who succeeded them there three hundred years later, after the period of Alexander and the Seleucids. The powerful relief flanking the approach to the Apadana (audience hall) in the Palace at Persepolis illustrates the bringing of New-Year gifts to the Achaemenid ruler Darius, and shows the Scyths from the area beyond Samarkand among the twenty-eight tributary nations. The accompanying finds in Pazyryk V are shown by radio-carbon analysis and stylistic comparison (excluding foreign imports, such as the Chinese silk) with the grave goods in the kurgans of southern Russia to be datable to the beginning of the third century BC.

The good state of preservation of the textile, in spite of almost two and a half thousand years of age, is primarily due to grave robbers. Their activities, which may well have taken place during the week-long festivities of the funeral, enabled water to seep into the interior of the tomb where it froze. This preservative layer of ice was so protected by the insulation of the stone slabs covering the kurgan that it never melted again, even in summer.

The woollen carpet of Pazyryk is 200 × 183 cm. in size. It is made in Turkish knots at a density of 3,600 knots per square dm. Although the shape is almost square the relatively small central field is oblong because, as is known in the case of many later carpets of all provenances, the border is broader down the sides than across the top and bottom. The chequerboard pattern of the central field has four vertical rows of six squares, and in each is a floral cross extended by sword-shaped leaves to form a star. In the five-fold border the broader and outer of the two main bands has a frieze running from left to right containing twenty-eight stallions, pale on a red ground. The narrower band has a frieze running in the opposite direction showing grazing elk (red-deer stags, reindeer?) red on a light ground. The spotted elk bulls, six on each side, are depicted with the suggestion of internal organs drawn on shoulder and flank, like the winged bulls in the Achaemenid palaces of Darius in Susa and Persepolis. The splendidly harnessed stallions, seven on either side, each ridden or led by a man, have their manes and tails carefully plaited. Their saddle cloths have designs reminiscent of the patterns on Turcoman tent bands (*kibitka* strips) and are unlike the felt saddle covers from the same kurgan which are decorated in appliqué. The bottom stallion in the left side border is shorter than the others and suggests that the knotting was done following a model. Measured vertically the closeness of the knots is about 25 per cent greater than in the same distance in a horizontal direction. Since the maker began the design of the left side border with the same number of knots as the lower cross border, the horse turned out a quarter too short. The two friezes are separated by a band with a row of leaf stars like those in the centre field, reduced in size and not divided into fields. The border is completed both inside and out by a band with a row of griffin figures contained in almost square octagons.

An interpretation of the meaning of the figures will always remain guesswork. Is it a procession, an embassy with gift horses, a cult subject or pure decoration?

The elks might be red deer, with the exaggerated antlers which Scythian art renders in another fashion, or they may be reindeer, a memory of the reindeer-hunting and reindeer-breeding period which among some nomad peoples directly preceded the horse-riding warrior period.

Because of the interruptions in the three outer bands of the border — upper left with two rosettes, upper right with a cross band — Wiesner suggests the possibility that the whole carpet is marked out as a dice board. It is an ancient oriental custom to place game boards among grave gifts. Even chess, which originated in the East, was at first a dice game. The large format of almost four square metres does not necessarily exclude its use as a gaming board, for game pieces of corresponding size have been found for later periods.

In style the Pazyryk carpet differs so markedly from all the other examples of Scythian art — the steppe is no cultural waste — that it is justifiable to consider Iran as the area of its origin. The celadon green and even more the cochineal red characteristic of the Karabagh carpets point to Armenia. Armenia (Azerbaijan), whose people were celebrated by Herodotus for their talents in producing dyes and in dyeing cloth, had belonged to Persia since the early Iranian period. The style of representation of the men leading the horses resembles in many features that in the relief of Persepolis, where the theme of the handing over of the gift horses occurs four times. The ornament on the horses and the head-covering of the Armenian delegation — who, like all the emissaries of the twenty-eight tribute-paying peoples, wear the narrow tapered trousers characteristic of the steppe — are more like the drawing in the Pazyryk carpet than those of the other, likewise horse-leading, Scythian and probably Thracian delegations. The griffins are Achaemenid. The Pazyryk carpet has twenty-eight stallions: the number of the tributary peoples. Twenty-eight men bear the throne of Xerxes in Persepolis and at the entrance of the tomb chambers of the Achaemenid rulers at Naj-i Rustam near Persepolis. The Pazyryk carpet might well be an Achaemenid royal gift commissioned in Armenia.

Apart from the style there are practical reasons against the origin of the carpet being in Scythian art. If the Scythians had mastered the technique of knotting they would surely have used it, instead of the less-resistant felt, to make their saddle covers, which are subject to extremely hard wear. That the Scyths were aware of the hard-wearing qualities of knotted fabrics is shown by a find made by Rudenko in connection with his work in the Pazyryk valley. He excavated the great kurgans of Basadar, situated about 180 km. further west on a tributary of the Katun; the gigantic kurgan Basadar II, about one and a half centuries earlier than Pazyryk V, had a

The carpet from Kurgan V in the Pazyryk Valley in the Altai, South Siberia, 3rd century B C. c. 200 × 183 cm. c. 3,600 Turkish knots per sq. dm.

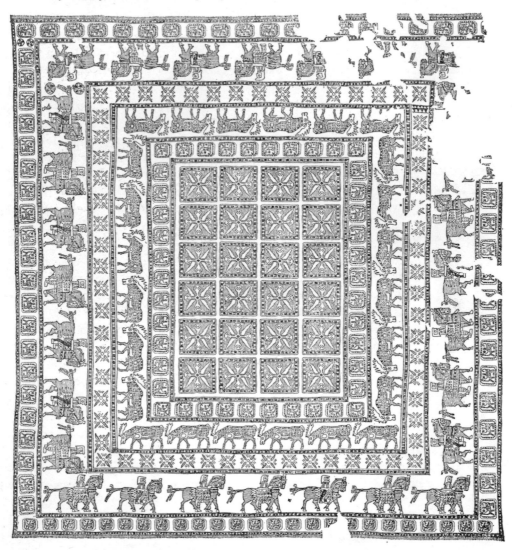

I. Detail of the Pazyryk carpet (complete illustration on p. 16), showing damaged portions.

circumference of approximately 200 m., with the tomb chamber dug more than 6 metres deep below it. Among other grave goods were fourteen horses. A piece of carpet had been used in the manufacture of one of the saddles. It has the unusually fine weave of about 7,000 Persian or Senna knots per square dm. The utilization of the better parts of worn-out carpets for horse, donkey and camel harness is still a general practice in the East. If the Scyths had made carpets themselves there would have been adequate material for these purposes and its use would have been the rule instead of an exception. Furthermore the use of two different methods of knotting in the same tribe is extremely improbable.

There is no lack of early documentary reference to the production of carpets, or to trade in them. It begins with the Bible — Exodus 36, VIII, and Acts 18, III, where the Apostle Paul is referred to as a carpet-maker — and includes the praises of the Greeks and Romans for the 'Babylonian' carpets, continuing with the description of the 'Spring of Chosrau', a mighty garden carpet which in winter furnished the Palace of Chosroes I (531—79) in Ctesiphon and was cut up by the Arab conquerers in 637 so that this unique piece of booty could be shared. Unfortunately the method of production is never mentioned in any of the sources. Further important finds are improbable because of the perishable nature of the material.

Before the discovery of the finds at Pazyryk and Basadar the oldest examples of knotted carpets were a few modest fragments from eastern Turkestan. They came from the Turfan expeditions of the Berlin Museum of 1906—8, from Sir Aurel Stein, and from the excavations of Le Coq in 1913.

Carpet fragments from Turfan, 5th—6th century. c. 500 knots per sq.dm.

It is disappointing that no fragment gives any indication of the designs on the carpets, beyond the use of the 'running dog' motif and small diamonds in half-drop arrangement. They all date from the fifth to sixth century and have a density of about 500 knots to the square dm.; it was assumed from them that the beginnings of knotting technique lay in the few centuries before the beginning of our era. The lucky chance of the preservation of the Pazyryk and Basadar finds has made it possible to put back this date by one or even two millenia; and the highly advanced technique presupposes a long period of development. The origin of the knotted carpet is lost in the mists of antiquity before then.

It was probably pastoral nomads who first inserted tufts of wool into textiles or mats as a protection against rising cold in their dwellings. Hunting nomads would use skins for this purpose, but the shepherd was concerned to maintain his stock, and the skins which he needed for his tents, boots, water carriers and other utensils could only be acquired by slaughtering his herds. Wool on the other hand was available in quantity at every shearing. The knotted carpet originated in the mountain-traversed steppe belt of Asia, between roughly the thirtieth and forty-fifth latitude. South of that the climate dictated the use of mats, and in the northern forests wild beasts provided the required floor covering. The urge to decorate, an innate aesthetic sense, led to the ordering of the various natural wool colours into primitive patterns. The next step will have been the addition of coloured tufts or threads; a further step, the greatest possible uniformity of the ground so as to show up the pattern, for until now it will have looked like shaggy fur. It was still a long way to the carpets of Basadar and Pazyryk.

After the kurgans of Central Asia there is a wide gap in the history of the carpet, apart from the Turfan fragments, until Fostat (Old Cairo) and the Ala-ed-Din mosque in Konya, central Anatolia. In the eleventh century AD the Seljuks broke westwards out of eastern Turkestan; they conquered Merv in 1036 and soon were the rulers of the Middle East. Carpet knotting seems to have followed in their train and spread widely in Asia Minor. The Seljuk carpets from Konya (now in the Türk-ve-Islam Eserleri Museum, Istanbul) are designed on the same principle as the contemporary fragments discovered in the Eshrefoglu mosque of Beyshehir in 1929, with a diaper of half-drop rows on the central field. This is either achieved by an

Konya, 13th century. Fragment 183 × 130 cm.

Konya, 13th century. Detail from a Seljuk carpet of 608 × 240 cm.

endless repetition of the same isolated motif (octagon, hooked lozenge) or by a lattice-like arrangement of lozenges or star rosettes connected by strongly linear interlaced stems which gives the effect of an independent motif (fig. 5 on p. 59).

The dominant motifs are almost always in lighter tones of the dark blue, red or dark red-brown ground of the central field.

Characteristic of the broad borders are heavy wedge-shaped hooks derived from the stylization of Kufic script (fig. 1 on p. 57) or rows of rosettes geometricized to squares (fig. 5 on p. 59).

Konya, 13th century.
Fragment 17 × 17 cm.

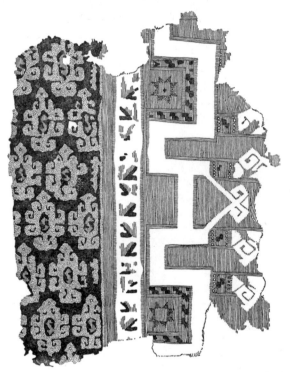

Konya, 13th—14th century. Fragment 91 × 74 cm.

Beyshehir, 13th century. Fragment 49 × 116 cm.

The designs of Seljuk carpets are not conceived purely from the decorative point of view. In the oriental imagination the border creates a frame round a little detail of the infinite that is flowing on freely without beginning or end. The way the border cuts through single motifs of the central field implies that the field is imagined as endless. These Seljuk carpets certainly started no later than the thirteenth century because one appears in a fresco by Giotto in the Arena chapel in Padua, painted in 1304.

We are again indebted to Italian painters for our knowledge of another type which inspired them, not much later in date. It has linear representations of birds standing either singly or in pairs in large almost square octagons. Representations of animals in early Turkish carpets come to an end with the phoenix-dragon motif in the fifteenth century (drawings on p. 22). Moschkowa has drawn attention to their resemblance to the birds on the oldest surviving khalyks preserved in some museums in Central Asia. (The khalyk is a small rug decorating the chest of the bride's camel at a wedding.)

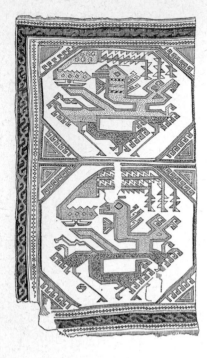

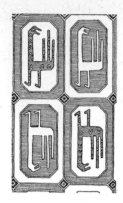

Two details from Anatolian carpets of the 14th century with bird patterns, from contemporary European paintings.

Fragment of carpet with dragon-phoenix motif, 161×91 cm. c. 800 knots per sq. dm. From contemporary paintings with this motif this fragment has also been attributed to Anatolia about 1400, but the author's examination of the structure and material has established that the piece (now in the Staatliche Museen, Berlin) cannot be earlier than 1700.

Rashid ad Din, an author of the fourteenth century, gives in his *Jami at-Tawarich* a list of the totems of the Ogusi tribe, also used by them for marking cattle. They are falcon, eagle, hawk, an eagle clasping a hare in its claws, etc. Similar birds in pairs are found as a repeat motif in Byzantine textiles of the tenth and eleventh centuries. All early Anatolian carpets known to us are of a relatively coarse weave (from 342 knots to the square dm. upwards) and the weft is always dyed red. The only exception is one fragment of a small carpet, from Fostat. It also has a red weft but has a density of almost 2,000 Turkish knots to the square dm. The dimensions reaching up to 520 × 285 cm. show that they were the product of an efficiently organized industry. Marco Polo in his journey through the Seljuk empire at the end of the thirteenth century reports that the best and finest carpets were produced in Konya.

Seljuk carpets can be seen as the direct descendants of the Turfan fragments, but not of the Pazyryk and Basadar carpets. These latter are twenty times denser in knot count, and the designs include naturalistic representations of animals and a much more delicate stylization of the floral motifs. In Anatolia on the other hand the colour sense is perhaps more subtle, but the animal drawing is extremely primitive. The style of the central field and borders is quite different. The Pazyryk carpet and the Basadar fragment are perhaps to be classified as the beginning of the development of the Persian carpet (Armenia). But there are no Persian carpets surviving from the period before the sixteenth century. Persian miniatures of the thirteenth century show carpets with similar features to those on Anatolian carpets and they betray no influence from the fine textiles which appear in the clothing portrayed in the same miniatures. The innumerable upheavals endured by Persia, her history of wars and revolutions, caused by such cataclysms as the campaigns of Alexander, the rise and fall of the Roman empire, the assaults of the Arabs (Islam) and then the Mongols, are perhaps to blame for a general decline in the art of knotting. The art of the nomads — though there is no proof of this — may have been an exception because nomad art is always proof against political and economic reversals. From the Caucasus region which lay open to Persian influences the earliest examples are the 'Armenian dragon carpets', alleged to date from the fifteenth century.

There was no evidence of the use of knotting in Egyptian carpet-making as long as the Fostat (Old Cairo) finds discovered by C. J. Lamm in 1935–6 were considered as cut, velvet, weft loop pile. Nonetheless the high standard of the individual Mamluk style of the carpets coming from the great Cairo manufactories in 1500 was unthinkable without a long tradition. The kaleidoscopic arrangement, of octagons and stars of different sizes and the thin slender leaf and other small motifs, shows the same specifically Arab striving to dematerialize the surface which is manifest in the iridescent faience facings of the mosques.

The Fostat finds show that Egypt very early took its own way in the development of knotting technique. The results of the closer examination which has been made of the Fostat finds should be sufficient proof of their Egyptian origin, apart from those made with non-Egyptian material or in Turkish knots. Of the seven fragments from Fostat in the Museum of Islamic Art in Cairo there is one entirely of left (z) spun, right (s) plied wool in Turkish knots (34 in height, 58 in width equals 1972 knots to the square dm.); it stands out at once as an import. The violet which is used prolifically here is to be found in Anatolian carpets. The curious treatment of the weft in this piece is unprecedented: of the four, five or six wefts only one goes firmly and sinuously in and out of each warp thread; the others, shifting along at each thread, go under every three warp threads very loosely, and after threading round the front of the next one go round the next three again from behind. If it is rightly dated to the ninth century by an inscription in Kufic script: 'Abd-rachman-ibn-sudaik' (according to the Head Curator of the Museum, Mrs Waffiya Ezzi, this is the name of a high court judge of Cairo in the ninth century) it is the only large fragment of carpet from the first millenium of our era; with its fine knotting it casts the first ray of light on the darkness shrouding the problem of hand-knotting in western Asia in the pre-Seljuk period. This would mean that, contrary to accepted opinion, the Middle East must have had a highly developed technique of hand-knotting long before its conquest by the Seljuks.

All the other six fragments (fig. 145—8), of which two seem to belong to one of the group of small carpets of apparently unusually small dimensions, continue the tradition of Egyptian carpets in towel technique, deriving from the Roman period (fig. 143), so far as their linen warp and the weft arrangement (straight and tight through a double warp) are concerned. This tradition can be traced back to the surviving 3,000 year-old small carpets which belonged to the priests of Amun in the Sixteenth Dynasty. Their structure will be dealt with in more detail in the following chapter.

The pile is produced by introducing woollen V loops round every second warp thread. The frugal use of these loops and their careful bedding between numerous weft threads justifies the proposition that the loops were put in singly and are not a looped weft thread woven in by laying a rod along the warp threads and subsequently cut. The right spin and left ply of all the material used shows it to be Egyptian. An inscription referring to the investiture of the son of Abssy as *maule* (head of finance or police in the ninth century) by the Caliph, and the Hijra year 202 (AD 818) on the border of another fragment dates them both to the ninth century; these fragments thus support the earlier theory that the Mamluk carpets (in Persian knots) of 600 years later were not the first carpets knotted in Egypt.

India did not produce hand-knotted carpets until the arrival of the Moghul emperors and at their orders. Because of the climate, the carpet was never adopted by the population. It served for regal display and later for export. In spite of the sometimes extreme naturalism of its patterns it never achieved emancipation from its Persian models. It was killed artistically in the nineteenth century by being given to prisoners to produce.

Eastern Asia evidently did not begin the production of hand-knotted carpets until much later. The manufactories started in many countries of Europe were mostly imitators or, in the Balkans, subsidiaries of Asia Minor and need not concern us here. Spain alone found its own style, in a divergent technique, and will be treated in a special section.

Production, structure and material

The knotted carpet (farsh, ghali, in Turkish halil) is produced by a combination of weaving and knotting: the short knotting threads are introduced during the weaving of the ground fabric out of warp (tun, chälä) and weft (pud, argach). The protruding regularly held brush-like ends of the knotting threads together form the pile (takhtä). The knotting process is always the same, whether the producers are

    nomads or semi-nomads,
    sedentary rural or urban families,
    working on their own account or for commission, or
    manufactories employing wage earners.

The looms (dasgah) on which the work is carried out are in principle rigid rectangular frames round which the warp threads are stretched vertically. A simple arrangement allows all the even threads (2, 4, 6 etc.) and all the uneven threads (1, 3, 5 etc.) to be pulled forward alternately so that the horizontal weft or woof threads can be drawn between them. The simplest forms of loom are used by the nomads, since they need to fold up their work and loom each time they move. They do sometimes use a vertical loom with a collapsible frame, but usually prefer the primitive horizontal loom without side beams.

Side beams are not necessary on the horizontal loom because the transverse beams over which the warp threads are drawn are held in a horizontal position by stakes driven into the ground. Thus the warp is held under tension in a very simple, but far from perfect, manner. A tripod of lashed rods is placed over the loom. On it hang the skeins of wool for the knots, while below is placed the mechanism for

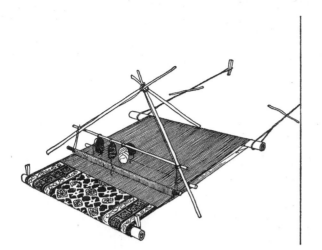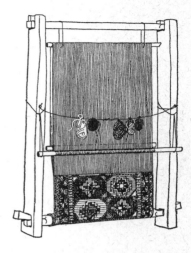

Horizontal and vertical nomad looms.

making the shed, which also presses back the lower warp threads into a level with the upper warp threads when the row of knots is done.

At first the knotter squats in front of the end of the loom, later largish stones are placed on either side of the warp as a support for a board laid across them on which she squats over her work. If she has to stop because of a migration or a storm the stakes are pulled up and the front cross beam with the beginning of the carpet on it and the free remaining warp threads are rolled up to the rear cross beam.

On the collapsible vertical loom the finished work is rolled onto the lower cross beam as the work proceeds so that the knotter squatting on the ground in front of the loom always has the row of knots she is doing at a convenient height. In this case the warp cannot be fixed on to the upper cross beam. It is held by a warp bar which hangs from the upper cross beam and can be let down as the finished fabric is wound on to the lower cloth beam. The sketch on this page shows the usual manner in which the warp is set up: its threads run unbroken round the lower and upper warp beams and turn back each time it has run round a cross bar. The carpet is begun close to the bar. From time to time the tension is slackened (by loosening the wedges) and the finished part of the carpet is pulled, together with the warp and bar, either downwards or up the back. When the carpet is complete the warp threads above the upper end are cut off and are usually either plaited or knotted. The loops of warp left after withdrawing the bar at the lower end are subsequently filled up with wefts or they twist up on their own.

With these methods it is practically impossible to set the warp threads back in the same position and tension after each interruption. Hence a nomad carpet nearly always has considerable variations in its width and sometimes in its length as well. Having to be light so that it can be transported, the loom is seldom very stable, and this limits the width of carpet the nomads can produce. They can reach considerable dimensions in length, because the warp can be made as long as they wish — stretched out on the horizontal loom, or wound round the warp bar on the vertical.

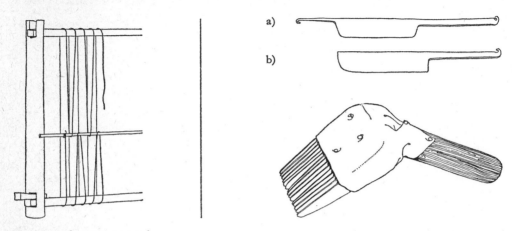

Mounting of warp over a rod.
Knife (tikh) with Tabriz knotting hook (a) and without knotting hook (b), right below, comb (daffeh, daftun).

The manufactories are freer of these limitations. The heavy, stable construction of the looms allows the fabrication of wide carpets. There is no difficulty in slackening the cloth beam so as to pull down the warp evenly along its whole width and pull up a section of the knotted surface behind the work, and then setting the warp again in its previous position and tension by driving in the loosened wedges. To avoid having to perform this time-consuming operation too often, the board on which the knotters squat shoulder to shoulder can be placed at either end on the rungs of a ladder, and lifted up a rung from time to time. With the simplest looms which allow of no movement of the warp the sitting board has inevitably to be raised as the work goes on. These lengthy interruptions are eliminated with looms that have rotating warp and cloth beams, and with the modern steel looms such as those developed in central Europe, where before the first war (as in Germany too) knotted-carpet manufacturers tried in vain to compensate for the higher wages they had to pay by a much higher degree of rationalization.

The knotting. After a band of webbing has been formed by shooting the weft back and forth alternately over and under the taut warp threads (Kilim, Gilimä, Gilim Baf) across the whole breadth of the carpet, the first row of knotting is started: the knotter cuts a piece of yarn about 50 cm. long from the hanks hanging above her with a knife (tikh) that never leaves her hand while she is working. (Pre-cut yarns of this length are also usual.) She loops this yarn round two adjacent warp threads so as to make the right-hand end protrude the thickness of a thumb, pulls the loop firmly downwards and as she does so she cuts off the yarn at the height of the projecting end. Her deft hands are already busy with the next pair of warp threads to make the next knot. So the work goes on. An experienced knotter leaves out the knots of another colour and fills them in afterwards. In some regions there is a special knife for the Turkish knot. It has a little hook at the point which holds the right-hand warp thread and also pulls through the right half of the knot (Tabriz knotting hook).

The nomad knotter chooses the colour of the wool by instinct, keeping the design in her head, or she finds her inspiration in a model carpet lying beside her. In the manufactories there is a drawing of the pattern (nagzh). This is drawn out by the designers and every single knot is indicated.

After each row of knots one or more wefts are woven in. A comb-like instrument (daffeh or daftun) beats the weft and the row of knots firmly downwards, and generally the ends of the knots are cut off with large scissors (gäichi) to the required height at the same time. If the shearing is left until the end of the day's work then the tufts of wool are combed out hard after each row with an iron comb (Chameh) to make the pattern plainer. The next row of knotting can then be proceeded with, followed again by weft threads etc. until the carpet is finished off at the upper edge with a plain woven border (kilim).

The knots and sometimes even the weft as well are not taken to the very outermost pairs of warp threads. Before the warp is set up these are twisted together to make specially thick strands. To protect them they are wrapped quite thickly with wool, cotton, goat hair or (very rarely) with silk of one or more colours (shirazi, shirasa) each time the weft turns.

The carpet is taken down from the loom. The ends of the warp threads may be left as twisted loops or cut up, but they are usually knotted together. Many nomads plait them into cross bands or braids that can be knotted together into a net. In some regions they prefer the bands of webbing to form the edge and in some nomad tribes these are given pretty woven or embroidered patterns, without a fringe (gabeh). Sometimes the plain woven band is turned back and hemmed down. Usually the upper end is finished differently from the bottom (for methods of finishing off a carpet see index). Knotted pieces with tassels at the bottom end are not intended for the floor (see fig. 104 on p. 217).

In the manufactories the grosser irregularities in the pile are levelled off by experienced master shearers (perdakhchi); these are craftsmen who enjoy much respect. At the final brushing of the carpet there is a last check up and any irregularities are ironed out with steam. A new piece is only washed if it has been soiled. For export certain carpets are always given a wash.

A good knotter can tie up to 1,000 knots an hour; with simple and familiar patterns or single colours even more. The finer the knots and the more complicated the pattern, the slower the work. The cost of labour for a carpet with 3,000 knots per square dm. is thus more than double that for one of the same size with 1,500 knots.

As a rule in the East it is women and girls who do the knotting, though boys and men sometimes do it too, especially in the manufactories in segregated halls. The romantic-seeming atmosphere of many workshops (kar-haneh), with little children playing round the looms and lying in cradles, cannot disguise the fact that much use is made of child labour. They squat before their work with the seriousness of adults. While the ten-year-old may lack practice and experience, the hands of the twelve-year-old fly over the warp with such speed that even the sharpest eye cannot distinguish the various phases of the process.

The most important man in a workshop is the master knotter. He supervises the accurate and careful work on two or three looms, and himself puts in the correct knots in the important places for the pattern. He is in charge of the material for the knots, and it is still the custom for him to engage the personnel for his looms and pay them according to their day's work.

Structure

The height of the pile depends on the pattern and on the wishes of the buyer. In many old pieces and in the luxury carpets of the court manufactories it is especially short, so as to show off the delicacy of the design to the best advantage. Right into the twentieth century the saying holds: 'The thinner his carpet, the richer the Persian.' The Persian custom of exchanging the thin 'summer carpet' for a thicker one in the cold season or of covering it with a felt carpet (namad) is no more current now than the gathering of the family round the charcoal brazier (mangal) under the gigantic round padded coverlet (lahaf).

The nomad carpet, especially in the mountain regions, fulfils its function of insulation against the cold better if its pile is long — no matter if the outlines of the pattern be blurred. Some very thin nomad pieces are made, however, especially in western Turkestan.

Two principal kinds of knotting are used:

a) The Turkish (Ghiordes) knot. The region of its use includes a number of areas besides Turkey.

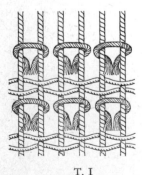 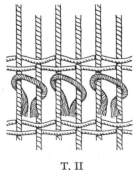 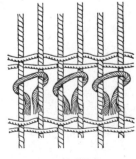

T. I   T. II   T. III

Turkish or Ghiordes knots

28

b) The Sehna (Sanandaj) or Persian knot. In the region of Sehna, modern Sanandaj, however, nearly all the carpets are done with Turkish knots. On the other hand the Persian knot is used over most of Persia, western Turkestan, India and China, and in Sparta (Isparta) in Turkey.

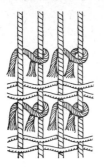  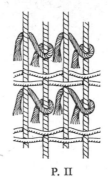 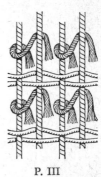

P. I   P. II   P. III

Persian or Sehna knots

Both methods have their advantages and disadvantages: the Turkish knot is firmer. The Persian knot enables fine contours to be kept more flowing, because the ends do not come up together. But if the warp is on two levels, one series of threads lying obliquely or vertically above the other, then the ends of the pile are pressed so close together out of the ground weave that very delicate designs can be achieved with either method.

Other methods of knotting, such as that round only one warp thread (see below) are confined to Spain or were only used sporadically in the East. We mention two in passing: Chufti, which knots round four warp threads, so that the knot loops round two pairs instead of two threads, and a nomadic use of Turkish knots for their ornamental bands over three warp threads (fig. 120).

Bidjar is not a different kind of knotting but uses an extremely thick, sometimes moist weft thread (argach) between strongly depressed warp threads. The second, thin, weft thread (pud) then runs in and out of every warp thread in a very sinuous movement. Bidjar in a very refined form is found in most carpets from the old established centres (Sivas, Tabriz, Saruk, Kashan, Kirman, Isfahan).

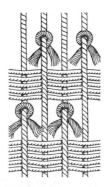 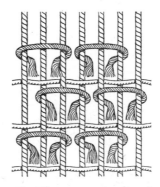 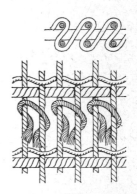

Spanish knot   Knotting over 3 warp threads   Bidyar weave

Towel or terry weave and single loop techniques are both important in the history of the development of the Middle Eastern carpet.

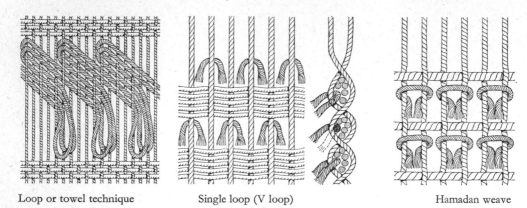

Loop or towel technique   Single loop (V loop)   Hamadan weave

In the Egyptian carpets of the Roman period executed in towel or terry weave the warp, weft and white pile loops all consist of right spun linen. Right spun wool was used for all the coloured pile loops. Warp: linen S-spun single ply, undyed up to 80 warp threads per dm. Weft: linen S-spun single ply, uncoloured. Three wefts alternating straight, so tight that they remain almost invisible. Pile loops: wool S-spun, two strands untwisted, coloured, and linen S-spun untwisted, uncoloured light. The pattern thread was carried in front across five warp threads, then brought back to the right in the shed between three front and three hinder warp threads leaving a loop about 1 cm. long above the ground weave. Then the free end of the pattern thread was led on over five warp threads to begin the next loop. Density: up to ten rows of loops in one vertical dm.

The Egyptian single-loop technique reserves linen as the material for the ground weave. The loops forming the pattern are always of wool except the white loops, for which linen or cotton was used. Warp: linen, Z-plied, two strands twisted, undyed light. Weft: linen S-spun, five to seven strands, untwisted — one Z-plied, two strands slightly twisted — undyed light. The five, six or seven strands of weft, each of three strands left-plied, were straight. Pile: wool S-spun, single, or else cotton or linen for white loops. Single loops round every other warp thread lifted by Hamadan weave, and alternating with the next row. The loops are hardly visible on the back. Density: up to about 2,700 loops per square dm. Although only every other warp thread takes a loop the horizontal density is always greater than the vertical because of the thick weft threads.

A technique used only sporadically and rarely in south Persia and Tabriz binds in a third warp thread on the back of the carpet at every other weft (so that these pieces seem to be overlaid by a close mat of vertical threads). It no more needs a special knot than the very rare 'two-faced' reversible carpet, which shows the pile on both sides because every other row of knots is put in on the underside (see fig. 71 a, b, p. 169).

As can be seen from the drawings, the knot is not literally tied; it is rather wrapped round the warp threads. It is made firm simply by pressing the weft close against it.

The ends of the yarn in the Turkish knot come up together between the warp threads and incline slightly towards the starting end of the carpet. This produces the lie or set of the pile. The ends of the Persian knot are separate, since the knot only wraps round one warp thread completely and does not come round the front of the second. Depending on whether this second warp thread is the left- or right-hand one of the pair, the pile inclines downwards to the left or right. Senna knots are termed either right-handed (S Ib, S III) or left handed (S Ia, S II). The right-handed knot (S Ib, S III, T III) is rarer because the knife has to be held in the left hand and is thus more suitable for left-handed people.

To ascertain the kind of knotting, the carpet is folded back parallel to a line of the weft. If the horizontal part of the knotting yarn covers both warp threads and its ends appear together, it is a Turkish knot. If the warp thread can be seen between the two ends of the knot it is a Persian knot. If the knot is moistened it makes it easier to see. It is difficult if the knotting is very close and the warps are on two levels, and if it is not wished to sacrifice one of the knots then the only way is to examine the first or last row of knots from the side. Even then there is room for error because sometimes Persian knotted carpets have the end rows in Turkish knots to make them firmer. For this reason a carpet must be examined at several different places to make sure.

If the warp threads lie side by side at the same level in the knot (T I, P Ia, P Ib) it appears on the back of the carpet as two humps, identical in the Turkish knot and almost identical in the Persian. If the knot count and thus the density is to be increased for the same breadth, the warp threads instead of lying side by side are held one above the other, depressed or on two levels (T II, T III, P II, P III). For this the first weft thread instead of running sinuously in an undulation, in and out of the warp threads, alternating with the return thread (P Ia, P Ib, T I), runs straight between them. The warp is depressed, or on two levels. On the back the second hump of each knot appears in a vertical groove.

The depression of the warp can be as much as ninety degrees: in this extreme case the two warp threads of each pair lie directly one above the other; on the back only one hump is visible. The knotting is now twice as dense across the breadth as with the warp on one level. The density of the knots along the length is unaffected by the depression and depends on the thickness of the knotting yarn, the thickness and number of the weft threads and on how hard and close they are beaten together.

A special weft weave was used predominantly in the region of Hamadan and in other areas of (especially west) Iran. As in *haute lisse* only a single thick weft thread is pulled through straight, so that every other warp thread is exposed at the back while its neighbour disappears behind the weft. In the weft row following the next row of knots the weft raises the warp threads which it had pressed down in the previous row. The most usual term for this procedure is Hamadan.

The density of the knots, the count or gauge, is expressed in the number of knots per square decimetre. It can range from less than a hundred to 8,000 in wool carpets, and in silk carpets it may be as much as 15,000 or even much more in special cases. It is reckoned by multiplying the number of knots in a square of ten centimetres along the length by ten centimetres across. To make the count a square of ten centimetres is measured or marked off on the back. Having made sure that there is no ninety-degree depression by examining a place in the pattern which is only one knot thick, the humps on the back are counted. Lengthways one hump is always one knot, but crossways this is only so if there is a ninety-degree depression, otherwise there are always two humps to a knot. It is more convenient to count the humps along a card ten centimetres long or, even simpler, to read them off in either direction on a thread counter with an aperture 2.5 $\times$ 2.5 cms., and multiply each result by four before multiplying them together.

Normally there is a higher knot count lengthways, but when the weft is thick, the warp threads thin and strongly depressed, it may be higher horizontally than vertically.

The following grading is recommended to describe density or gauge of a carpet:

up to c. 500 knots per sq. dm.	very coarse
from c. 500 to 900 knots per sq. dm.	coarse
from c. 900 to 1,800 knots per sq. dm.	medium fine
from c. 1,800 to 2,500 knots per sq. dm.	fine
from c. 2,500 to 4,500 knots per sq. dm.	very fine
over 45,000 knots per sq. dm.	exceptionally fine

In Persia the count is expressed according to the number of knots on a gireh — exactly seven centimetres of the warp — e.g. 30 Regh = 30 knots to the gireh = 45 to the sq. dm.

For a very dense structure the weft yarn may be so fine and the beating so strong that the weft is almost invisible on the back. The details of the design are then more clearly seen on the back than in the pile. On the other hand the pattern of very coarse carpets is often unrecognizable on the back because of loose knotting and thick weft rows.

Besides knotted pieces (pile weaves) there are in the East textiles with separate parts of the pattern knotted in (see Tekke fig. 120 and Shiraz fig. 104) and carpets and blankets without pile. The brocaded carpets theoretically belong in the category of textiles with patches of knotting (nimbaf = half knots, golbaryasteh = rising flowers, cf. fig. 102). These were made in Turkey, Persia (Polish carpets), India and East Turkestan with metal threads (thin gold or silver leaf wrapped round silk) woven into the areas between the knotted designs (see fig. 70).

Weaving was highly developed in the East long before knotting and reached its zenith in the fine brocades.

Other Weaves

The more or less coarse plain-weave textiles rarely appear in Europe except as the backing walls of all kinds of knotted bags and cushions. In the trade, woven or embroidered textiles, apart from cloth, appear as Palas, Kelim and Soumak, Verneh (shadda), Sileh and pieces produced in Djidjim technique native to the Caucasus. All these textiles have in common that the pattern is formed by coloured weft threads running over an invisible monochrome warp. Only in some ornamental strips (see fig. 118) does the monochrome weft, visible only at the selvedge, create the pattern by bringing up multicoloured warp threads.

In Palas it is only possible to make stripes across the whole breadth. Gelim (gilim) is the general word for textile in the Middle East. In the West we understand by Kelim (kilim) a particular technique of weaving. In the Anatolian (see fig. 23), Caucasian and Persian Kelim (and also in the Balkan Kelim) each weft thread of a particular colour is carried to and fro in the area of its own part of the pattern while another colour continues the pattern from the adjacent warp thread. Since no weft threads run the whole breadth of the piece this process creates vertical slits between the elements of the pattern which occur side by side. These slits are kept as small as possible by indenting the outlines of the design. The design of the Kelim is as clear on the back as at the front. Because of the small size of the looms older pieces of larger format are made of two narrow widths sewn together. Of the Anatolian Kelims the *kis-Kelims* are considered the best. They are called Karamani (Karamanli) in the trade, after the province of Karaman, and are woven by brides for their dowry (see fig. 27). The finest Kelims are the Sehna Kelims woven by Kurds, who do especially fine ones on silk warps. They are said to be so fine because they were used by the ladies in the bath houses (hamam), and they competed with each other there in their modest luxuries.

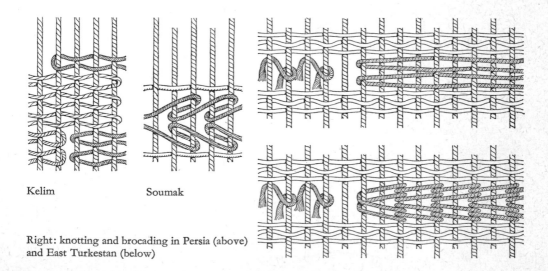

Kelim   Soumak

Right: knotting and brocading in Persia (above) and East Turkestan (below)

The Soumak (sumach, soumakh) carpet (see fig. 61) is named after the town of Sumakh (Shemakha) in the eastern Caucasus. The better quality goes under the name of Kuba-Soumak, the more flimsy are called Derbend-Soumak. In the Soumak the coloured pattern wefts, showing obliquely on the upper side, run continuously in each part of the pattern of the same colour over four warp threads in front, and are brought back behind two, in the contrary direction. The next part of the pattern is begun with a yarn of the new colour. The ends of the threads are not cut off. They hang in a tangle at the back and help to make the carpet more proof against cold and less liable to slip on the floor. After every other row, or at most every third of these rows, an invisible straight weft of wool or cotton is introduced across the whole breadth and beaten down firmly, as in the knotted carpet. The next rows of pattern run obliquely in the opposite direction from those before. This produces a herring-bone effect. Soumak technique occurs on the Phrygian fragments of textile of the early seventh century found in Gordion, Central Anatolia.

Dyeddyim (Djidjim, Jejim, Dyiyum, Jijim) are not to be confused with the coarse eastern Anatolian Dyiyum textiles which were common on the European market in the early twentieth century. They are a refined version of Soumak technique: the pattern threads run obliquely upwards, but almost always in the same direction, over two warp threads above and back round one behind. Herring-bone appears at only a few places or not at all. After every row of pattern a straight thin weft is run across the whole breadth, usually consisting of unplied wool. The back of the Djidjim weave resembles the back of a knotted carpet, except for the thread ends that hang down or are carried along to the next part of the pattern of the same colour.

The Sileh (see fig. 66) also comes from the southern Caucasus and its southern and south-eastern foothills (Karabagh, Kasak, Baku). Its structure resembles that of the Djidjim, but the pattern thread runs over four warp threads in front and backwards round two behind. The most beautiful sileh are those with scrolls stylized to large massive S and Z motifs. As can be seen from earlier pieces with designs that are more naturalistic, these are not dragons with a thin head curve and rudimentary claws. For the formats of about 280 × 200 cm. two vertical widths are usually sewn together. For the white parts of the pattern cotton is always used.

Verneh are native to the districts of Karabagh and Kasak. While the background weave remains invisible in Soumak, Sileh and Djidjim, the Verneh takes its characteristic aspect from the brick-red, yellow-brown, brown-black or dark yellow background weave. The solitary motif is woven in and sometimes finished with embroidery.

The Shadda (Shedde, Shaddah) blankets from the Karabagh are also Vernehs.

All these textiles are made entirely of wool, except that many Sileh, Verneh, Djidjim and Soumak use an undyed cotton weft for the white parts of the pattern. Only the Soumak is suitable for the floor.

The following should also be mentioned:
the blankets decorated with much embroidery and skilful appliqué for which Reshd — near the Caspian Sea — is famous;
the flat embroideries of the Karabagh;

the Susanshird pieces which came from Farsa (previously Basa-Sir), south of Shira, during the sixteenth to eighteenth centuries;

the old embroidered 'western stuffs' for the finest Persian clothing;

the Bukhara embroideries in red, blue and green on a white ground;

the coloured embroidered or appliqué felt carpets; and

the hangings made in Persia before the eighteenth century, on which the pattern was made by impressions of coloured wax onto a cloth. These are the precursors of the handprinted blankets and cloths (kalemkar) now exported from there in considerable quantity.

The Material

The most usual materials for oriental carpets are: sheep's wool, cotton, goat hair, silk and (formerly) linen. Camel hair is hardly used at all today because of its high price. Hemp or jute only occurs in the cheapest products, mostly knotted in Southeast Asia, which are not suitable for European use. In Tibet the hairs of the yak are said to have been used.

Originally all carpets were made entirely of wool (pashm. Turkish: yün). Being an insulator against cold and a damp repellant it fulfils the functional requirements of the carpet. According to region and breed, sheep's wool shows considerable differences. The newly washed sheep are sheared once or twice during the summer season. Only shorn wool is good; the best comes from the neck, shoulders, flanks and thighs. Wool from dead animals, skin wool or even plucked wool are of little value. Repeated, careful washing with soap and other alkalis frees the remaining dirt and the superfluous fat which hinders dyeing, while leaving each fibre with its natural fat content. With some kinds of wools certain dyes take better if the wool is washed in water alone.

After drying and sorting the wool is spun — by nomads still with a simple hand spindle — with a left-hand twist. Only in Egypt is it usual to spin to the right and ply to the left. The wool for the pile is dyed on the spot or given to the dyer. For the underweave the warp wool is very rarely dyed (see fig. 104) and the weft wool only in some regions.

For the warp, which lends the carpets its durability, almost always two or three, sometimes even four strands of wool are firmly twisted together in a Z-ply. For the weft, which is used principally to secure the knots, the strands are generally only slightly plied, or twisted round each other so loosely that it can hardly be called a ply. This means that on the one hand the yarn remains soft, while on the other it is easier to manipulate when the threads are not entirely separate and untwisted. For the pile too the spun threads are twisted round each other only enough to keep them together so that the knotter can tie the knot in one action. Plied knotting wool, such as is now sometimes found in Russian carpets, gives the pile an ugly crumpled appearance and destroys its lustre. The yarn of the pile, and in many regions the weft yarn too, looks unplied on the carpet when seen under the magnifying glass.

Camel hair is the best cold insulator. Less elastic than sheep's wool, it is easier to manipulate, but it does not hold colours so well. It used to be preferred undyed with its lovely natural gradations of colour, or mixed with sheep's wool. Goat hair (muh) is unsuitable for knotting except for the fine hairs of the kashmir (in the famous kashmir shawls) and angora goats, because it resists spinning and plying and the knots tend to undo. On the other hand it is valued by nomads and peasants for warps, selvedges and (less often) for the weft. Angora or kashmir goat hair is mixed into special knotting wools in a proportion of 1 : 10, because of its silky sheen.

Cotton (pambe. Turkish: pamuk) from the flight hairs of the seeds of the cotton plant, spins and plies well. Very firm and not prone to stretch, it is useful for making the ground weave firm. In the manufactories it has taken the place of wool in the warp and often in the weft too. Linen is even firmer and has at times been used for the warp, but it is too expensive. A considerable proportion of semi-nomadic and peasant knotted goods use cotton for the weft and extensively for the warp as well. It is not very water-repellent, and must be guarded against mould, which quickly makes it fragile. It is unsuitable as a knotting yarn because it tends to felt. It is used in western Turkestan and Anatolia (even in antique and older pieces) solely for the white knots because of its brilliance.

Silk (abrishan. Turkish: ipek) is obtained by winding off the thread spun by the silk-worm for its cocoon; it is very fine and about half a kilometre long. Being very resistant to stretching it is highly suitable as a warp for specially finely knotted carpets. More rarely the weft is of silk. As a knotting yarn it allows the finest gauge. Its sheen lends a lustre to the pile which is much prized, but this is a matter of taste, since its iridescence detracts from the force of the pattern. It is so lacking in elasticity that every footstep shows, and thus it is more suitable for luxury articles. Jap silk is made from the ends and short pieces of damaged cocoon silk. It is much inferior in quality — particularly when spun together with cotton — and is inclined to become brittle with age. These inferior yarns are found, like artificial silk and cotton made glossy by mercerisation, in cheap silk and souvenir carpets (see Anatolia).

To ascertain whether wool, cotton, hair or silk has been used only the eye and hand are needed if the area of the pile is large enough.

Wool is warm and woolly to the touch, cotton cool and felty, hair hard, prickly and coarse, silk fine and smooth. With small areas of pile and for the underweave a magnifying glass is needed; for a burning test, a match to apply to a portion of material removed from the piece.

Wool looks wavy; it shrivels when burnt, and fuses together into a dark lump which smells of burnt hair or horn. Hair when magnified looks stiff like wire, when spun, like a thin wire rope, and the ends of the warp threads look like a small brush. It smells and behaves like wool when burnt.

Cotton appears fluffy and leaves behind when burnt a grey white thread of ash which smells slightly of burnt wood and disintegrates when touched.

Silk is shiny and flexible. It burns with a slight smell of singed wool, and in the same way as wool.

Even more than by its designs, the oriental carpet enchants us with its colours and their combinations.

Colours are *effects of light*.

White is the sum of all the colours. They have various wave lengths. White light is broken up by a prism into a spectrum of red, orange, yellow, green, blue, indigo and violet, and brought together again as white. Even two colours like red and blue-green, yellow and violet-blue can be reunited as white (complementary colours). Under strong illumination a complementary colour evokes in the eye its contrary as a contrast; in other light conditions they may extinguish and darken each other. For all these reasons the colour effect of a carpet should be tried out, not in the open air, but only in the room for which it is destined.

In contrast to the exceptional gift of the Orient for design, their colour sense does not seem to us to be any more developed than the western. If old carpets combine colours which are otherwise considered to clash (even complementary colours), with apparently unerring certainty for the final effect, into a soft and rhythmical harmony without any disturbing dissonances, this lies more in the quality of the natural dyes, the material and the patina of age than in the colour composition itself. Hand-spun wool is irregular in thickness and does not take dye uniformly. The natural colouring agents only penetrate into the outer layers of the individual fibres, and their colour is diluted when the pile is shorn and the undyed centres become visible. In addition the wool breaks up the light rays in its different layers and thus varies the tones of colour. Thus while the knotter thinks he is placing full areas of colour side by side, in fact he has made areas which without any addition from him contain a broad scale of colour, a sum of gradations of tone, which combine harmoniously in the eye into a milder, warmer, quieter tone. The softened contrasts, as in impressionist painting, allow intermediary tones to arise from the harmonization of neighbouring areas of colour in the eye. One can often see with astonishment how what seemed at first to be a plethora of colours in a carpet is in fact composed from only four, five, six or seven basic colours.

Synthetic colours revealed the weakness of many combinations. These dyes penetrate the fibres intensively and produce standard colours in the knotting material. Thus when really fully coloured areas stood side by side they were often particularly painful to the eye if they happened to be in complimentary colours.

In the number of colours and in the mastery of their combinations there is naturally a difference between the court and the commercial manufactories (up to two dozen colours), the domestic and peasant pieces, and the products of the nomads whose usual four to seven colours sometimes seem to have been juxtaposed without any selection (e. g. Yuruk, see fig. 25) without in any way detracting from the rustic charm of the piece. Of the main colours red, blue and brown tones usually predominate. White can be added to these. Yellow with few exceptions (Milas, Khotan) is used more rarely; and green equally so, particularly in all areas with a Sunnite population. The tones of the colours range from pale and light through medium, deep and full to dark and sombre. As a rule the colour scheme of the oriental carpet is warm.

The pattern designers of the great manufactories early began to use half tones as well as the basic colours. Since every colour is dependent for its effect on its context, i.e. the neighbouring colours, they divided up the areas of colour. Renouncing the contrast of light and shade they repeated the same motif or parts of a motif in another colour, put in delicate outlines to soften the obvious decorative contrasts and kept the borders in different colours. Without the borders to balance them many of the designs would be unbearable.

Here too age and patina were needed to add to the harmonization of the colours. To the eyes of those who admire the Polish carpets for the somewhat decadent grey lustre which time has given them they would have appeared unpleasantly harsh when they were made. By chance the author was able to discover the original colours under the sewn-on silver fringe of one of these carpets. Canary yellow and grass green can hardly have made a soft effect with the gold and silver areas of the brocading which are now dark with oxidation.

Patina is created both by chemical and physical means: the colours change chemically through the year-long effects of light, air, sun and sometimes washing. The physical alteration of the pile surface is a result of the soft rubbing and polishing of the fibre ends by woollen socks and slippers. (The oriental would never tread on his carpet with shoes in the old days.) These processes bring about a comparatively regular alteration of the colours; only where there is a mixed dye can the balance be destroyed because one colour fades more quickly.

In almost every area where carpets are made synthetic dyes preponderate today. The natural dyes are being increasingly superseded, for their laborious extraction and the process of using them increase the costs of dyeing tenfold. Even in the smallest dye-works catering for the nomads the cans from the great European chemical works are stacked up to the ceiling. Industrial dyes are at least the equal of natural dyes for durability (light-, friction- and wash-proof) and have long since recovered from the teething troubles of their beginnings ('aniline period'). In using them the aim is to achieve as far as possible the advantages of the natural colours. By the use of half and quarter tones attempts are made to reach the colour schemes of older, natural-dyed carpets. Where the patterns remain more or less constant, as in Kashan, it was soon possible to gain sufficient experience. In carpets with frequently changing designs, as in Tabriz, they succeeded so little that the knotters in the neighbouring town of Heris kept for many years to natural-dyed wools for any carpets not destined for export. Anything up to seven of the good modern synthetic dyes may be mixed for the between tones, and this process needs much care, but results in durable tones which are hardly subject at all to alteration by the ageing of their separate constituents. Patina is very rare in carpets produced from material dyed with these colours. There is thus no objection to a gentle wash, sparing the depth of the weave, with chemicals that slightly corrode the ends of the pile and soften the colours.

Good dyeing with synthetic dyes is better than bad with natural dyes. Industrial colours cannot equal the effect of the best dyeing with natural colours. For this reason many carpet lovers will always prefer natural dyes.

Until the appearance of industrial dyes the oriental extracted his colours from the materials offered by nature. The nomad, insofar as he dyes for himself, immerses the hanks of wool into boiling water in which the dyes are dissolved. Besides the irregularity in the thickness of the handspun wool the nomad also has to contend with differences in the nature of the water (especially its lime and mineral content) and the wool (first and second shearing) as well as other hazards of his wandering life, so that it is unlikely he will achieve a uniform result with his dyes. He therefore expects nuances in the pile of the carpet in areas of the same colour (raghä, abrash). This shading, appreciated by the western connoisseur, is only tolerated by the eastern merchant in nomad products, while he demands perfection from the carpet made in a manufactory. With few means of comparison he is not aware that the perfection of industrial products is a questionable advantage.

The professional dyer dyed in the vat according to old recipes, abiding meticulously by them; sometimes he only dyed in one colour, and this in masterly fashion. The vat is a clay tub the height of a man, barrel-shaped and glazed on the inside, with an average diameter of 50 cm., equipped with a heating chamber at its foot. In recent years the vat has had to give place to copper washing boilers.

In spite of modest equipment and limited means the art of the oriental dyer was outstanding; it was based purely on empiricism. He was completely ignorant of the chemical processes which took place.

Natural dyes are derived both from plants and minerals. The only important source from the animal kingdom is different varieties of cochineal. The kermes louse which lives on the kermes oak is native to the Orient; it is added to the dye bath, dried and ground up, to produce the Armenian karabagh red (crimson) typical of Azerbaijan carpets. A similar purplish red comes from the coccus which was introduced into the Orient, together with its cactus host, through Spain from Mexico, after the discovery of America.

A much more important source of red is the root of the wild madder which needs no cultivation. According to its age the dried and crushed root gives light red or dark bluish red tones. Madder belongs to the mordant dyes: the yarn must first be prepared for dyeing with alum, tartaric acid, egg white, glycerine or metal oxide mordants, so that the tendency of the colour and fibre to unite is increased to make an indissoluble combination.

Blue is obtained from the indigo plant which grows in India and other tropical countries. The use of indigo is attested for at least the past 5,000 years, although it has to undergo a complicated process in the fermentation vat because its dye, indigotin, which is not water-soluble, does not colour directly: honey, resins or dates are fermented in the vat, and by addition of an alkali, indigo is transformed into indigo white. When after about twenty-four hours the yarn is immersed, it keeps its natural colour until it is again exposed to the air when it absorbs oxygen and turns blue. The darker the blue is to be, the more frequently is the material plunged into the vat, so that the dye is only gradually deposited on the fibre and can penetrate it better. Otherwise it would wear off badly by friction. Natural indigo is never completely fast to rubbing.

For yellow there are many native materials. The noblest, saffron from the stigma of the crocus, is very laborious to obtain and too dear. Isperek, a kind of milkwort, when fixed with alum becomes a clear full yellow with a slight greenish tinge. The yellow from pomegranate skins is not as clear as that from isperek or vine leaves, but can be converted by subsequent treatment with metal salts, to olive and greenish tones. Buckthorn and dyer's woad are other yellow dyes. Turmeric produces a yellow that is not very fast.

A certain green represents the colour of the Prophet for the Sunnites, and must not be trodden underfoot. Thus it occurs very rarely in large areas on Anatolian carpets. Green dye is extracted from ripe turmeric berries. The green derived from mixing blue and yellow discolours more easily; the same is true of purple from blue and red. Celadon green from treatment with metal salts affects the wool and corrodes it (Ferrahan carpets). In the same way black, brown-black and blue-black to grey, obtained from Brazil or logwood with iron salt, is corrosive. Thus it was preferred to use natural grades of brown from fawn to black for the brown tones, because in time the wool is destroyed right down to the under-weave.

Greys and browns are given by nut shells, oak bark and oak galls.

The roots of the henna (alkana) plant provide a light red, its leaves a yellowish red which is still used in the East as a hair dye for ladies. White is not produced by dyeing. It is usually ivory-coloured natural wool. True white, if cotton be not used, rouses a suspicion of bleaching and thereby damage to the quality of the wool. The particular cream colour of Turcoman tent equipment is white wool cured in the hearth smoke. All colours, even the dark ones, are brighter if they are dyed on light-coloured wool.

The symbolic meaning of the different colours in the East varies according to region and is not of importance in carpet-making.

The eastern carpet is generally designed with a central field and a border. Borders usually consist of a main border and narrower bands beside it which are called guard stripes.

The pattern in the central field may arise in a variety of ways: by multiple repeats of a similar motif; systems of flower scrolls with the stems running in one direction (e.g. vase carpets); a medallion; the prayer niche (mihrab); or other ways (e.g. carpets with pictures or portraits). By filling in the corners of the central field, often with a quarter of the main motif (e.g. medallion) they become corner pieces.

Repetition may occur either in simple rows or in half-drops, horizontal, vertical or diagonal rows, lattices or lozenges (see fig. 56).

The form of the prayer niche is very different in different regions. Prayer rugs made in manufactories have often lost the original sense of the prayer niche, and it is used only decoratively. The border, except in carpets from western Turkestan and eastern Turkestan, is usually predominantly of a different colour from the central field. It may be decorated with rows of a single motif (see fig. 59), stripes (see p. 150), cartouches (see fig. 76), and stems or scrolls, from the most primitive geometricized, often fragmented form to a detailed and naturalistic complex system with elaborate palmettes and even animals (see fig. 90).

The nomads, with their limited resources, make more modest designs: simple and half-drop rows of unpretentious elements and other uncomplicated repeats. The colour scheme may range from a variation between two colours to great multiplicity. If the medallion is used it appears either alone or repeated without any organic connection or interplay, alongside or over the ground pattern (e.g. p. 150).

The manufactories employ their own designers and dyers as well as their own master knotters and shearers.

The designers adapt models from ceramics and book illustrations into patterns suitable for carpets — with some influence from the style of the period to mitigate the force of tradition. Maintaining a duktus in keeping with the material and an equilibrium between the main pattern and the infilling, the design is tied together organically by superimposed drawings. The resulting record, in which every knot is noted on graph paper, then becomes the final reference for the work of the knotter. The master knotter lays down the structure of the under-weave for achieving the desired effect, according to the local technique.

The master shearer brings the pattern out to its full effect by his expert shearing. Too high a pile would waste the time expended on the fine pattern, too low would affect the durability of the carpet.

The master dyer must be able to judge the colour values according to their significance in the pattern. The choice of too strong a tone could destroy the pattern by making one part of the pattern or motif too prominent.

The design of the oriental carpet must necessarily remain a mystery to the westerner, since his mind works so differently from that of the oriental. In spite of his developed faculty for abstract thought, witness the contributions of the Orient to mathematics and astronomy, the oriental apprehends reality through thoughts and feelings which to the westerner seem quite unreal.

Religion, mythology, superstition, legend and astrology, society and the tribe with its traditions, especially for nomadic and peasant populations, seem to have affected his art more than the development and expression of the individuality of the artist.

The prohibition on the representation of living creatures, which was not enunciated by Muhammad himself but arose at the time of the schism, has had far-reaching effects. It was more strictly followed by the Sunnites in Asia Minor than by the Shi'ites in the other regions where carpets were made. It was responsible for a heightened development of ornament: the reduction, abstraction and geometricization of living creatures and plants into components of design, a process which the Turfan finds show was already happening in Central Asia before Islam; and with it that most original creation of the Islamic world, the arabesque. This element of decoration should also be seen as essentially ornament and not loaded with irrelevant symbolism, except in a few exceptional cases. Designers may in the first place have increased their repertoire of ornamental elements by adopting motifs with a symbolic significance from the culture and the cults of their own or other peoples (e.g. the cloud band from China), but they used them purely as forms of decoration. In the large manufactories in Persia the naturalistic design derived from the plant world and extended by the addition of animals was carried to perfection. Erdmann rightly appraises this development not as the climax but as an offshoot of the evolution of the carpet, and not to be set above the powerful stylization along which the art developed in other regions. In every oriental there lies dormant the memory of his ancestors' nomadic life. Even today he likes to pass his leisure hours sitting on a carpet like the Sasanian kings portrayed on ancient silver dishes. Life on cushions and mattresses gives the floor quite another meaning from our rooms with their furniture, in which the wall counts for more than the floor. It is not fortuitous that in the West it was wall hangings (gobelins) that were perfected while in the East it was floor carpets.

The carpet covering the ground signifies for the oriental a little fragment of infinity, where time and space flow together. Time itself is for him primarily eternal, unmeasured: cyclical. The carpet then must be confined within aesthetic limits, and the material and techniques used be in keeping with textile criteria. The vision of the oriental is not spontaneously naturalistic, and these limits are rarely in danger of being overstepped. Where exaggerated modelling and illusionistic perspective have nonetheless impinged there may occur pieces which have lost true character, with the qualities of painting or architecture inappropriately dominant.

Of course the westerner can appreciate and understand the rules of composition of a pattern, but he will never penetrate its deepest meaning or that of its constituents, in spite of his intellectual comprehension. Yet it is this mystery, this unattainable secret which exercizes such a spell upon him over and above the aesthetic appeal. He is even able to distinguish the true from the false. As long as the patterns have their origin in the domain of the spirit he feels himself drawn towards them, even when superstition is manifest in them. The Anatolian Yuruk weave tufts against the evil eye into the prayer rugs that they make to glorify Allah, while the Persian nomads represent huge beasts of prey which almost burst apart the design, as a protection against the forces of nightmare, fear and terror (see fig. 101). It is only sentimental designs, such as the drinking faun, which evoke that unfortunate after-taste of trash, that regret at the waste of so much skill and careful work and costly material. Unsatisfactory and bloodless too are the 'nomad patterns' constructed from tracings or sketches, entirely devoid of any original, earthy power — quite apart from the inadequacy of the understanding and imitation of the designs — and again those patterns inappropriate either to textiles or carpets in which other influences, such as miniature paintings or European patterns, predominate.

Exchange and admixture of patterns have always occurred as a result of migrations, wars, commissions from rulers, emigration or deportation of knotters into manufactories, tribes that migrate over vast distances, or marriage. They have been balanced by the instinct and conservatism of the peoples and tribes. In these days when large manufactories see it as their task to copy popular designs which originated thousands of kilometres away, even their best work can never transcend the quality of an imitation.

An exhaustive study of the motifs and symbols used in Caucasian carpets is in hand by L. Kerimov; a description and explanation of the hand-knotted and Kelim collections of the Turk-ve-Islam Museum is in progress. It is to be hoped that Iranian scholarship will set up similar studies for the Persian area. There is of course a dilemma, in that the original meaning of the motifs and symbols has become lost over the generations. In the twentieth century the designers and knotters are not all conversant with their significance. Where they do still remember, or did until recently, as in western and eastern Turkestan and China, close investigations are being made.

Here it is sufficient to give a survey of the most important motifs, patterns and symbols. For many of them, especially in so far as concerns the borders, European terms have become usual. While they allow a relatively exact definition they of course bear no relation whatever to the real content.

Animal combat, symplegma, especially on Persian and Indian manufactory carpets.
Arabesque. Linear interlaced

or looped, systematically ordered decorative elements, with or without the addition of plant motifs.
Ashkali. Frequent ornament

on old Shiraz carpets.
Bamboo. (See chapters on eastern Turkestan and China.)
Barber's Pole. A pattern of adjacent oblique stripes appearing in the border and also in geometric medallions. Named after the English barber's pole.
Bat. (See chapter on China.)
Bird, already stylized on early knotted work of Turkish tribes, and also on carpets from other areas, naturalistic or stylized.
Boteh, bota, mir-i botar or boteh miri, also called almond and pear or palm top or Indian pear, and when very small, humorously, flea pattern. It is the most extensively employed leaf motif: a leaf, with an inclined crest top which in geometric form is bent at an angle, and some-

times with little feet as well, in innumerable variations. Contrary to the opinion that it is a symbol of the flame of the fire worshippers (Parsees), or of the ruler's seal showing the outer edge of his hand dipped in blood, it is proved by its appearance in the borders of early carpets to be purely of floral origin.
Buddha's Fingers. (See chapters on eastern Turkestan and China.) Finger-shaped citrus fruit.
Buddha's knot (fig. 143). Endless knots representing fate or fortune (see chapters on eastern Turkestan and China).
Buffalo occasionally appears in animal carpets.
Butterfly. On Indian and Persian carpets, and particularly frequent on Chinese (see chapter on China).
Camel, on nomad carpets; Shaddah and Djidjim (fig. 63).
Crows Foot or goosefoot pattern (trade description).

Cartouche, in main borders, more rarely in the central field.
Chess board pattern, division of the central field into squares (fig. 41); already

appears on the Pazyryk carpet (p. 16).
Clouds, cloud band, originating in China (see chapter on China), appears on Turcoman, Persian, Caucasian (fig. 39) and on old Anatolian carpets.
Crane. (See chapter on China.)
Crenellation, medakhyl. A reciprocal pattern derived from a row of pinnacles, spear points or lily-like motifs.
Date. (See chapter on dating.)
Do-Gul =two blossoms: a pattern of two flowers in regular alternation appearing mainly in north-west Persia.
Dragon. (See p. 281 and chapter on China.)
Dragon-Phoenix motif (Ming emblem), on Turkish carpets of the fifteenth century and Caucasian 'dragon' carpets of the seventeenth.
Duck (p. 191). Mostly on Persian and the oldest Caucasian carpets.
Eagle, also double eagle. Geometricized in western Turkestan. The Caucasian 'Eagle' (fig. 43) is a geometricized plant motif.
Elephant. Rare, only on Persian, Indian and Chinese carpets.
'Ewer and Comb'. On carpets destined as prayer mats.
Fish. On Persian and the oldest Caucasian carpets, also Chinese.
Flowers and Blossoms. Naturalistic, particularly in India and Persia, stylized in all other regions to strict geometricization in the Caucasus and western Turkestan. Especially favoured are tulip, carnation, lily, narcissus, rose, lotus, peony and chrysan-

themum (see China). Small flowerheads often appear edging the mihrab in Turkish prayer rugs.

Fo lion (see chapter on China and fig. 136) — Chinese lion.

Forked scrolls or stems. Characteristic ornament on

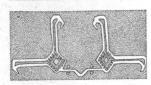

Persian and Caucasian carpets (fig. 49).

Goblet border, also called Oak or Acanthus leaf or Cup and leaf border. (Trade descriptions. fig. 38, 46). Description of the borders of Caucasian carpets with wineglass or goblet-like geometricized flowers between indented stylized leaves.

Graveyard motif. On Anatolian prayer rugs (fig. 22).

Griffon, winged mythical

beast, appearing already on the Pazyryk carpet.

Gul and Gol. (See chapter on western Turkestan.)

Haj = cross (see chapter on western Turkestan.)

Hand. On many (especially Caucasian) prayer rugs (fig. 34).

Hanging Lamp. Often on prayer rugs hanging from the arch of the mihrab. On Persian carpets attached above and below the medallion.

Herati or Ferrahan pattern. Also called Mahi-to-hos (fish

in pond) from the lanceolate leaves arranged symmetrically round each lozenge formed of stems.

Heron. (See chapter on China.)

Hexagon, particularly frequent on Turcoman carpets.

Horse, main motif on the Pazyryk carpet (p. 16); stylized on nomad carpets, naturalistic on Persian and Chinese picture carpets.

Hound. Extensively used in stylized form on nomad carpets; naturalistic as an elegant hunting dog or tame hunting leopard on hunting carpets.

Hourglass border (Trade

description). Geometric fragmented scroll motif with hourglass-like components.

Humans, stylized on nomad carpets (p. 171) or naturalistic on manufactory carpets (p. 191).

Inscriptions in Kufic, Nakshi or Talik script, referring to the subjects depicted in the carpet, the patron or the knotter, or with texts from the Koran.

Khilin. Adopted from the Chinese symbolic repertoire

for Persian and Caucasian carpets, a fabulous beast like a stag.

Kufic script (see **inscriptions**). Ornamentally stylized Kufic characters round a border (fig. 1).

Leaves. Almost always stylized, and geometricized past recognition in many nomad carpets (see also under **boteh** and the chapter on China).

Leopard. On hunting and animal carpets, usually preying on another animal.

Lion. Symbol of power.

Lozenge. Smooth, stepped, indented, serrated, fronded or with hooks, in every size from scatter to main motif, in nomad carpets of every provenance.

Lozenge or diamond lattice. Especially on Caucasian carpets.

Luck circle, luck knots, character for Good Luck. (See chapters on eastern Turkestan and China.)

Meander, especially frequent in the border of eastern Turkestan and Chinese carpets.

Medallion, single or repeated as the main motif in the central field.

Mihrab. Prayer niche on prayer mats.

Mina khani. Manifold repetition of large flowers, each

with four small flowers arranged round it to form a lozenge pattern.

Mountains. (See chapters on eastern Turkestan and China.)

Numbers. (See chapters on dating and Turkish carpets.)

Octagon. The most frequently occurring polygon.
Palmette. Most frequent on Persian and antique Caucasian

carpets, large flowers, in side view or in long section, stylized into a circular form.
Peacock, geometric on Caucasian (p. 131), naturalistic on Persian and Indian carpets.
Phoenix. (See chapter on China.)
Pomegranate. (See chapters on eastern Turkestan and China.)
Prayer niche and arch (see under mihrab).
Rosette, an ornament appearing on the majority of carpets.
'Running Dog', subsidiary border design; a stem scroll

reduced to a hook-like motif.

S border, and S figure. More or less geometricized scrolls or single motifs, from very small to very large (fig. 66).
Shekiri (sugary) border, especially in Sehna and Serabend) with delicate angled wave scroll, carrying soft boteh.
Stag or elk. Dominant motif on the Pazyryk carpet (p. 17, see also chapter on China).
Stars of all kinds, isolated, in rows or filling polygons.
Stem, stem scroll. Innumerable variations, naturalistic, stylized or geometric, continuous or reduced to a single component, on almost every carpet in some form.
Swastika, hooked cross which appears in many variants as an ornament or symbol, in all cultures; especially frequent in East Turkestan and Chinese carpets.
T pattern, T border, also appears in rows of double Ts on Turkestan and Chinese carpets (fig. 132).
Thunder and lightning. (See chapters on eastern Turkestan and China.)
Trees. Naturalistic (fig. 90), stylized (fig. 127), and often extremely geometricized (fig. 102).
Turcoman line, special form

of the angular wave scroll on Turcoman carpets.
V hook, ancient Seljuk geometric motif (fig. 12).
Vase, single or in groups with tall flower and twig pattern (p. 271, see also chapter on China).
Volute calyx, in different

forms on carpets of every provenance.
Water, on garden carpets in the form of canals, streams and ponds (p. 191), in China in the sea-water-cloud motif.
Wave scroll, in different forms, frequent on borders.
X hook, geometricized scroll component, single or in rows on nomad work.
Y motif, derived from forked scroll or a pair of birds' heads, specially frequent in the Hatchlu (p. 231, see also chapter on western Turkestan).
Zig-zag border, also triangular or seam border, the

most usual design for the edging between guard stripes.

Names and terms for carpets

A carpet is usually called after the village or the more or less closely limited area of its origin, or after the tribe which knotted it. There are also many other kinds of appellation.

According to the country of origin:
Turkish, Irano-Persian, Russian, Afghan, Chinese, Indian, Pakistan, Egyptian, Spanish, Portuguese, Greek, Bulgarian, Romanian, Hungarian carpets, etc.

According to region or province:
Anatolian, Karaman, Levantine, Caucasian, Reffahan, Khorassan, Turcoman, Turkestan, North African (Mahgrebi), Balkan carpets.

According to the trading centre:
e.g. Mossul, Bokhara, Khiva, Kerki, Samarkand.

According to the find-place:
Pazyryk, Polish, Siebenbürgen (Transylvania), Ardebil carpets, etc.

According to painters whose pictures show certain types of carpet particularly often:
Holbein, Lotto carpets.

Carpets that cannot be attributed to a particular region of their country of origin:
Anatol, Sultan for thick, Yuruk-like, east Anatolian and north Iraqi carpets.

According to format:
Charhad for the smallest scraps of carpet, charpay (= 4 ft.) for formats up to 10 × 80 cm.
Namaseh (Namaza), prayer rug; formats up to about 100 × 80 cm.
Sejedey (Sedjadeh), formats from about 180 to 230 cm × 125—150 cm.
Sarquart (= 1¼ saer. 1 saer = about 106 cm., but not always the same), pieces of about 130 cm. in length.
Sarenim, Sar-i-nim or sar-andaz (= 1½ saer), pieces of about 150 × 100 cm.
Dosar (= 2 saer), large and relatively narrow pieces about 220 cm. in length.
Kenareh (= shore, edge. See chapter on laying out and care), long narrow pieces (runners).
Keley, Keleï (Ghali, Kali), carpets of 150—200 cm.

wide and at least twice the length.
Ghalijeh (Keleyghi), smaller carpets the same shape as Ghali = Keley.
Mianeh (= half). Added to the designation of size.
Exotics, Viennese trade term for Keley from about 180 cm in width.

According to method of fabrication:
Turkbaff (Turkish knots), carpets knotted in Khorassan (north-east Iran) in Turkish knots.
Farsibaff (Persian knots), carpets from the south Iranian province of Fars.
Harun, carpets (specially from Kashan) which are not very carefully knotted and thus do not show the pattern as clearly on the back as to qualify for a name by provenance.
Gabeh (= unclipped), in the Shiraz region for rustic carpets with a long pile and patterns mostly of undyed wool; also for carpets without a fringe.
Kendirli, Turkish (especially Kula) carpets with sporadically thicker wefts.
Nimbaff (= half knots) or Golbaryesteh (= projecting flowers), for woven pieces with patches of knotting (fig. 104). Reversible carpets: the pile is knotted both in the front and back (fig. 71).

According to place of production:
Manufactory, court manufactory, domestic, prison, orphanage carpets.

For indicating different qualities from the same provenances:
For example, Meshed, Kuduani and Arab for Baluchi carpets. Bibibaff (after the princess Bibi Hanum) for the best kinds of Baktiari carpets.
For indicating (often allegedly) better quality:
For example, Mecca-Shiraz, Meshed-Baluchi, Saruk-Mahal, Laxer-Tabriz, Eski- (Turkish, old) Kirman.

After dynasties or rulers:
Seljuk, Ottoman, Saffavid, Mamluk, Shah Abbas carpets etc.

After producers or patrons:

For example, Petag, Hotz, Ziegler, O. C. M. (Oriental Carpet Manufacturers), Mayer-Pünther carpets.

According to the pattern:

Adler carpets, Allover. (Trade term for carpets with endless repeat and no prominent motif.)

Bastard carpets (see Caucasus).

Tree carpets, trees predominate in the pattern.

Picture carpets, carpets decorated with a picture.

'Bouquet' carpets. The pattern consists of a repeat of bunches of flowers.

Dragon carpets (see chapters on Caucasus, eastern Turkestan and China).

'Elephant foot' (trade term), the large octagon pattern on Turcoman carpets.

Do-guleh (= 'two flowers'). The pattern consists of the repetition of two different flowers.

Djuft (Djoft = pair). Two carpets of the same size with the same pattern.

Findighan (Findig = hazelnut). Especially Shirwan carpets with a scatter pattern of small stylized blossoms.

'Flea' carpet. Trade term for Mir carpets with small boteh (Indian pear) pattern.

Garden carpets, with representation of a park either horizontal or vertical.

Self-colour carpets. Trade term for carpets with large monochrome areas on the central field.

Hatchlu, Hachly or Kachly (see Turkmenia and p. 231).

Court scene carpets, with court scenes adapted from miniature painting.

Inscription carpets. Inscriptions (usually from the Koran) predominant in the border or over the whole carpet.

Hunting carpets, with hunting scenes.

Season carpets, with allegorical representations of the seasons of the year.

Cartouche carpets. The central field is divided into cartouches.

Yaçibedir) carpets, with a sombre effect from the Bergamo region.

Suite. Auctioner's term. One broad and two narrower carpets of the same length and pattern.

Conference carpets (trade term). The three carpets belonging to a suite with a Ghalidshed across the whole breadth of the three, knotted in one piece.

Badge of Tamerlane. In the central field the shintamani (three balls, 'badge of Tamerlane', see fig. 8) in endless repeat.

Landscape carpets, with representations of a landscape.

Medallion carpets. One or more medallions dominate the pattern.

Millefleurs (= 1,000 flowers). Small-scale flower pattern.

Paradise (= Persian garden) carpets, with naturalistic flowering trees and animals.

Portrait carpets, with portraits of personalities.

Sheikh Sefi carpets, with the pattern of the historic Ardebil carpet.

Set. Four carpets of different sizes in the same pattern, with which the orientals lay out a room.

Sinekli (= fly) carpets. Turkish prayer rugs, the mihrab, covered with identical very small stylized flowerheads.

Striped carpet. The pattern consists of narrow stripes.

Ter-Mustuphi carpets with allegedly French rose or flower pattern; also called nachl-i-frangh (= European pattern).

Picture carpets with scenes from history, literature or saga.

Animal carpets. Animals predominate in the pattern.

Vase carpets. Vases with flowers in multiple repeat or sprays rising out of vases form the pattern.

Armorial carpets with the emblem of the patron or the recipient.

Cloud-band carpets. Cloud bands dominate the pattern. Self-colour carpet.

According to use and custom:

Knotting is done primarily for floor carpets, prayer rugs, cushions, bags, saddle covers and for decorating the dwelling.

Souvenir carpets, cheap carpets, often artificially aged, intended for the unsuspecting tourist. These articles are mass-produced in Turkey and Iran, mostly as prayer rugs or carpets for family or communal prayer (saph), in wool or spun silk on a cotton ground-weave.

Ayatly, Turcoman burial carpet.

Bride's carpet, see under kis carpet.

Khalyk, formerly a Turcoman term for small carpets decorating the front of the bride's camel at the wedding.

Khourdjin (= Khordshin, Khurjin), see under bags.

Dip Khali, Turcoman for the floor carpet in a tent.

Engsi, Enessy, Turcoman carpet serving as a door flap at the entrance to the tent (fig. 119).

Graveyard carpets (Turbelik, Mazarlik), Turkish carpets reserved for burial ceremonies, in which the motif of a little house flanked by a cypress and weeping willow is repeated vertically inside the mihrab (fig. 22).

Prayer rugs with niches (mihrab) or without, on which the believer performs his devotions in the direction of Mecca: Manazlik (Turkish), Jainamaz (Persian), Sajada = Sejadeh (Arabic), Salachak (Turcoman).

Germetch. Turcoman carpet lying at the tent entrance.

Yastik (Turkish), Pushti (Persian). Small carpets

up to 80 cm. long, which served originally as bolsters for leaning against and sitting on.

Kapunnuk, Saryk Turcoman. Lambrequin-like decoration at the tent entrance.

Kibitka slaps. See under tent band.

Kis carpets, Kis Kelim (Kis = bride, girl). Carpets knotted by the bride herself for her dowry (fig. 17), or woven kelims (fig. 27). The term kis-Ghiordes is particularly well known.

Cushion, small: bolesh-motaka, Serin (Kurd); large: Motaka, Doshak (Kurd).

Nani, small carpet used by the Gashgais like a hammock as a cradle.

Ojalyk (Turkish), prayer rug, large pieces with a medallion looking like a mihrab, with a gable at either end (fig. 16).

Osmolduk. Five-sided carpet to decorate the camel's flanks.

Pushti, see under Yastik.

Communal prayer carpet, see under saph.

Rupalani, saddle cover (p. 201), also called Gashya.

Rutakali (= on the back), ass and horse rug (fig. 106).

Saph, communal prayer carpet or family prayer rug with a row or two rows of niches side by side (mihrabs).

Pillar carpet. Without side borders, made in China to hang round pillars (p. 281).

Serin, see under cushion.

Sineban, knotted breast-band for horses and asses.

Tainakcha. Turcoman horse rug (p. 241).

Bags. Smallest, for money: tantye (tanche, fig. 100), for pipes: kailandan (fig. 105);

small: torba for spoons, chenche torba, for salt, dis-torba;

long: tobreh;

for the saddle, and double bags: khurdjin (kurtchin), also namagdin or nemagdum; Turkish, heybeh (fig. 29).

large: choval, chuval (fig. 117), mafrash (Caucasian), also for box-like paniers.

Turbelik, see under graveyard carpets.

Tent band or strip, kibitka strip (Turkish: chadir sheridi, Turcoman: yolami and bou), up to 15 m. long, woven decorative bands for the tent, with embroidered or knotted patterns (fig. 120).

I. Bergamo c 1800. 176 × 149 cm. (p. 51).

Warp: W. Z-spun, two strands S-plied undyed ivory.

Weft: W. Z-spun, single strand dyed red. Two wefts alternating sinuous.

Pile: W. Z-spun. 2–3 strands T.I: h. 24, w. 22 = 528 per dm².

Upper end: A few wefts remaining of a W. kilim, red.

Lower end: –. Sides: W. shirazi red not original.

Touch: soft, medium heavy, coarse flat granulated.

Colours: 6, *red, blue, blue-green, ivory*, orange-brown, dark brown.

Pattern: in the red central field a large motif cut off by the side borders is arranged vertically so that the red ground appears in the form of the same motif. These large motifs are clamped together with volute hook attachments. All the motifs are scattered over with a symmetrical arrangement of X hooks and geometric flowers. The main border has a row of large geometric flowers on ivory ground; down the long sides this is of a simpler form than across the ends. The guard stripes are very insignificant, consisting of a dotted seam of red and white accompanying a narrow band of oblique stripes.

Geography and history

Turkey is the classic point of contact between West and East, the bridge between Europe and Asia.

Only three per cent of its territory lies in Europe (including Istanbul). The Asian part of Turkey is what is called Asia Minor, with its capital at Ankara; this is the large Anatolian peninsula, its shores washed by four seas, the Mediterranean, the Aegean, the Sea of Marmara and the Black Sea.

Anatolia is a high plateau interspersed with mountains. It flattens out to the west and is hemmed in by mountain barriers rising to more than 3,000 metres to the north (Pontic mountains) and south (Taurus). The west is the most fertile part of the country; the east is mainly mountainous. The highest mountain, 5,165 metres, is Ararat, on which Noah's ark is supposed to have landed. Round Lake Van alone are two dozen peaks more than 3,000 metres high. In the east, too, rise the Tigris and Euphrates. On the coasts the climate is mild; at the eastern end of the Black Sea it is even tropical (in the Rize district tea is cultivated), and the surrounding mountains provide abundant rainfall (but in the south only in winter). On the plateau of the interior with its violent changes of temperature most of the rivers dry up in summer because of insufficient rainfall; the winter brings heavy snow.

Following the dictates of geography and climate, the important carpet industries developed in west and central Anatolia. Nomads are the main competitors for the small quantity produced in the east. The best wool comes from the west Anatolian districts of Balikeshir, Ushak and Kütahya. The main supply of silk comes from Bursa (Brussa). The most important cotton-growing area lies in the south-east, on the gulf of Iskenderum.

The Hittites were the first people to form a state in Anatolia. Their kingdom was the leading power in the Near East in the seventeenth century BC, and its influence reached as far as Babylon. In the thirteenth century BC they had a resurgence of power after defeating the attacks of the Egyptians, and the king's daughter became queen of Egypt. The changeable history of the Hittites was followed by the rule of the Phrygians, an Indo-European people. Their king Midas ruled at the end of the eighth century over a mighty empire with its capital city at Gordion. Here were found the fragments of textiles in Soumak technique belonging to this period.

After the Cimmerians defeated Midas, the Lydians, another Indo-European people, gained control of western Anatolia. The Lydians were an industrious mercantile folk who were famous for their highly developed dyeing industry. One of their kings was Croesus, who ranked as the richest monarch on earth until he was defeated in 546 by Cyrus, the Persian Great King. Then Lydia and the flourishing small coastal states, which had been developing since the second millenium BC through the migrations of the Greeks, were annexed to the Persian empire. These small Greek states with their rich cultural background reached the apex of their development later, with the expedition of Alexander and the series of his generals, or Diadochi, which followed it. The second and first centuries BC saw Roman rule.

Byzantium, also a Greek foundation, was raised in status to be the new capital of the Roman empire by the great Roman emperor Constantine I in AD 330. For centuries, while Rome was suffering the threats of the barbarians, and her power and prosperity were diminishing, Byzantium remained the centre of power and the guardian of western culture. But differences over dogma created a gulf between East and West. In the seventh century 'Eastern Rome', having just won a series of victories over the Persians, had to contend with the rise of the Slav states in the Balkans which threatened her rear, and at the same time had to meet the onrush of the Arab armies of Islam right at her very gates. Of all her empire only Asia Minor and Greece remained. By the eleventh century she had recovered, defeated Bulgaria, and once more annexed Syria and Mesopotamia, but then the Seljuk advance began. The Seljuk Turks began their campaign of conquest from Turkestan and did not stop until they had overrun Asia Minor. There they disseminated the Seljuk culture. Konya (Iconium) became the most important Muslim residence and attracted scholars, architects and craftsmen from Persia, Armenia and Byzantium. The Seljuk carpets from Konya are the earliest surviving large carpets of the Near East. Though the crusaders freed a few regions of Asia Minor they caused dire upheavals in Byzantium in addition, and twice occupied the city of Constantinople. The army of occupation was led by Venice, who possessed preferential trading rights in Byzantium. Oriental carpets were among the goods imported into Europe by Venetian merchants.

Another tribe of Turks, set in motion by Genghis Khan's incursions into Turkestan, followed the same route as the Seljuks had done earlier, and in the thirteenth century managed to acquire the succession to the throne of Asia Minor by right of inheritance. They assumed the name of their first ruler Osman, and were called the Osmanli or Ottoman Turks. They conducted an expansive foreign policy, overran the Balkans in the fourteenth and fifteenth centuries, and in spite of military defeat survived the Mongol storm under Timur.

Byzantium new consisted of nothing more than Constantinople. The Eastern and Western Churches were irreconcilable, and their mutual animosity made it impossible to save it. In 1453 the city was conquered and transformed into the oriental city of Istanbul, capital of the Ottoman empire. This empire then annexed Syria, north-west Persia (1514) and Egypt (1517), and a fine civilisation developed. The Sultan was now able to summon the best carpet-makers from north-west Persia and Egypt to attend his court, and he had at his disposal the great manufactories of Cairo.

The chequered history of the Ottoman empire — defeat outside Vienna in 1683 (many carpets fell into the hands of the victors), in the nineteenth century the secession of Egypt which became independent, victory in the Crimea against Russia, loss of the Balkans — came to an end with the loss of the territories of Arabia, Palestine, Mesopotamia, Syria and the Lebanon in the First World War. From its truncated remains Kemal Atatürk created the new Turkish state, and abolished the Sultanate (1922). The Turkish government is attempting to increase the export of carpets, which had fallen off badly because of decline in quality and high prices. The craft of knotting is encouraged and the state Sümerbank undertakes the export of the products of many of the manufactories, especially for Sparta and Hereke. It also assists the small carpet industries in outlying districts with financial loans and puts their products on the market.

Sheeps' wool, for fine pieces mixed with ten per cent of angora, is the principal material for the pile. Good silk for special pieces, jap silk for souvenir pieces, and cotton for white piles are less important, while the high price of camel hair makes its use impossible; the utilisation of synthetic fibres is also being considered. Increasing use is being made of cotton for the ground weave, though wool and goat hair (nomads) are still the standard materials.

In Izmir and Demirçi have been set up the first looms in Turkey for broadloom weaving, but they afford no competition to the hand-knotted carpets.

Turkish carpets from the thirteenth to the eighteenth centuries

The earliest known Seljuk carpets all had patterns with rows of motifs arranged in diaper (half-drops) (p. 21). The slightly later carpets with animals have quartering or rows of squares. The Ottomans were averse to representations of living creatures in art, however, and this type came to a sudden end in the fifteenth century, with its final version, the phoenix-dragon motif (p. 22). Fragments of Seljuk carpets of the fifteenth century found in Fostat by C. J. Lamm show motifs very similar to the Turcoman guls in diaper arrangement. In a fragment from Beysheshir the diaper of large gul-like medallions is overlaid by a thin lattice of squares, a device which is typical of Tekke Turcoman carpets even today. Diaper and quartering were the principal pattern elements in the designs of all Anatolian carpets except prayer rugs until the eighteenth and nineteenth centuries. Even when the patterns of Persian carpets were revolutionised in the fifteenth century (see p. 155) by stressing the centre with a medallion, in Anatolia this new idea was immediately subordinated to the old schemes.

In using the niche (mihrab) as its primary motif the prayer rug was taking over an architectural element alien to carpet design. Here religious rather than aesthetic considerations were dominant. In the mosque the richly decorated mihrab shows the worshipper the direction of Mecca, towards which he faces as he kneels, repeatedly prostrating himself, to recite the prescribed prayers (Sunnites five times, Shi'ites usually three times daily). If he prays outside the mosque he must seek a clean piece of ground. Thus it was a natural thing to spread out a mat for prayer, from which developed the easily transportable prayer rug with a pattern showing the prayer niche to the worshipper as he prays. Not all carpets designed for prayer show the niche, however. These rugs are subject to much hard wear, but a few rugs for communal prayer (saphs) of the fifteenth century, having been made for mosques, have been relatively well preserved (figs. 3 and 4). In the *saph* several niches are arranged side by side in a row or in two rows one above the other. The niches in these early examples are drawn like frames over a ground which is either continuous (fig. 3) or divided into fields (fig. 4).

Early Ottoman carpets can be divided into three principal pattern types: in the fifteenth century they had rows of squares, each containing a large octagon, a pattern which still appears on Bergamo carpets at the present day (fig. 13), or a diaper of octagons linking outlines with lozenges formed of pairs of arabesque leaves (fig. 6). This type disappears in the seventeenth century. In the sixteenth century the Ushak manufactories produced a design related, in spite of the different effect it creates, to the second group, with rows of two arabesque scroll motifs (fig. 9). This pattern, usually in yellow on a red ground, had a life of 200 years when it was eliminated by the expansion of the border, which only allowed room for one motif of the

1. **Seljuk carpet. Konya, 13th century.** 520 × 285 cm. (detail). (page 57 left above.)
Warp: W. S-plied, 2 strands, twisted, undyed.
Weft: W. 2-spun, single, dyed red, 3 shoots alternating, sinuous.
Pile: W. Z-spun, 2 strands, untwisted. Knots I.: h. 18, w. 19 = 342 per sq. dm.
Upper end: —. Lower end: —. Selvedges: —. Quality: dry, soft, flabby, coarse.
Colours: 7, *dark wine red, dugh, dark blue,* light greenish blue, light brown, ivory, dark greenish blue.

2. **Seljuk carpet, Konya, 13th century.** Fragment 125 × 226 cm. (detail). (p. 57 right above.)
Warp: W. S plied, 2 strands twisted, undyed.
Weft: W. Z-spun, single, dyed red. 2 shoots alternating, sinuous, and 3 shoots: 1 contrary to 2 and 3.
Pile: W. Z-spun, 2 strands untwisted. Knots T. I.: h. 28, w. 25 = 700 per sq. dm.
Upper end: —. Lower end: —. Selvedges: —. Quality: dry, flabby, medium thick, coarse.
Colours: 7, *dark blue, pale blue, red,* brownish yellow, light olive, rust, dark brown.

3. **Communal prayer rug (saph). Anatolia, 15th century.** 128 × 311 cm. (page 57 middle).
Warp: W. S-plied, 2 strands, twisted undyed light.
Weft: W. Z-spun, single, dyed red. 3 and 2 shoots alternating, sometimes 2. and 3. together, hamail (zig-zag on underside).
Pile: W. Z-spun, 2 strands, untwisted. Knots T. I: h. 30, w. 28 = 840 sq. dm. per Drection of work from left to right.
Upper end: remains of a W. kilim, red. Lower end: —.
Quality: hard, coarse.
Colours: *dark blue, violet,* light blue, red, ivory, some light green, yellow, light and dark brown.
Pattern: two rows each of 8 mihrabs drawn as frames over the dark blue ground. After the first pair of mihrabs the design is continued in reduced size. In the border an early form of inleilaced Kufic. In the guard stripe at the beginning, another pattern.

4. **Communal prayer rug (saph). Anatolia, 15th century.** 120 × 425 cm. (page 57 below).
Warp: W. S-plied, 2 strands, twisted, undyed light.
Weft: W. Z-spun, single, dyed red, 3 shoots alternating, sinuous.
Pile: W. Z-spun, 2 strands untwisted. Knots T. I: h. 23, w. 23 = 529 per sq. dm. Direction of work from left to right.
Upper end: —. lower end: remains of a broad W. kilim, red.
Selvedges: —. Quality: dry, coarse.
Colours: 7, *ivory, red, dark blue,* light blue, some dark green, dark brown and olive brown.
Pattern: mihrab design developed from the Kufi border (cf. drawing on p. 20) used as a frame with attached lamps and a tilted square edge ending in arrow heads, in 5 light rectangular panels. In the central mihrab the wedge right above is missing and the arrow heads round the square. The design of the octagons in the main border is a precursor of outline interlacery. Both in and outside the niches are two triangles edged with hooks along the hypotenuse, such as are still found today on Anatolian (especially Konya and Bergama) and Caucasian carpets.

ground pattern. The design of the border consisted at first of a monochrome looped ribbon pattern derived from a figure of Kufic script, later of curling cloud bands with attached stems alternating with rosettes, or of rosettes alternating with palmettes. The name of Holbein carpets given to this type is misleading in that no painting by Hans Holbein the Younger is known which represents a carpet of this kind. On the other hand there are clear depictions of this type in the paintings of Lorenzo Lotto.

The geometric patterns of Ottoman carpets long remained impervious to the new Persian patterns of the fifteenth century, in which the ground pattern is subordinated to a medallion that emphasises the centre. Then suddenly the palace or court manufactories of the sixteenth century show a style of pattern which until then had been entirely alien to Turkish carpets (fig. 151). Naturalistically drawn motifs from palmettes and rosebuds, spiral scrolls and over-emphasised frondy lanceolate leaves are characteristic of this group. But these motifs, usually in half-drop rows, are predominantly a ground pattern, while the medallions, often rather paltry, and approximating to a circular form, are laid over it either singly or again in half-drop rows, without any organic connection with the ground pattern. This type, known as Cairene, was widespread even in Europe in the sixteenth and seventeenth centuries. It is without precedent in Seljuk and early Ottoman carpets and seems to have been based by the court designers on Ottoman textile and ceramic patterns. The strong Persian influence in the pattern and the Persian knots used for the fine drawing perhaps suggest the work of knotters deported from north-west Persia. The right-spun, left-plied material, and the colours as well as the appearance of Mamluk elements in early examples prove the rightly named Cairene carpets to be products of the great Cairo manufactories. The eleven master carpet-makers ordered from Cairo with '30 cantar of coloured thread' to the Ottoman court by Sultan Murad III in 1585 can hardly have produced very much there with such a small quantity of material. They were presumably requisitioned there for one particular task.

5. Seljuk carpet. Konya, 13th century. 320 × 240 cm. (detail). (p. 59 above).
Warp: W. S-plied, 2 strands, twisted, undyed.
Weft: W. Z-spun, single, dyed red. 2 shoots contrary, sinuous.
Pile: W. Z-spun, 2 strands, untwisted. Knots T. I: b. 30 w. 28 = 840 per sq. dm.
Upper end: —. Lower end: —. Selvedges: —. Quality: dry, flabby, coarse.
Colours: 7, *medium blue, pale blue, light red, wine red,* medium brown, grey-green.

6. Holbein carpet. Anatolia, 15th—16th century. 264 × 124 cm. (p. 59 below).
Warp: W. S-plied, 2 strands, twisted, undyed light.
Weft: W. Z-spun, single, dyed red. 2 shoots alternating, sinuous. In the right half hamail four times.
Pile: W. Z-spun, 2 strands, untwisted. Knots T. I: h. 38 w. 25 = 950 sq. dm.
Upper end: —. Lower end: —. Selvedges: —. quality: dry, flabby, thin, slightly ribbed.
Colours: 7, bright *red, ivory,* light blue, dark green, rust, some olive yellow, medium blue. Brownish black outlines have fallen out.
Pattern: octagons with outline interlacery in alternate rows with lozenges formed from paired arabesque leaves. Interlaced Kufi band in the main border.

The most important manufactories of Anatolia at that time lay in the region of Ushak. That they were also known in Europe and received commissions from there is shown by the 'Lotto carpets' with European coats of arms knotted into the pattern. In Ushak also they came to terms with the new Persian patterns. The medallion now dominates in Ushak carpets as against the stylised small floral all-over pattern which becomes no more than a filling. But the medallion is generally set in half-drop rows. This is either arranged with one vertical row of medallions down the centre of the carpet and half medallions in the spaces at either side (Medallion Ushak) or by a half-drop of horizontal rows, with star-shaped medallions alternating with a rather smaller motif (Star Ushak, p. 61). Both patterns are in red on a blue ground or vice versa. The main borders have loops of cloud-band with attached stem scrolls alternating with rosettes, stylized scrolls with palmettes or an arabesque scroll with leaves like cockscombs — and these cloud-bands surround palmettes in their convolutions (p. 61). Star Ushaks are seldom longer than four metres, Medallion Ushaks may be twice as long. Both these types continued in the seventeenth and eighteenth centuries.

'White Ushaks' appeared at the same period: the 'bird' and 'badge of Tamerlane' carpets. Their structure and border patterns are of the same origin; but the carpets have a light ground and for the first time use undyed light wool for the weft instead of the red dyed wool which had hitherto been universal in Anatolia. The bird-like motifs on the carpets with a light ground (fig. 7) are geometric linear scrolls radiating in fours from a rosette and continuing the pattern with the next rosette. The second group has an endless repeat of three circles in a triangle over two waves arranged in half-drop rows. This is probably a decorative derivation from the Chinese symbol chintamani. This pattern is not limited either to carpets with a white ground or to Ushak. It appears both on red and blue grounds and in carpets of other provenances. The Turk-ve-Islam Eserleri Museum possesses an example of the first group in the format 510 × 245 cm, and of the second, one with a red ground of even larger proportions.

During these centuries the production of the smaller manufactories in other regions of Anatolia was developing, but little of it was exported. Konya and Bergamo continued the crude geometric patterns of the early Ottoman carpets, based on rows of large squares, and the peasant and nomad peoples went on knotting for their own use.

III. Ushak, early 17th century. 'Star Ushak'. 335 × 190 cm.
Warp: W. S-plied, 2 strands, twisted, undyed light.
Weft: W. Z-spun, single, dyed reddish. 2 shoots: 1. straight, 2. sinuous. Strong hamail.
Pile: W. Z-spun, 2 strands, untwisted. Knots T. II (c. 20%): h. 39, w. 26 = 1,014 per sq.dm.
Upper end: —. Lower end: —. Selvedges: —. Quality: dry, hard, thin, ribbed.
Colours: 7, *brick-geranium red, blue-black, green, yellow*, dark brown, navy blue, light blue.
Pattern: on the red ground a fragment of the continous repetition of half-drop rows of large arabesque stars and large cruciform cartouches. Filling pattern of delicate angular flower scrolls. The border has two guard stripes. The relatively wide main border has an arabesque wave scroll containing tree-like floral motifs in its interstices. These alternate regularly between red and green in contrast to the colour of the leaves of the scroll surrounding them.

In the eighteenth century the prayer rug gradually becomes the main item of production, particularly as it was also taken up in Europe at this period.

Communal prayer rugs of the seventeenth century from Ushak have the curved Persian nichearch of the elegant 'Cairene' prayer rugs. From each arch hangs a lamp. The usually blue or red ground of the niche may be covered with naturalistic flower or lanceolate leaf scrolls unconnected, with a medallion laid over them, or the place for the feet of the worshipper is marked by a single arabesque in the ground of the niche. The spandrels are filled with stylized angular scrolls in the manner of the ground pattern of the large Ushak carpets of this period. This scroll filling of the spandrels is also adopted by the early Ghiordes prayer rugs, whose curved niche arches are supported by pillars.

The niche, light in colour almost without exception, remains empty, except for the lamp which occurs on many pieces. In these Ghiordes prayer rugs of the seventeenth century cotton appears for the first time as a knotting material for white parts of the pattern, while cotton is not found in the ground weave before the eighteenth century.

The majority of the Siebenbürger or Transylvanian carpets are to be dated to the seventeenth century. They are so-called because of their frequent occurrence in the churches of this region, which was under Turkish rule from 1526 to 1699. Most of these carpets, with or without niches, must be referable to the workshops of Anatolia, since all the current Anatolian patterns of the period, including the 'bird' motif, are found on them. A striking characteristic is the frequent occurrence of rows of cartouche-like geometric stems in the main border. This type of border pattern is also characteristic of early Ladik prayer rugs whose triple arch is supported by thin pairs of columns (Column Ladik, fig. 10). In the panel above the niche there is often a series of flowers on rigid stalks with paired leaves (tulips?). These rows of flowers have given the name 'Tulip Ladik' to the eighteenth-century carpets. The niche was be now rather simplified, with a stepped arch and no pillars (fig. 21). Usually the border pattern is a tulip held in a fork of leaves, in regular alternation with a rosette.

In the eighteenth century niches become smaller, the arch angular and stepped. The pillars, reduced to hanging floral mouldings, have often disappeared altogether, or remain as the rudiments of candelabra. The coarsened spandrel and border patterns break up into single components and often become repeats of the same stylised or geometric leaf motif (p. 81).

The region of Konya not far from Ladik continues the Column Ladik in a rougher, more angular form and also uses the tulip motif. Early prayer rugs also survive from here, the pattern dominated by a speckled motif reminiscent of a light-coloured animal pelt on a darker ground.

In Kula the border is reduced to stripes (shobokli = pipe) (fig. 18) or nine identical stylised flowers are combined in the same orientation and colour into a quadrilateral, creating an effect like tiles. Strings of flowers are the favourite form of filling the niche. The mutual influences of the patterns of Kula on the one side and Ghiordes on the other were so great that their carpets can often only be recognised by points of structure. These mixtures of pattern are to be explained by the common direction under which both manufactories worked during the eighteenth century. The 'grave-yard Kulas' show a particular form of pattern for the niche: the motif, arranged in straight vertical and horizontal rows, of a little house flanked by two trees. These 'graveyard' carpets (mazarlik, turbelik) also come in fact from Ladik, Ghiordes and Kirshehir (fig. 22). The charming and peaceful Mudjur prayer rugs (p. 91) with their green, red and yellow colour harmony also divide up the border with a tile effect.

Influences from Ushak and Ghiordes can be seen in the Milas prayer rugs, with their more rustic designs related to Bergamo (p. 71). The niche has an angular construction below the arch. Carpets without niches mostly give the effect of being built up of many borders ('Striped Milas', fig. 14).

Typical of most of the Turkish prayer rugs are the rows of flower heads arranged along the inner edge of the mihrab and the multiple contour of the arch.

The wool for the warp of Anatolian carpets, right into the twentieth century, is a right-plied two-ply; for the weft it is single, with a few exceptions (especially Kula), untwisted and usually dyed; for the pile, two-ply untwisted, only very seldom single. In doubtful cases the single unplyed weft wool of Bergam carpets is the most certain diagnostic as against Kasak carpets.

Cotton has been used since the end of the seventeenth century for white knots (Turkish) and from the last third of the eighteenth century for the weft, two-ply, and later sometimes in the warp too, with two or three strands plied together.

7. Ushak or Siebenbürgen (Transylvanian), 17th—18th century. Bird carpet. 235 × 138 cm. (detail) (p. 65 left above).
Warp: W. (left spun) Z-plied, 2 strands twisted, undyed light.
Weft: W. Z-spun, single, undyed light. 2 shoots: 1. straight, 2. sinuous.
Pile: W. Z-spun, 2-ply untwisted. Knots T. II (25%): h. 52, w. 44. = 2,288 per sq. dm. Upper end: —.
    Lower end: —.
Selvedges: — no original strengthening. Quality: dry, hard, thin, ribbed.
Colours: 6, *ivory, rust red, pale blue,* olive, light olive, dark red-brown.
Pattern: the border with two guard stripes divides the central field off from the white ground. It is covered with the 'bird' pattern; this is a continuous repetition of a flower which has been geometricized to a rectangle, to which 4 bird-like geometric scrolls have been attached radially, in alternate rows with a stylized rectangular flower.

8. Ushak, 17th century. Badge of Tamerlane 6 (detail) (p. 65 right above).
Pattern: the chintamani in half-drop rows on a light ground. In the main border a double scroll with arabesque cloud band loops and stylised flowers.

9. 'Lotto Carpet'. Ushak, 16th—17th century. 215 × 133 cm. (p. 65 below).
Warp: W. S-plied, 2 strands, twisted, undyed, light.
Weft: W. Z-spun, single dyed red. 2 shoots alternating sinuous. Hamail in both halves.
Pile: W. Z spun, 2 strands untwisted. Knots T. I: h. 34, w. 30 = 1,020 per sq. dm.
Upper end: 2 cm remaining of a wool kilim, light blue.
Lower end: as upper end: —. Selvedges: W. shirazi blue round 4 warp threads.
Quality: dry, not quite soft and thin, slightly ribbed.
Colours: 5, *dark rust red, olive yellow, cornflower blue,* ivory, blue-red, dark brown outlines rather corroded.
Pattern: yellow, arabesque, cruciform lozenges and drapes, octagons in alternate rows on a red ground.

Turkish carpets of the nineteenth and twentieth centuries

Istanbul became Turkish in 1453. The Turk-ve-Islam Eserleri Museum preserves the most important collection of Seljuk and early Ottoman carpets. Istanbul developed no tradition in carpet production. In the seventeenth century there was a knotting school in a madrasah near the Fatih mosque, which made among other things the so-called Polish carpets with gold and silver brocading. In the nineteenth century an orphanage produced good quality carpets of no individual character after Persian and Ottoman models: the Istanbul Darüliçise (fig. 11). In the early twentieth century Zareh Penyamin, who had been a designer in the Hereke manufactory, opened a workshop in the Top Kapu quarter, which functioned until about twenty years ago. His most famous carpets were an 'Isfahan' of silk, forty metres square, with 10,000 knots per square dm., and a silk prayer rug with about 40,000 knots per square dm., which was clipped so short that it could be folded together like a scarf and put in the pocket. At the same time Nahabet Keçiçyan from Kayseri maintained a workshop in the Kum Kapu quarter. He had given up his workshop in Panderma and came to make Panderma carpets in Istanbul.

The story of Nahabet's great wager is still told in the Istanbul bazaar: he declared to a group of friends that he could imitate an antique carpet and give it an antique patina so skilfully that even the most experienced connoisseur would not see that it was a fake. So as to be sure of winning the bet against Nahabet his friends waited, after the carpet was finished, for the visit of an old American dealer who came every year to Istanbul to buy antique carpets, and was considered to be the greatest of connoisseurs. He came, gave the piece a lengthy examination, and bought it. Nahabet won his bet. He thereupon went and explained to his client and returned him the purchase money.

The manufactory of HEREKE, sixty kilometres from Istanbul on the Gulf of Izmit, was founded in 1844. Its present building was put up at the order of Sultan Abdul Hamid for the Ottoman manufactory. It developed no style of its own. Looking through the pages of their old pattern books, one can see how they imitated everything good and expensive be it from Turkestan, Persia or Ghiordes. On a visit to the factory we saw on the looms two 'Bird carpets' (wool on a cotton warp) copying an historical model and a small silk carpet with a count of 10,000 knots per square dm. All formats, at a count of about 3,600, 4,900, 6,400 and 10,000, are knotted carefully and with good materials. In the pavilion which was erected beside the manufactory for the visit of Kaiser Wilhelm II lie large carpets with Persian patterns bearing the sign of Hereke (see Glossary).

Carpets of no particular note, which show the inscription 'Imrale' at the upper end, come from the prison on Imrali island on the Sea of Marmora.

BRUSSA (now Bursa) is the centre of Turkish silk production. 'Brussa carpets' receive laudatory mention as early as 1474. The more modern silk and jap silk carpets known under this name do not come from Brussa, where there is no carpet industry.

In PANDERMA (now Bandirma) on the Sea of Marmora, copies of ancient Turkish and Persian patterns were produced, mostly with prayer niches, in good and less

10. Ladik, 17th century. 'Column Ladik'. Prayer rug (namazlik). Now c. 162 × 125 cm.

Warp: W. S-plied, 2 strands, twisted, undyed light.

Weft: W. Z-spun, single, undyed light. 2 shoots: 1. straight, 2. sinuous.

Pile: W. Z-spun, 2 strands, untwisted. Knots T. II: h. 40, w. 28 = 1120 per sq.dm. Direction of work against that of the pattern.

Upper end: —. Lower end: —. Selvedges: —.

Quality: now dry, almost thin, ribbed.

Colours: 6, *Terracotta, ivory, light blue, olive-yellow* light brown, black, brown fallen out.

Pattern: in the red central field two twin columns support the triple arch of the mihrab. In the light blue spandrel are large pairs of leaves. In the broad main border hexagonal cartouches with rosettes flanked by arabesque scrolls. Triangular chequers between the cartouches.

11. Istanbul Darülaçise, 19th-century. Prayer rug (namazlik) 156×115 cm.

Warp: C. S-pied, 3 strands, twisted, undyed white.

Weft: C. S-plied, 3 strands, twisted, dyed reddish, violet and blue and undyed light. 2 to 4 shoots, either 1. straight, 2. sinuous or 1. and 2. straight, 3. and 4. sinuous. Direction of work contrary to that of mihrab.

Pile: W. Z-spun, 1 and 2 strands, untwisted, silk Z-spun, white. Knots T. III (up to 50°): h. 50, w. 51 = 2,550 per sq. dm.

Upper end: —. Lower end: 1 cm. wool kilim red remaining.

Selvedges: W. shirazi red 3 cord. Thick shirazi over it not original.

Quality: Like thick velvet, fine, granular.

Colours: 9, *brown-red, light olive, rust,* violet, yellow-brown, olive-brown, pale greenish blue, cream, some orange-yellow.

Pattern: in the light olive central field a red mihrab with curved arch, filled by a flower lamp from which a second lamp hangs down on a long chain. Symmetrical to this an elegant pair of rudimentary columns and a pair of ewers. A broad main border patterned with the 'candlestick' motif.

68

12. Yaçebedir (formerly Yahçibei, Bergama district). 'Charcoal' carpet, 19th century. (126—139)
132×104 cm. W a r p: W. S-plied, 2 strands, twisted, undyed light. W e f t: W. Z-spun, single, dyed red,
2—5 shoots alternating, sinuous. Double shoots, and in the archway of the mihrab up to five shoots carried
forward and back from the sides for about 30 cm. P i l e: W. Z-spun, two strands, untwisted; cotton for
some pink knots. K n o t s: T. I and T. II (in the left half up to about 20°): h. 46, w. 28 = 1,288 per sq. dm.
U p p e r e n d: 1—3 shoots remaining of a red wool kilim. L o w e r e n d: as upper end. S e l v e d g e s: w.
shirazi blue 4 cord. Q u a l i t y: smooth, almost thin, hard, granular. C o l o u r s: 11, *dark red, navy blue,
white,* olive brown, olive, black, some light yellow-green, light olive-green, blue green and olive-yellow,
very little pink. P a t t e r n: a blue frame divides off the central field from the over-all red ground. The
squat blue mihrab stands in the central field above a broad panel. It has a small-stepped arch ending in a
V hook. The niche is filled with stars with added stems, V hooks and flower heads. The border has
guard stripes, the main border has toothed leaves of different colours in irregular order.

69

good quality silk, wool or wool and cotton mixture, nearly always on a cotton ground weave. 'Pandermas' are often artificially aged by rubbing down with bricks and by darning. Many of these 'antique' carpets can be recognised by the grey cotton shirazi. The production of Panderma was smaller than is generally supposed. The 'Silk Panderma' comes mostly from Kayseri, where the best quality range is styled 'Panderma'.

The term BERGAMO includes rustic carpets from the wide area spreading from the east to the north-west of the town — classical Pergamon. They are of good wool on a wool or goat hair ground weave with a red dyed weft, and coarse to medium fine knotted. They reach sizes approximately square of three to four square metres. Pieces from Canakkale, ancient Troy on the Dardanelles, are often larger. The patterns are geometric and sometimes reminiscent of Caucasian carpets from the Kasak-Gendje area. Of the classic pieces the finer were made in Ezine (fig. 13), the thicker in Avonya near the Dardanelles. Good smallish pieces with a rustic charm come mostly from Soma, forty kilometres east of Bergamo. The Yaçebedir, a more sombre type with lovely blue black and dark red, is also knotted by nomads (fig. 12). Others of the same style are called Yün Yürük (wool yürük) after the nomad people, or Balikeshir after the town situated in the north of their region of origin. The red used for the pile of these pieces sometimes has the peculiarity of corroding the wool so that the pile has a relief effect. Particularly original are the magic signs knotted into the upper edge by the peasants and nomads against the evil eye. In Bergamo, which now lies on the asphalt European road no. 104, no carpets are made. Its ethnological museum contains nothing of importance.

The district of SMYRNA (now Izmir) was still carrying on the traditional patterns of 'Cairene' carpets in the nineteenth century. Its rapid degeneration was described on p. 10.

At the turn of the century they attempted to disguise the loose knotting by the over-long, unusually flat pile. Knotting is no longer practised in Smyrna. Machine-woven wares come from there.

IV. Milas, c. 1800. **Prayer rug** = namazlik (250—256) 253 × 157 (154—160) cm.
Warp: W. S-plied, 2 strands, twisted, undyed light.
Weft: W. Z-spun, single, dyed red. 2—4 shoots alternating, sinuous.
Pile: W. Z-spun, 2 strands, untwisted. Knots T. I: h. 24, w. 26 = 624 per sq.dm.
Upper end: remains of a red W. shirazi.
Lower end: not original. Selvedges: not original.
Quality: soft, thick, coarse.
Colours: *Olive-yellow, brick red, ivory,* navy-blue, violet, black-brown, dark brown, pale blue-green.
Pattern: the ten-fold border leaves only a narrow central field free; ratio of border to central field: 106:
   51. The mihrab with typical Milas outline hardly reaches the upper third of the central field, the large remaining area is patterned symmetrically with horizontal rows of leaves.

In MILAS and its surroundings yellow is preferred as the second colour with red instead of the blue usual in Anatolia. The light central field is long and narrow in relation to the border which encroaches on it, and the niche inside it is unusually short. The niche has an angular waist beneath an arch which is not stepped (p. 71). If there is no niche, the central field is divided up into stripes, unless it holds a simple stepped medallion, or it is reduced to a narrow panel by an exceptionally wide border of many stripes.

Three types are distinguished: Ada-Milas (= island milas, named after the off-shore island), Tahtaçi Milas (= wood milas), and Milas Karaova (a village 30 km. south-west of Milas). Milas carpets are coarse to medium fine and worked entirely in wool. The wool of the weft is nearly always dyed red. The kilims are often wide, red like Bergamo carpets, or yellow. The formats are not large and go up to about 300 × 200 cm.

At the south-west tip of Anatolia lies MEGRI (now Fethiye) on the site of ancient Telmessos. Megri carpets, also called Rhodes carpets (after the off-shore island) are mostly small prayer rugs with a central field either holding a niche — often with a lamp, and with candelabra standing at the base of the field — or divided into two almost always different fields along the length, sometimes in the ground colour (fig. 15). These fields may be waisted in several places by protruding wedge shapes, and each field has a different geometric floral design; in one field it is always denticulated lozenges arranged along a bar. Megri carpets are all worked entirely in wool, coarse to medium fine. Goat hair sometimes occurs in the ground-weave. The weft is dyed red.

GHIORDES, about 200 kilometres north-east of Izmir, has given its name to the Turkish knot which is often called the Ghiordes knot. Its production consists almost exclusively of prayer rugs. The arch became angled in the eighteenth century, and the borders, spandrels and panels were increased in importance, reducing the prayer niche itself to little more than half the length of the narrow central field (p. 81). The remaining central field above the arch is filled with rows of geometric leaves. The broad bands of the border have floral patterns and the rows of gigantic carnations typical of Ghiordes. The shobokli (= pipe) border of Kula carpets (fig. 18) that splits up the border into narrow stripes, was also adopted. In the carpets with an angular medallion (fig. 16), a pattern that could equally well come from Kula, the border again is disproportionate to the remaining central field. The broad angular wave band of the border, taken over from the kis-Ghiordes, encloses stylized flowers in its loops. In the small square kis Ghiordes (fig. 17), these spaces alternate in colour. These simple kis Ghiordes, faithful for two generations to their five-colour patterns, have a lasting charm no less than the other Ghiordes carpets with their cooler colour schemes. The pile is of wool, rarely of silk. Cotton is usually chosen for white knots. The gauge ranges from medium fine to very fine (silk). In the eighteenth century cotton was increasingly adopted for the weft; it is rarer in the warp.

The new Ghiordes carpets appearing on the market today, some with the early pillared niches, are mostly not from Ghiordes, which from the turn of the century has produced only mediocre wares.

13. Ezine, Bergamo district. Early 19th century. (144—153) 149×153 cm.

Warp: W. S-plied, 2 strands, twisted, undyed light.

Weft: W. Z-spun, single, red dyed. 2—4 shoots alternating, sinuous.

Pile: W. Z-spun, 2 strands, untwisted. Knots T. I: h. 40, w. 22 = 880 per sq. dm.

Upper end: —. Lower end: —. Selvedges: —.

Quality: soft, medium thick.

Colours: 7, *ivory, rust red, dark blue,* navy blue, faded purple, light brown-red, dark brown.

Pattern: the meander-like guard strike divides up the carpet into central field and border, both with the same red ground. In the central field two heavy stars composed of cross beams in white octagons, following an old pattern scheme of the 15th century; the horizontal border running between the two octagons which created a square lattice has been omitted here. Some of the hooked motifs on the crossed beams are reminiscent of the 'phoenix-dragon' motif.

14. Milas-Karaova. 'Striped Milas'. 2nd quarter 19th century. c. 150×118 cm.

Warp: W. S-plied, 2 strands, twisted, undyed light, and dark brown.

Weft: W. Z-spun, single, dyed red. 2 shoots alternating, sinuous.

Pile: W. Z-spun, two strands, untwisted. Knots: T. I: h. 36, w. 30 = 1,080 per sq.dm.

Upper end: —. Lower end: —.

Selvedges: W. shirazi light red-brown 3 cord.

Quality: dry, thin, coarse, granular.

Pattern: the pattern consists entirely of border, except for the narrow yellow panel with geometric stem which is all that remains of the central field. The design of the main border shows an angular stem derived from early Ushaks and often used later in Milas and Bergama, with cock's-comb-like arabesque attachments.

15. Megri (also called 'Rhodes carpet'). 19th century. (169—173) 171 × 128 (125—131) cm.

Warp: W. S-plied, 2 strands, twisted, undyed light and light with dark brown.

Weft: W. Z-spun, single, dyed red. 2 shoots alternating, sinuous.

Pile: W. Z-spun, 2 strands, untwisted. Kots: T. I: h. 28, w. 24 = 672 per sq. dm.

Upper end: a few shoots remaining of a blue W. kilim.

Lower end: as upper end.

Selvedges: W. shirazi blue-red round 8 warp threads.

Quality: soft, fleecy, thick, rather coarse.

Colours: 8, *dark blue, red, orange, white,* light blue, green, dark brown, some rust-brown.

Pattern: In the yellow central field two large elongated blue octagons, each with three indentations along
  either side. The left hand one has serrated lozenges joined by a serrated band, the right hand lozenges and
  rosettes. In the rest of the central field, above the dark brown panel, is a survival of an old Seljuk motif:
  a geometric element facing inwards alternating top and bottom.

16. Ghiordes. 2nd quarter 19th century. c. 200 × 106 cm.
(above).

Warp: W. S-plied, 2 strands, twisted, undyed.

Weft: Cotton. Z-spun, single, undyed. 2—5 shoots:
1. straight, 2. sinuous or 1. and 2. straight, 3.—5. sinuous.
hamail at the corners of the ground.

Pile: W. Z-spun, single. Cotton. Z-spun, 2 strands,
untwisted, white. Knots: T. II (c 20°): h. 36, w.
26 = 936 per sq. dm.

Upper end: —. Lower end: —. Selvedges: W.
shirazi not original.

Quality: dry, medium firm, thin, slightly ribbed.

Colours: 12, *navy blue, cream, pale green,* green-blue,
light blue, brown-black, light brown, red-brown,
dark brown, blue-green, olive-green, olive-yellow.

Pattern: from the point of view of pattern this
Ghiordes could be a Kula. In the relatively narrow
olive-green central field (borders : central field =
62 : 44) lies a blue centre piece. Carpets with this
arrangement are sometimes called 'Prayer rugs with
opposed niches' (= odshalyk). The corners are
decorated with the 'sinekli' (= 'fly') pattern. In both
panels a large arabesque cloud band, adopted from
Ushak carpets of the 16th—18th century.

17. Ghiordes, late 18th century. Kiss-Ghiordes (104—110) 107 × 109 cm. (below).

Warp: W. S-plied, two strands, twisted, undyed light.

Weft: C. S-plied, 2 strands, slightly twisted, undyed light. 2 shoots alternating sinuous.

Pile: W. Z-spun, single. Knots T. I: h. 48, w. 33 = 1584 per sq. dm.

Upper end: —. Lower end: —. Selvedges: silk shirazi not original.

Quality: now thin, flabby.

Colours: 5, *cream, navy blue, blue-green, red,* dark brown.

Pattern: there is a small blue-green central field framed by the broad border, containing a centre piece like
a flayed animal pelt and on it a horizontally placed medallion. From the upper and lower end a lamp hangs
into the centre piece. The main border contains a light zig-zag formed by hooked lozenges alternately
based on the outer and inner edges. 6 guard stripes.

18. Kula, c. 1800. Prayer rug. c. 179 × 126 cm. In structure a so-called Kendirli-Kula.

Warp: W. S-plied, 2 strands, twisted, undyed light.

Weft: W. S-plied, 2 strands, twisted, undyed light and dark brown. W. Z-spun, single, dyed, olive-yellow.
  2 shoots: 1. straight, 2. sinuous. Some 2–4 strand shoots straight (Kendirli). Additional thick cotton
  shoots introduced up to 40 cms. inwards and back from the sides. Hamail occurs at one place.

Pile: W. Z-spun, single. Knots G. II (ca. 30°): h. 32, w. 28 = 896 per sq. dm. Direction of work contrary to
  that of mihrab.

Upper end: up to 1.5 cm. remaining of a W. kilim, olive green. Lower end: as upper end, then warp
  threads looped and twisted. Selvedges: bright coloured W. shirazi 2 cord, only partly original.

Quality: soft, medium firm, coarsely ribbed.

Colours: 9, *apricot brown, light blue, white,* light blue-green, green, pale blue, olive-yellow, sand, brown-black.

Pattern: two floral bands fill the apricot brown mihrab, the arch of the mihrab is flattened and gently
  stepped. The rest of the light blue central field has diagonal rows of leaves. The main border is itself divided
  up into stripes (shobokli), the two guard stripes have the 'alligator scroll', making nine bands of border.

19. Demirçi, 19th century. 'Cömürçi-Kula', prayer rug. (156—164) 160×124 (122—126) cm.
Warp: W. S-plied, 2 strands, twisted, undyed light.
Weft: W. Z-spun, single, undyed light in the lower sixth and dyed purple to brownish. In light W. 1 shoot straight with 2 shoots sinuous, in dyed W. 2 shoots straight with 3 shoots sinuous.
Pile: W. Z-spun, single. Knots T. I and T. II (10°): h. 38, w. 32 = 1216 per sq. dm.
Upper end: remains of a W. kilim purple. Lower end: remains of a W. kilim, brown, blue-green.
Selvedges: W. shirazi 3 cord.
Quality: soft, thick, smooth.
Colours: 15, *black, bright blue, green, cherry red,* pea-green, blue, dark blue, white, some green, dark olive, cinnamon, dark brown, pink, dark green, purple.
Pattern: the shallow arched mihrab is drawn into the black ground by a band rolled up at the base. A flowering tree fills the niche. The main border (5 guard stripes) has a row of large flowers called 'Apple' in Ghiordes (carnation?).

KULA, about seventy kilometres south-east of Ghiordes, and the surrounding district has produced prayer rugs in large numbers. Their colour scheme is very discreet. Large ropes of flowers on a blue, red or apricot brown ground are preferred to decorate the niche, which has a flat arch, often slightly stepped (fig. 18), unless it is covered with an endless repeat of a very small stylised flower (sinekli pattern). In the niche of the 'graveyard' Kula the little house flanked by two different trees of the Mazarli (= grave) motif is repeated. Mazarlik, or graveyard carpets are also made in Ladik, Ghiordes and Kirshehir (fig. 22).

The strings of flowers are a development of the floral pillars which support the more finely drawn and higher arch in the pattern of the eighteenth century Kula carpet. The spandrels were even then filled with flower sprays, and the borders with continuous palmette scrolls. By 1800 the borders were being broken down into stripes (fig. 18) or divided up like tiles. This tile effect is created entirely by the colour and alignment, similar motifs being arranged in squares, without any square outlines.

Pile and ground-weave are of wool. The count is coarse to medium fine. Unlike other Turkish carpets, the weft of old Kulas is often a twisted two-ply. Many Kula have wefts three and four strands thick at irregular intervals, and are called Kendirli Kula; if these wefts are less thick they are called Yaremkendirli.

Demirçi prayer mats (fifty kilometres north-east of Ghiordes) combined the patterns of Ghiordes and Kula (fig. 19). They are harder than Ghiordes and Kula carpets in tone. In structure they are closer to Kula. Today Demirçi produces very coarse carpets of Smyrna type and machine-woven wares.

Simav also produces new carpets of poor quality.

USHAK and district was the home of the most famous manufactories of the Ottoman period until the middle of the eighteenth century. None of the greatness of Ushak's past is to be found in the wares mass-produced there today. They are mostly coarse, with Persian patterns.

The old Ushaks are entirely of wool and of high quality, the counts being from coarse to medium fine. Classical Ushak carpets (p. 61) already show a peculiarity

V. Ghiordes, late 18th century. Prayer rug (namazlik) 158 × 125 cm. (120—131).
Warp: W. S-plied, 2 strands, twisted, undyed light.
Weft: C. Z-spun, 2 strands, untwisted, undyed. 2 shoots alternating sinuous. Strong hamail.
Pile: W. and C. (white) Z-spun, 2 strands, untwisted. Knots T. I/II: h. 48, w. 34 = 1,632 per sq. dm. Direction of work contrary to that of mihrab.
Upper end: —. Lower end: —. Selvedges: —.
Quality: dry, thin, granular.
Colours: 5, red, white, olive-yellow, black-brown, olive-grey.
Pattern: narrow central field (side borders : central field = 3 : 2) with squat olive-yellow mihrab. At its base opposed arabesque flowers. In the spandrels 'yaprak' (= leaf of cinar tree) in rows. Both panels dominated by a heavy arabesque cloud band. Kula floral band in the main border. Seven guard stripes, two of which have the large flower called 'apple' motif.

in the ground-weave which appears later in many Anatolian carpets, including smaller ones, particularly in Kula and Ghiordes: the so-called *hamail*. At the back of the carpet this appears as a diagonal line in alternating directions. It is brought about because the wefts are not taken right across the breadth of the carpet but return from the centre, staggering the return at each row so as not to make a slit along the length. This curious proceeding was not chosen to make it easier to work out the design or to make the carpet lie better on the ground, but so that a knotter who worked quickly was not held up by a slower workmate and did not need to wait for her before putting in the next weft thread.

SPARTA (now Isparta) and Burdur and the surrounding district now form the centre of Turkish carpet production. In contrast with the rest of Turkey the Sehna knot is used in this region, though it certainly is not really necessary for the long-piled wares produced by the metre or for the thick and coarse 'Smyrna' carpets. They will make any pattern to order in any size, even the very largest. Many picture carpets also come from Isparta. Carpets are made in the prison in Isparta. Only some of them are marked C. E. (abbreviation for Cezaevi = prison).

From Cal come some old rather coarse column prayer rugs.

Doçemealti (south of Isparta, near the Bay of Antalya) is known for good woollen carpets, dark in colour.

In Eskishehir (a hundred and fifty kilometres south-east of Bursa) interesting carpets used to be made. Then they went over to inferior-quality copying of Persian and Chinese patterns.

The Machliç carpets, called after the town of Mihaliçcik (ninety kilometres east of Eskishehir) are better. The name is also given in Turkey to the carpets, known in Europe as Tuzla prayer rugs, which come from the villages and nomads of the broad region round the Lake of Tuzla. They have a characteristic large white octagon in the wide panel above the mihrab.

KONYA had the oldest tradition of hand-knotting in Anatolia. The great Seljuk carpets were made there and some of those from the early Ottoman period with geometric patterns that continued almost unchanged for centuries. Its museum preserves important pieces from both periods. Distinctions are made according to the villages, which may be anything up to ninety kilometres from Konya; there are Karapinar, Davac, Obruk and Tashpinar Konyas. The Konya Ladik reproduces Ladik patterns in more sombre colours. From the eighteenth century there are prayer rugs with a pattern reminiscent of a brindled animal pelt. The work reproduced in fig. 20, which is a peasant product for home consumption, may come from this large region. Old Konya carpets often have an additional band in the border at the upper and lower ends with a motif rather like a small gabled house placed separately over the whole width of the carpet. The connexion of this edging motif with that still used in western Turkestan in the nineteenth century in the Kisil Ayak (cf. fig. 112) should not go unnoticed. The weft is dyed red, though in peasant pieces it is also made of undyed brown wool or goat hair. The count is medium fine. Konya and the province of Karaman are famous for their beautiful Kelims. Although Kelims were woven in all parts of Anatolia they were for a long time all called Karamani. The

20. Konya, 18th century. Konya-Karapinar. 217 × 102 (97—107) cm.

Warp: W. S-plied, 2 strands, twisted, undyed light.

Weft: W. Z-spun, single, undyed dark brown. 2—4 shoots alternating sinuous.

Pile: W. Z-plied, 2 strands, untwisted. Knots T. I: h. 31, w. 31 = 961 per sq. dm.

Upper end: —. Lower end: —. Selvedges: —.

Quality: soft, thin.

Colours: 11, *terracotta, sand, dark blue,* light blue, green-blue, yellow-green, blue-green, white, dark brown, cinnabar red, dark purple-brown.

Pattern: red central field with asymmetrical arrangement of 4 geometric stems like large birds in flight. This is a characteristic motif in the border of early Ghiordes carpets, and in Turkey is called 'kafale' (= head) pattern. The main border is sand colour with quatrefoil rosettes on a thin straight stem.

84

21. Ladik, dated 1771. Prayer rug. 'Tulip Ladik'. 187 × 113 cm.

Warp: W. S-plied, 2 strand, twisted, undyed light.

Weft: W. Z-spun, single, undyed brown.

Pile: W. Z-spun, 2 strands, untwisted. Knots T. II (25°): h. 52, w. 32 = 1,664 per sq. dm.

Upper end: W. kilim red. Lower end: as upper end. Selvedges: W. shirazi red 2 cord.

Quality: dry, almost thin, ribbed.

Colours: 2, *red, dark blue, olive-yellow, green-blue,* light blue, ivory, black-brown, pale violet, vermilion.

Pattern: the typical pattern of the 'Tulip Ladik': the red mihrab lies in the relatively narrow central field.
It has a six-stepped arch, ending in a double hook, bearing the inscription 'Tarih sene 1185' (= date year
1185). Geometric leaves and flowers in the green-blue spandrels. An almost square panel has five lilies
hanging from three inverted arches from a line of niches. The dark blue main border has geometric flowers
alternating regularly with a tulip between a rectangular fork of leaves.

best are the prayer (fig. 23) and kis-Kelims (fig. 27). In the kis-Kelims intended for their dowry the girls sometimes weave parts of the pattern in silver thread. Today the province of Karaman produces carpets commercially.

LADIK liked stronger colours than Ghiordes or Kula. Strong blue and red are the main colours. Carpets other than prayer rugs are rare. Instead of the three-arched niche, supported by graceful pairs of pillars, of the 'Column Ladik', appeared the single, usually stepped, arch frequently diminished in size by the relatively wider border. Sometimes it has a second smaller niche drawn inside it. The tulips — and other flowers too — facing either up or down above or below the mihrab have thin straight stalks with paired leaves. The pile and ground-weave are of the best wool, apart from the extremely rare occurrence of cotton for the warp. The weft is dyed red. The count is medium fine to fine (figs. 10 and 21).

Nigde, about two hundred kilometres east of Konya, produces many good commercial wares. The arches of the prayer rugs are steep and have large steps.

In Bor near Nigde there was a Greek school of knotting which went on into the twentieth century. They imitated mainly early Ladik, Ghiordes and Kula prayer rugs. The rugs all have the name Bor and a number knotted into the upper end.

Aksaray (Ak-Serail), known in the Middle Ages for its fine carpets, has not produced any for a long time.

KIRSHEHIR (a hundred and eighty kilometres south-east of Ankara) has a tradition of carpet production. The arch of the prayer rugs often ends in a little crest. The drawing of the mihrab is often no more than a frame on a green, white or more rarely a yellow ground. A large proportion of the 'Medjid' (Mejidieh) carpets named after the Sultan Abd el Madyid (1839—61) was produced in Kirshehir. Usually they have loose floral patterns influenced by the European roccoco, on a white ground. They were also popular in Ghiordes and Kula. Fig. 22 shows a Kirshehir graveyard carpet (mazarlik). Cherry red and grass green are noticeable in the colour scheme of Kirshehirs. In more recent Kirshehir carpets these colours are often too harsh. Pile and ground-weave are of wool. The weft is usually red, but sometimes yellow or greenish. The count is medium fine.

The prayer rugs from MUDJUR (Muçur) have the richest range of colours of all Turkish prayer rugs (p. 91). Eleven or thirteen colours are no rarity in the older pieces. Bright red, pea green, olive-yellow and light blue are dominant. Usually the niche is plain with multifold outlines ending in a closely stepped arch with a crest. This crest reappears in rows as the filling of the panel above the arch. The main band of the broad border is divided into tiles bearing star rosettes geometricised into lozenges. The carpets are nearly square, the pile is of wool with a rich sheen. The count is medium fine. The ground-weave is wool and the weft dyed red.

KAYSERI (Caeseria) in central Anatolia has been known since the end of the nineteenth century for the large quantities of silk (mainly jap silk) carpets which it produces for export in sizes up to 300 × 200 cm. The best quality bore the designation Panderma. Old Anatolian and Persian patterns were copied. It has never developed a style of its own. Among the light colours a pistachio green is the most remarkable. The Kayseri region also produces woollen carpets.

22. Kirshehir, 19th century. 'Graveyard carpet' = **mazarlik.** (161—165) 163 × 109 (106—112) cm.
Warp: W. S-plied, 2 strands, twisted, undyed light.
Weft: W. Z-spun, single, dyed red. 2 shoots alternating sinuous. Hamail.
Pile: W. Z-spun, 2 strands, untwisted. Knots T. I: h. 42, w. 28 = 1,176 per sq.dm.
Upper end: c. 2 cm. W. kilim, grey-olive.
Lower end: c. 1 cm. W. kilim, yellow-olive.
Selvedges: W. shirazi grey-olive and yellow-olive 2 cord.
Quality: soft, medium firm, dry.
Colours: 8, *cherry red, bright blue-green,* yellow, white, brown-black, purple, geranium-red, yellow-olive.
Pattern: in the red mihrab a pale blue-green band, turned up at the bottom, containing geometric twining
 stem and flower heads encloses the graveyard motif (mäzarli), three times repeated vertically. In the
 spandrels and in the innermost of the 5 guard stripes a carnation is repeated in side view. In the other two
 principal stripes of the border S-scrolls or fragmented geometric stems.

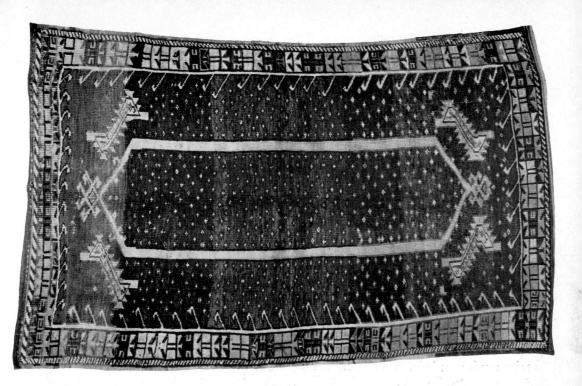

23. Konya-Obruk, 19th century. Prayer kelim. 173×120 (116—124) cm. (p. 88).
Warp: W. S-plied, 2 strands, twisted, undyed light grey. 50 threads per dm.
Weft: W. Z-spun, single, and S-plied 3 strands, slightly twisted (white). 100 threads per dm.
Upper end: 4 cm. added W. kilim dark red-brown, the warp threads originally looped and twisted, knotted into a fringe in tens. Lower end: as upper end.
Selvedges: no strengthening. The shoots of the brown parts of the pattern were not led round the outermost warp threads, so that these remain visible here.
Colours: 9, *red, blue-green, white,* medium blue, light blue, olive-yellow, olive-green, purple, dark olive-brown.
Pattern: the red mihrab is drawn into the green central field with a zig-zag band. It has a steep arch crested with hooks, and crowned by a large tree composed of volute calyxes superimposed. A similar tree in each spandrel. Within the mihrab linear fish-bone stems; on the central one 2 large rosettes. The main border is red, with geometricised hexagon scrolls. Most outlines are indented so as to keep the slits engendered by the kelim technique as small as possible. 3 guard stripes.

24. Sivas, 19—20th century. 'Village Sivas'. (147—157) 152×96 (93—99) cm. (above).
Warp: W. S-plied, 2 strands, twisted, undyed light.
Weft: W. Z-spun, single, undyed light to dark brown. 2 shoots alternating sinuous.
Pile: W. Z-plied, 2 strands, untwisted. Knots T. I: h. 48, w. 23 = 1,104 per sq. dm. Upper end: W. kilim light olive, orange, red, dark brown turned down underneath and sewn.
Lower end: as upper end, but only light olive, red.
Selvedges: W. shirazi coloured, 4 cord.
Quality: soft, fleshy, thick, smooth.
Colours: 7, *wine red, yellow,* pale green, dark brown, purple, orange, white.
Pattern: central field is red, enclosed in a hooked band. On it a frame with arches either end, ending in a hooked lozenge and flanked by a pair of broad geometric leaf scrolls. The border is only a narrow band with a fragmented geometric scroll.

Outside Kayseri itself the most important production centres are Bünyan (for fine quality), Inçesu and Ürgüp. Very handsome runners used formerly to come from Inçesu, which now produces the coarser Kayseri quality. From Yahyali (eighty kilometres south of Kayseri) comes one of the most felicitous examples of modern Turkish carpets (fig. 26). The quiet colours of its good wool are still partially obtained with vegetables dyes.

The carpets from SIVAS (four hundred kilometres east of Ankara) must be divided into 'Manufactory' and 'Village' sivas. The manufactories produce the larger carpets up to formats of 600 × 400 cm. They look Persian in design and fabrication. They may be excellently made and in this case are difficult to distinguish from Persian carpets. Carpets with the inscription 'Sivas C. E.' (abbreviation for Cezaevi [= prison]), and a number near the top end are the work of prisoners.

The sivas from the villages (fig. 24) has a rustic and geometric pattern. Wine-red is dominant. The wool of the thick pile is of very good quality, the count is medium fine. The ground-weave is of wool. Goat hair is sometimes used in combination.

Carpets from Zara, seventy kilometres east of Sivas, are similar to these.

The nomads in the extensive region round Sivas make the Kurd sivas. Its patterns are sometimes based on the Kirshehir mazarlik. Hence it sometimes happens that the misunderstood 'graveyard' pattern is knotted in upside down. A rather unattractive artificial orange-yellow often appears in the borders. The coarse ground-weave contains much goat hair.

VI. Mudjur (Muçur), early 19th century. Prayer rug (namazlik). 156 × 135 (132—138) cm. (page 91).
Warp: W. S-plied, 2 strands, twisted, undyed light.
Weft: W. Z-spun, single, dyed red, occasionally dark brown. 2 shoots alternating sinuous, sometimes 3—4 shoots alternating—and round 2 warp threads each—sinuous.
Pile: W. Z-spun, single and 2 strands, untwisted. Knots T. I: h. 38, w. 30 = 1,140 per sq. dm. Direction of work contrary to mihrab.
Upper end: —. Lower end: —. Selvedges: W. shirazi 3 cord.
Quality: Now soft, flabby, thin, smooth.
Colours: 13, *terracotta, light blue, olive-green, yellow*, bright red, medium blue, pale blue, pea-green, yellow-brown, purple, black, white, dark brown.
Pattern: red mihrab with four-fold outline and 7-stepped arch with small crest. It is empty apart from flower heads protruding inwards from the outline and a hooked V in the crest. Typical Mudyur ewers in the spandrels. In the panel the 'ainale' (= mirror) pattern, a row of crests as over the arch. Main border with 5 guard stripes is divided into tiles with star rosettes on lozenges.

Egin produces carpets with Persian patterns. Maden has become known for its small carpets of no particular note.

Orfa, near the Syrian border, produced among other carpets the 'Urfa Set' at the turn of the century. This meant a set of one broad and two similar narrow carpets, all of the same length and the same pattern (usually shiraz and boteh).

From Kars, close to the Russian frontier, come carpets of both good and inferior quality with Caucasian patterns in vegetable and synthetic dyes.

YURUK means pastoral nomad. The nomads and semi-nomads of Anatolia have been knotting for many generations. For them the prime importance of a carpet is that it should be a good insulator against the cold. For this reason their carpets are thicker than those of domestic and workshop fabrication. Scattered about in the nomad pieces, even in prayer rugs, one finds longer tufts of wool or hair knotted in against the evil eye, and also now and again glass beads knotted into the kilims.

The term Yuruk applies to all Anatolian nomad carpets. However the pieces knotted by the Kurds who also lead a nomadic or semi-nomadic life in the east of Anatolia are called Kurd. Yuruks (fig. 25) are knotted throughout in good quality wool, coarse but firm. They often have strikingly thick wefts. The height of the pile varies. It may be so long that the patterns are blurred and the carpet looks like a fur. Much goat hair is used in the ground-weave. The wefts may be dyed in bright colours. To correspond with the height of the pile the geometric patterns are simple and large scale. Diamonds, lozenges, squares and octagons — in rows or concentrically one inside the other — are hooked or have zig-zag outlines. Inspiration from Bergamo, Konya and the Caucasus can be seen in many Yuruk patterns. The zig-zag line plays a large role. The patterns may be simple and noble, and primitive and wild as well. Synthetic colours were not adopted until late. Sultan is a trade name for thick Yuruk and Kurd carpets from eastern Anatolia and northern Iraq. The main centres for assembling and trading in Yuruk carpets are Adana near the Gulf of Iskenderun in the north-east corner of the Mediterranean and Kütahya in the centre of western Anatolia. Here the handsome Darçeçili Yuruk carpets are also traded.

The Anatolian KURD (Kürd) carpets have all the characteristics of the nomad carpet. They are all darker and more discreet in colouring and never as long in pile as some of the Yuruk carpets. The most important depots for Kurd carpets are Bayazid on the Turkish Persian frontier, Malatya in the western part of eastern Anatolia and Kagizman, south of Kars, on the Turco-Russian border. From the region round Kagizman there also came especially handsome kelims, some with silver thread woven in. Probably no other Turkish provenance has so many carpets with swellings in the weave, a fault that reduces wear. Very few pieces look flat.

Kelims are woven in many parts of Anatolia (figs. 23 and 27). The knotting of Yastiks, the smallest carpets up to about 50 × 90 cms. originally intended as cushion covers, and Heybeh, saddle bags (fig. 29), is not confined to particular areas.

25. **Yuruk, Anatolia, 19th—20th century. 'Konya Yuruk'.** (179—185) 182 × 113 (110—116) cm. (above).

Warp: W. S-plied, 2 strands, twisted, undyed light.

Weft: W. Z-spun, single, dyed red, olive-yellow, grey-brown, orange, green-blue, olive. The number of shoots (6—14 alternating sinuous) often increases towards the middle after separating slightly in places. Colour and weft weave show that the left half of the carpet was partly knotted together with the right.

Pile: W. Z-spun, 2 strands, untwisted. Knots T. I: h. 23, w. 22 = 506 per sq. dm.

Upper end: 4 cm. W. kilim grey-brown, orange. Lower end: —.

Selvedges: W. shirazi in the weft colours 4 cord.

Quality: soft, shaggy, thick, coarse.

Colours: 7, *red, olive-yellow, purple,* yellow-brown, orange, blue-black, ivory.

Pattern: the primitive atavistic design in strong colours suits the coarse knotting of this shaggy thick carpet.

26. Yahyali (southern Kayseri), mid-20th century. Prayer rug. 144 × 86 cm. (p. 94 below).

Warp: C. S-plied, 5 strands, twisted, undyed white.

Weft: W. and hair. S-plied, 2 strands, slightly twisted, undyed light brown to black. 2 shoots: 1. straight, 2. sinuous.

Pile: W. Z-spun, 2 strands, untwisted. Knots T. II (50°): h. 44, w. 28 = 1,232 per sq. dm.

Upper end: 1 cm. W.—C.—kilim, black and white blended, then fringe left.

Lower end: as upper end, then warp loops plaited into a diagonal braid.

Selvedges: W. shirazi 3 cord.

Quality: dry, thick, coarse ribbing

Colours: 9, *dark red, surmey (indigo black), brown-orange,* olive, green, black, some yellow, white and grey.

Pattern: the arch of the niche is three-fold. The central part with seven steps reaches to the upper panel. The central field is blackish-blue. The supporting pillars are replaced by flower bands. The mihrab and spandrels each have a hanging lamp. Both panels have large geometric flowers in alternating directions. There are similar flowers on the brown-orange main border. 2 guard stripes.

27. Konya, 19th century. 'Kiss-kilim'. 188 × 103 cm.

Technique: kelim with silver brocading.

Warp: C. S-plied, 3 strands, twisted, undyed white, 64 threads per dm.

Weft: W. S-plied, 2 strands and C. (white) S-plied, 3 strands, twisted. C. 3 strands, wrapped in silver foil. 120 shoots per dm.

Upper end: about every 20 warp threads twisted into two plaits which are knotted together at top and bottom.

Lower end: as upper end.

Colours: 7, *white, red, dark blue,* olive-green, rust-red, light blue, silver.

Pattern: large diamonds, their vertical ends terminating in arrow heads, are arranged concentrically one inside the other. The vertical sides have a border with a line of hooked stepped polygons joined by a straight stem; the narrow sides rosettes with X crosses in a row.

28. Anatolia, 19th century. Kurd tent band — 'Chadir-Sheridi'. 415 × 8 cm. (detail) (above).
W a r p : forms the pattern; W. S-plied, 2 strands, twisted, undyed and dyed in all the colours of the pattern.
80 threads per dm. W e f t : goat hair. Slight S-ply, 2 strands, undyed brown. 44 shoots per dm. The band
is worked on a double warp at two superimposed levels.

29. Yahyali, 19th—20th century. Heybeh—saddle bag. 135 × 45 cm. Knots T. I, 1,394 per sq. dm.
(middle).

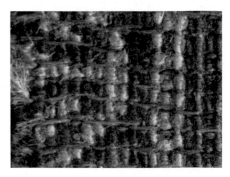

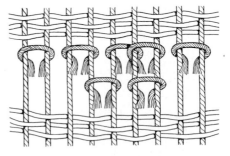

Caucasian carpets

Geography and History

The great fold of the Caucasus mountains stretches for a length of 1,100 km. at a breadth of 100 to 160 km. from the north-east shore of the Black Sea south-eastwards to the Caspian. The highest peaks are the extinct volcano of Elbrus (5,633 m.) and Kasbek (5,047 m). Parallel to the Caucasus and to the south runs the Lesser Caucasus which forms the northern boundary of the hilly territory of Armenia, bounded on the south by the course of the Arax (Araxes). The Lesser Caucasus has many extinct volcanoes rising to heights of 4,000 metres. Abundant snow and rainfall in the western Caucasus provides a wealth of forest and so of wild animals for the central and western Caucasus. In eastern Caucasus where there is less rain there are fewer woods, but, as on the hills of Armenia, the good pasturage encourages extensive sheep breeding. While the plain round the Rion on the Black Sea coast, hemmed in by the Great and the Lesser Caucasus, has a climate favourable to the cultivation of grapes and citrus fruits, the steppes peopled by nomads stretch out north and southwards from the eastern Caucasus (Shirvan and Mogan steppe). As a consequence of these climatic and geographical conditions the focus of carpet production lies in the eastern half of the Caucasus. The cotton grown in Shirvan was introduced into the carpets of this region. Shirvan and Karabagh have cultivated silk for centuries.

The main routes of communication run on either side of the impassable Caucasus — the few north-south connections through the mountains have to cross passes at

30. a. b. Anatolia, 9th century. (?). Fragment from Fostat (Old Cairo) c. 12 × 10 cm.
Warp: W. z-spun, two strands s-plied undyed light.
Weft: W. z-spun, single strand dyed red. Three welts alternating sinuous, alternately behind 3—4 warp threads.
Pile: W. z-spun. 2—4 strands. T. I.: h. 52, w. 54 = 2,808 per dm².
Upper end: — lower end: —. Sides: remains of W. shirazi red round 3 × 1 and 2 × 1 warp threads.
Touch: silky, thin, firm, smooth.
Colours: 7, *red, dark blue, yellow-olive*, ivory, light blue, dark brown, light yellow-olive.
Pattern: Fragment is from right hand borders. On the red field of the main border runs a delicate, twisting, ivory/olive stem with geometrical flowers crosswise; the border separated from the yellow-olive edging by a dark brown thread (2 knots round three warp threads). Flowers are set at every two or three twists of the stem and alternate with small lozenges from which shoot small forked flowers with a third of the main flower combined with a voluted, cup-shaped geometrical vegetable motif. In the spandrels, half-lozenges containing a three-leaved flower at the tip and a crosswise flower in the centre. On the light olive-yellow field of the guard stripe appears a row of stylized flowers on a blue background, which is found almost unchanged in fine Turkmenian carpets until the 20th century. The spandrels in the interstices under the flowers are red flecked with ivory. All the pattern details are worked in colours that do not provide strong contrast.

heights of almost 3,000 metres — and join in Baku on the Caspian. The mountains which fall away less steeply to the north-east do not reach to the coast. The narrow coastal strip has always been the point of contact between southern Russia and Persia. Much in the history of the Caucasus and the Armenian mountains remains to be investigated.

According to the reports of the anthropologist Radde, about three hundred and fifty tribes live in the Caucasus — among them Lesghians, Chechens, Cherkassians, Ossetans, Talysh, Mountain Jews, Karachais, Mountain Tartars and Kumüks — with approximately a hundred and fifty different languages. Apart from the languages of the later Indo-European and Turkish immigrants they can be classified into the West Caucasian, South Caucasian (including Georgian) and East Caucasian or Checheno-Lesghian languages. Among the Caucasian peoples the Georgians with their ancient written language were culturally the most important.

The inaccessibility of the mountain valleys (the only part that was more thickly populated was the less steep north-east Caucasus that sinks down to the Caspian) protected many tribes and fragments of tribes into the nineteenth century from complete annihilation by the Persians, Turcomans, Turks and Russians who have held the Caucasus in their respective spheres of power during past centuries. Because of their isolation several tribes retained the patterns for their knotting almost unchanged for generations, right until the beginning of the twentieth century.

It was probably towards the end of the eighteenth century BC that Indo-European tribes started to immigrate into the Armenian hills. In the eighth century BC the Indo-European Cimmerians and later the Scyths broke into the Transcaucasian region. The Medes conquered the land in about 600 BC and drove the Scyths back across the Caucasus. In the sixth century BC the Armenians immigrated into the hilly region that bears their name. They developed a high culture. Their skill in the extraction and use of dyes on wool doubtless contributed to the early mastery of the art of knotting in this area (p. 16). Seleucid governors founded independent Armenian kingdoms, and Greater Armenia at times reached to the Caspian. Parthians and Sasanids then bound Transcaucasia more firmly to the Persian Empire. Derbend is one of their frontier forts. About AD 300 the Armenian Christian church was founded.

In the thirteenth century the land was conquered by the Mongols, in the fifteenth century by the Persians, in the sixteenth the Turks laid it waste. In 1590 Abbas had to come to terms with the Turks, and Transcaucasia with Azerbaijan and Armenia were handed over to the Turks. Two thousand bales of silk from Karabagh and Shemakhe (Shirvan) were to be delivered yearly to the Turks. Large quantities of carpets were also included in the tribute, but there is no exact record of the numbers. In the independently governed provinces carpet knotting ceased almost entirely with the decline of the manufactories. In 1603 Julfa, the most prosperous and well planned of Armenian towns, greeted Shah Abbas once more as its deliverer. To receive him the city was decked out with tremendous splendour, in spite of the hard years of Turkish rule: gold-threaded carpets, brocades, satin, silks and golden vessels richly wrought. Situated at the crossing of the most important caravan routes on the southern salient of the Arax, Julfa based its wealth on the trade with Russia, Europe and China. Silk, carpets, vegetable dyes and horses.

Shah Abbas was determined to exploit the industry and skill of the population of Armenia to the advantage of Persia. 350,000 Armenians were deported into the interior of Persia, under the most cruel conditions. Under more humane conditions the burghers of Julfa were transported to New Julfa, built opposite the Persian capital of Isfahan, with a church where they could practise the Christian religion. There the industrious and able Julfians animated the flourishing carpet industry and developed a far-reaching export trade.

For two hundred years the Caucasus was once more the northern frontier of western Persia. In the re-won province fifteen khanates developed during the eighteenth century. The Khans, the nominal representatives of the central administration of Persia, were in fact autocrats. Stable social and legal relations were formed in this way which favoured economic life. The carpet workshops also recovered, especially since they served the prestige requirements of the khans, who influenced the style of carpets by their demand for Persian patterns. Innumerable Persian elements were introduced which are still to be found in Caucasian carpets, more or less stylised. The names of the khanates where carpet production was of importance still survive today in the carpet names of Gendje (Gyanza), Shirvan (Shemakha), Kuba, Erivan, Nakhichevan, Baku, Talish with Lenkoran and Karabagh with Shusha.

In the first quarter of the nineteenth century Russia finally seized Transcaucasia from Persia, together with Armenia and Azerbaijan. Towards the beginning of the twentieth century carpet knotting had become the chief source of revenue for certain districts, where more than half the population was engaged in it.

Today the region of the eastern Caucasus is politically organised into the Soviet Republics of Georgia, Armenia, Azerbaijan and Dagestan. The capitals of Tiflis, Yerewan (Erivan), Baku and Makhachkala are administrative and industrial centres. From Baku, the focus of oil production, the well towers have spread on both sides of the mountain range for 500 km. to the north-west. Coal and copper mines have been started, many water power stations utilise the mountain rivers. The sixty kilo-metre long Mingetshau reservoir at the confluence of the Kura and Alasari is also creating new agricultural possibilities. Carpet knotting is encouraged and guided by the state. It is done for the most part in modern cooperative workshops. While very few new home-made pieces have appeared in the export market over the past decades these have been offered for sale again more recently.

Caucasian carpets to the end of the eighteenth century

The history of the development of Caucasian carpets leaves more questions un-answered than that of any other oriental carpets. The hand-knotted work of this isolated area was not known in Europe until late, in any quantity, and has not found much response until recent decades for its individual formal abstract patterns.

The so-called dragon carpets (fig. 31) are patterned in lozenges in which vertically posed stylised dragon-like creatures and animal combat scenes alternate with gigantic palmette flowers. They were first thought by connoisseurs to be Anatolian, of fifteenth century date onwards, because a geometric 'phoenix and dragon combat' is the motif on the last of the Anatolian animal carpets (p. 22). Now they are all attributed, with the same dating, to the Caucasus region. The heavy division into lozenges by broad leaf stems is continued in the large Caucasian carpets of the seventeenth and eighteenth centuries, while the animal combats are gradually transmuted into floral motifs (fig. 32). Whether an earlier dating than the second half of the sixteenth century is justified has yet to be proved. Many details of the design suggest that sixteenth-century Persian patterns are as much an influence here as they were in the seventeenth and eighteenth centuries.

The Caucasus region was always open to new ideas; the result is always Caucasian, even when the models are apparent. Be it Herat, Djoushegan or medallion pattern, cloud band or dragon ornament, standing vases or a tree design, everything is fused into the one individuality with a seemingly boundless strength. The strict forms of the monumental patterns which threaten to swamp the narrow borders laid round them, are entirely original; their powerful ductus is much more fitting for carpets and textiles than their models. Thus it seems unjustified to speak of 'bastard carpets'.

Judging by the large formats that may reach eight metres in length, these carpets

VII. Caucasus, 18th century Soumak, 329 × 262 (250–274) cm. (p. 101).
Warp: W. Z-spun, 3 strands S-plied undyed ivory. C. 70 warp threads/cm.
Weft: W. Z-spun, 2 strands lightly plied, undyed ivory. 1 weft after each pattern row.
Pattern row: W. Z-spun, 4 strands S-plied. On the front carried over every two warp threads diagonally forward and on the back carried back in opposite direction over one warp thread. Direction of diagonal changed after each row, thus creating herring bone structure. (Technique: see p. 34)
Upper end: C. every 6 warp threads taken together in a honeycomb knot with six rows of knots.
Lower end: as upper end.
Sides: W. shirazi red round 4 warp threads.
Colours: 13, *red, ivory, dark green, dark blue, yellow,* brown-black, violet, blue, brown, dughi, light brown, olive green, light red-brown.
Pattern: The rising pattern of the red central field is in the 'dragon carpet' tradition (see fig. 31). Three large motifs along the length, each consisting of two weighty geometric pairs of leaves overlapping alternately, and containing a Caucasian palmette. To bind these monumental motifs a palmette held in two cup-like large blue leaves is placed between them. The traditional 'dragon fights' are reduced to 4 flat yellow shapes with geometric interior design. The double headed Russian imperial eagle bearing three crowns is introduced four times into the pattern, in symmetrical arrangement. The rest of the ground is, like the main motifs, almost symmetrically covered with stylized and geometric plant and floral motifs, rosettes, stars, bipeds and quadrupeds. The brown-black main border has along the long sides an alternation of lozenges and a motif similar to an angular figure eight along a thin straight stem. In the various sized spandrels thus left are rods with hooks on one side opposing each other. On the narrow sides the stylized stem known from the border of the 'dragon carpets', in which a geometric leaf similar to the main motif of the Turkish 'Bird' carpets alternates with a lozenge. The seven guard stripes form the double Caucasian stem on a blue ground. A band of 'running dog' round the edges.

31. Caucasus, 16th century. Dragon carpet. 678×230 cm. (detail).

Warp: W. S-plied, 3 strands, twisted, undyed light.

Weft: W. Z-spun, 2 strands, untwisted, undyed brown. 2 shoots: 1. straight, 2. sinuous.

Pile: W. Z-spun, 2 strands, untwisted. Knots: T. II: h. 32, w. 44 = 1,408 per sq. dm. Upper end:—. Lower end: —. Selvedges: —.

Quality: dry, medium heavy, coarse ribbing.

Colours: 7, *red, blue, sand,* brown, black-brown, pale blue-green, ivory.

Pattern: the blue central field is divided into a diamond diaper by broad red and sand-coloured lanceolate leaves with heavy Caucasian palmettes. Within the diamonds are 'dragons', animal combat groups, large Caucasian palmettes and trees, all in symmetrical arrangement. Ducks appear in the half diamonds at the lower edge. The border contains an angular wave stem with square rosettes and oblique palmettes.

32. Caucasus, 17th century. Dragon carpet. Fragment 572×268 cm. destroyed by fire in 1945. (left).
Pattern: the scheme corresponds to that of the 'dragon carpet'. The 'dragons' and animal combat groups,
   which in the previous example, earlier by a century, are predominantly animal rather than vegetable,
   are by now entirely floral in conception.

33. Kazakh, 19th—20th century. (224—230) 227×174 (170—178) cm. (detail) (right).
Warp: W. S-plied, 2 strands, twisted, undyed light.
Weft: W. S-plied, 2 strands, slightly twisted, dyed red. 2—4 shoots alternating sinuous.
Pile: W. Z-spun, 2 strands, untwisted. Knots T. I: h. 30, w. 32 = 960 per sq.dm. Upper end: 1 cm.
   remaining of a red W. kilim. Lower end: as upper end. Selvedges: W. shirazi coloured 2 cord.
Quality: soft, fleshy, heavy, oblique ribbing.
Colours: 6, *red, ivory,* medium blue, blue-green, olive-yellow, black-brown.
Pattern: red central field with large flat geometric stems running into volutes covered by light six-petalled
   rosettes and a second motif from the same rosette in half-drop rows with broadened diagonal stems.
   The main border has a heavy geometric scroll pattern on a light ground.

must have been made in manufactories, and judging by the variations in structure
— from the beginning of the eighteenth century cotton is even sometimes used in the
ground-weave — made in different areas of the Caucasus region. They cannot but be
the outcome of a sound tradition of hand-knotting. What designs can have preceded
them?
In some paintings of the fifteenth-century carpets are shown with simple lozenges
or a design with an octagon under a hooked stepped polygon in rows of squares.
The same pattern, never seen in Anatolia or Persia, still appears in Caucasian carpets
in the twentieth century. Very probably we are looking in these paintings at the
patterns of early Caucasian carpets.
In the eighteenth century the smaller format still retained the size of motif of the

34. Kazakh-Gendje, 19th century. Prayer rug. 138 × 86 cm.

Warp: W. S-plied, 3 strands, twisted, undyed light, also one thread light with 2 dark brown.

Weft: W. S-plied, 2 strands, twisted, dyed red. 2 shoots alternating sinuous. At short distances also 3—4 shoots.

Pile: W. Z-spun, 2 strands, untwisted. Knots T. I: h. 27, w. 24 = 648 per sq.dm.

Upper end: —. Lower end: 1 cm. W. kilim red. Warp threads looped and twisted.

Sides: W. shirazi in all pattern colours 2 cord.

Quality: soft, thick, coarse.

Colours: 12, *indigo, red, white,* black-brown, medium blue, light blue, green, light red-brown, brown, vermilion, orange, olive.

Pattern: the quadrangular arch divides the mihrab from the blue-black central field. The mihrab contains two large plant scrolls geometricised to diamonds in medium blue and blue-green. The spandrels contain hands. The middle one of the three border stripes has the Caucasian double stem pattern on a white ground.

large lozenge-patterned carpets — the same development here therefore as in Anatolia — giving rise to the medallion-like effect of a single large flower or palmette which is all that remains visible of the total imagined pattern. The medallion was not adopted *per se* until the end of the eighteenth century. It was usually repeated in rather a bizarre form in vertical rows or as a stepped polygon over a stylised floral ground pattern without making any integral connection with it (p. 151).

From the eighteenth century onwards the carpets of the Caucasus must be studied together with those of north-west Persia next door to the south, though we have no desire — as has sometimes been done — to claim these latter for the Caucasus.

The introduction of vertical and half-drop rows of identical flower or palmette motifs, making both simple and rising patterns, brought in a new type in the eighteenth century.

Caucasian carpets of the nineteenth and twentieth centuries

Domestic and nomadic work never ceased throughout the centuries. Their work shows elements of design taken from manufactory carpets, such as angular medallions and rows of stepped polygons (fig. 44) or star medallions gradually superceding the old patterns with their square divisions (fig. 41). Smaller elements from the patterns and motifs of large carpets are enlarged into principal motifs (fig. 43). Diagonals, (p. 111), vertical and half-drop rows on monochrome or striped grounds are popular. Floral Persian patterns are made Caucasian by stylisation, geometricisation and colour emphasis on individual parts of the pattern (especially the geometric forked scroll). In one-way patterns the forked scrolls are sometimes transformed into winged beasts (p. 131). Stylised animals and separate human figures may be dotted about in the filling, and filling or background patterns are much used as in all folk art, because of a *horror vacui*. Unpatterned central fields are rare (fig. 58). Borders become broader, sometimes to the point of excess (fig. 40). Their stem scrolls break up into geometric floral or Kufic components. In spite of endless variety everything is quite specifically Caucasian, even when the relation is patent to Chinese (fig. 39), Anatolian (fig. 61) or Turkestani and Turcoman patterns (cf. the lower main border in fig. 110 with its central design of the two medallion heads in fig. 36).

35. **Kazakh, 19th—20th century.** c. 230 × 142 cm. (p. 107)
Warp: W. S-plied, 3 strands, twisted, undyed light.
Weft: W. S-plied, 2 strands, twisted, undyed dark brown. 4 shoots alternating sinuous.
Pile: W. Z-spun, 2 strands, untwisted. Knots T. I: h. 29, w. 30 = 870 per sq.dm.
Upper end: —. Lower end: —. Selvedges: —. Quality: soft, medium-heavy oblique ribbing.
Colours: 6, *red, blue-green, blue,* ivory, pale yellow, dark brown.
Pattern: the red central field is dominated by a blue-green cross-shaped medallion outlined by a band with
  stars. In the centre is a floral square. On the blue ground of the main border are octagons with eight-
  pointed stars.

36. Kazak, 19th century. Prayer rug. 176 × 104 cm.

Warp: W. S-plied, 3 strands, twisted, undyed light, mostly 2 threads light with 1 dark brown, or vice versa.

Weft: W. S-spun, 2 strands, twisted, red, 2 shoots alternating sinuous.

Pile: W. Z-spun, 2—3 strands, untwisted, knots T. I: h. 36, w. 27 = 972 per sq. dm.

Upper end: 2 cm. red kilim. Lower end: as upper end, then warp threads looped and twisted.

Selvedges: W. shirazi red; on the left 3, on the right 2 cord.

Quality: fleshy, thick, firm.

Colours: 9, *terracolta, carmine, ivory,* dark blue, green-blue, light blue, black, olive-yellow, dughi (light red).

Pattern: the hooked band outlining the six-angled arch divides the mihrab from the red central field.
The mihrab is filled by a heavy medallion which has two waists. In the arch there is a small tablet with
an inscription for placing the prayer stone. Geometric scroll with S-shaped volutes in the light main
border.

108

37. Kazakh, c 1900. Borchaly-Kazakh. Prayer rug. c. 183 × 128 cm.

Warp: W. S-plied, 3 strands, twisted, undyed light, in places light with dark brown.

Weft: W. S-plied, 2 strands, twisted, dyed red. 2—4 shoots alternating sinuous.

Pile: W. Z-spun, 2 strands, untwisted. Knots T. I: h. 32, w. 26 = 832 per sq. dm.

Upper end: 2 cm. W. kilim red, warp threads closely knotted into 5 transverse rows and sewn down.

Lower end: 1 cm. W kilim red, warp threads looped and twisted.

Quality: soft, thick, coarse oblique ribs.

Colours: 7, *red, blue-green or pale green, white,* light olive-brown, dark blue, some dark brown and orange.

Pattern: the mihrab has a thin frame, turned into the base in a quadrangular loop. There is a five-sided arch. The central field is blue. The white ground of the main border has a clumsy reciprocal motif. Both guard stripes have reciprocal running-dog bands.

The numerous types of prayer rug are all unmistakably Caucasian as well. The drawing of the whole prayer niche as a frame over the patterned central field is exceptional. As a rule only the contour of an arch is given by a massive band. It suggests a head-shaped archway, with four, five or six angles (figs. 34, 36, 37). The ground pattern continues under the outline of the arch (fig. 56), or the spandrels are filled with a scatter pattern (fig. 47). Hands also occur sometimes in the spandrels (fig. 34). The arch itself may be filled with ornament indicating the place where the prayer stone is laid (a baked clay slab of holy earth).

From the nineteenth century several migrations of pattern can be established. The patterns typical of one area are adopted by others. Thus the true provenance of many pieces must be decided not by the pattern but only by structure, material and colour scheme. In the Caucasus, it is true, the Turkish knot is used exclusively and the woollen warp is almost always twisted three-ply; even so, many points of structure can be distinguished. These are therefore considered in detail in the general discussion of the various groups of Caucasian carpets.

A special group of patterns is represented, appearing in the first half of the nineteenth century, by those carpets from Karabagh, Kuba and Derbend which were knotted for the French-style furnishings of Russian and rich native patrons, with rows of little bunches of roses — often in medallion or rocaillerie frames.

A date is more frequently knotted into Caucasian carpets than in those from other provenances. They are given in Arabic numerals according to the Gregorian calendar by Armenian Christians, and in the years of the Hijra (or hejira) by Muslim knotters. Since Armenians and Muslims often lived together in the same village both dates are sometimes recorded on one carpet.

In Soviet Caucasian carpets the designers mix the old elements of pattern or they invent new ones. A new species for the Caucasus is the picture and portrait carpets, glorifying production with representations of oil-well towers and cornfields and historical personalities with portraits as close as possible to photographic realism.

VIII. **Kazakh, 19th century.** (180—188) 184×117 (113—121) cm. (p. 111).
Warp: W. S-plied, 2 strands, twisted, undyed light, light with light brown and light with dark brown.
Weft: W. S-plied, 2 strands, twisted, undyed light brown. 2—4 shoots alternating sinuous.
Pile: W. Z-spun, 2 strands, untwisted. Knots T. I: h. 28, w. 26 = 728 per sq. dm.
Upper end: W. kilim brown, turned back and sewn down.
Lower end: a few shoots remaining of a brown W. kilim.
Selvedges: W. shirazi, brown and yellow-olive 4 cord. Quality: soft, heavy, very thick, coarse.
Colours: 9, *red, green, blue, black-brown, yellow,* ivory, light olive, light red-brown, rust red.
Pattern: the central field is divided into broad diagonal stripes holding rows of large boteh with tops
   bent to the left. A few birds and small boteh as filling for the ends of the stripes and 2 very small S signs
   in the middle of the central stripe. In the light main border a stem scroll disintegrated into large squares
   with attached double hooks. Medakhyl bands for the 2 guard stripes.

Kerimov quotes one hundred and eleven names simply for Azerbaijan carpets, in the three main groups Gendje Kasak, Karabagh with Shusha and Jebrail, and Kuba Shirvan with Baku alone, classifying them according to the place of production and standard designs. This chapter restricts itself to mentioning the names of provenances of Caucasian carpets that are current in the West.

The KASAK GENDJE region embraces more or less that part of the Lesser Caucasus and the Armenian hills lying within the triangle formed by Tiflis, Yerevan (Erivan) and Kirovabad. Its carpets have the longest pile and the freest patterns of all Caucasian carpets. The designs are uncomplicated. The range of its clear basic colours is limited to between five and nine. Blue, red, ivory, green and yellow are the principal colours.

Kasak and Gendje carpets are very similar in structure as well: the warp is of undyed wool, three-ply twisted except in a few cases of two-ply twisting. The weft of natural brown or dyed reddish wool, occasionally blue, is twisted two-ply. Usually every row of knots is followed by two to four alternating sinuous weft rows. Elsewhere in the Caucasus two weft rows is the rule. With a length of pile of from 6 to 12 mm. and a gauge of 600 to 1,200 knots per square dm. these carpets are coarse to medium fine, but sturdily knotted. The ends are finished at top and bottom with a dissimilar narrow kilim as is the practice everywhere in the southern Caucasus region. While the warp loops are left twisted at the bottom, at the top end they are cut off and knotted or closely braided into several oblique rows of plaits. A characteristic termination unusual in other parts of the Caucasus is to turn over the kilim and stitch it down to the back of the carpet. Down the selvedges two or three pairs of warp threads are wrapped in wool (shirazi), either red, brown or in several colours. The formats go up to four, exceptionally to seven or ten square metres.

The simple and large-scale designs of the Kasak are rich in variants: cross-shaped (fig. 35) and other angular medallions (fig. 36), clumsy boteh, which may be arranged in diagonal stripes (p. 111), fan-shaped rosettes (fig. 33) and hooked lozenges are typical elements, as well as hooks on long stalks and curved crossed hooks.

Carpets from particular Kasak provenances have become generally known: Bordshaly (fig. 37). Mainly from the village of Chobanker. It uses light colours, including a characteristic bluish green. Diagnostic is a primitive reciprocal pattern in white and dark brown in the border.

Lori-Pambak (fig. 38) have slightly broken colours. They have a long pile and large geometric medallions. Karachop are mostly soft green in ground colour, on which a large light octagon is often the central motif, surrounded by four squares. These motifs are often thickly scattered with little star rosettes.

Lambalo (fig. 40) is a term by which the trade describes Kasaks in which the exceedingly wide border often leaves no more than a narrow dark panel for the central field.

Excellent Sileh and Verneh are also woven in the Caucasus region.

GENDJE carpets received their name from the former khanate of Gyanza with its capital at Gendje (now Kirovabad). They vary in quality and the pile on average is not so long as on the Kasak carpets which they resemble in structure except for

38. Kazakh, c. 1900. Lori-Pambak. c. 252 × 184 cm.

Warp: W. S-plied, 3 strands, twisted, undyed light, also light with dark brown.

Weft: W. S-plied, 2 strands, twisted, dyed reddish. 2—4 shoots alternating sinuous. Additional double shoots from the sides up to 40 cms. deep and in the middle of the carpet.

Pile: W. Z-spun, 2 strands, untwisted. Knots T. I and T. II: h. 32, w. 29 = 928 per sq. dm.

Upper end: 1 cm. W. kilim red, warp threads closely knotted into 2 transverse rows. Lower end: —.

Selvedges: W. shirazi red 2 cord.

Quality: fleshy, thick, coarsely granular.

Colours: 7, *red, white, olive-* to *pale olive-green, sand,* medium blue, some dark blue and dark brown.

Pattern: the pattern is rendered in broken colours, and dominated by the large octagon with its typical Lori-Pambak centre. Like the other two octagons, it is surrounded by a narrow band with large hooks on either side.

39. Karabagh, 19th century. Cloud band Karabagh. 164×106 cm.

Warp: W. S-plied, 2 strands, twisted, undyed light with dark brown or light brown.

Weft: W. S-plied, 2 strands, twisted, undyed black-brown. 2—4 shoots alternating sinuous.

Pile: W. Z-spun, 2 strands, untwisted. Knots T. I: h. 32, w. 22 = 704 per sq. dm. Upper end: —. Lower
end: —.

Selvedges: W. shirazi brown, 2 cord.

Quality: fleshy, thick, coarsely granular.

Colours: 5, *ivory, dark blue, rust red,* olive-yellow, brown-black.

Pattern: red central field with a large medallion surrounded by 2 large geometric scrolls in such a way
that the upper one creates an arch below the white panel. Within the medallion are 4 pairs of cloud bands
arranged symmetrically round a square containing a swastika.

40. Kazak, 19th century. Kazak-Lambalo. 226 × 127 (124—130) cm.
Warp: W. S-plied, 3 strands, twisted, undyed light.
Weft: W. S-plied, 2 strands, twisted, dyed red. 2—3 shoots alternating sinuous.
Pile: W. Z-spun, 2 strands, untwisted. Knots T. I: h. 28, w. 31 = 868 per sq. dm.
Upper end: —. Lower end: —. Selvedges: W. shirazi blue not original.
Quality: smooth, fleshy, coarse oblique ribbing.
Colours: 9, *red, indigo* (surmey), *ivory, yellow-olive,* medium blue, madder (dughi), brown-red, green-blue, dark brown.
Pattern: the excessively wide 6-fold border reduces the central field to a narrow indigo panel with a medakhyl surround. In it simply a few small motifs. The red main border has a plant scroll broken down into a scorpion-like ornament.

41. Gendje, 19th century. (152—158) 155 × 96 (94—98) cm. (p. 117 above).
Warp: W. S-plied, 2 strands, twisted, undyed light, also light with light brown.
Weft: W. S-plied, 2 strands, twisted, dyed reddish, brown and undyed brown. 2 shoots: 1. straight, 2. sinuous.
Pile: W. Z-spun, 2 strands, untwisted. Knots T. III (30°): h. 29, w. 28 = 812 per sq. dm.
Upper end: 2 cm. W. kilim reddish, warp threads looped and twisted. Lower end: 1 cm. remains of a light brown W. kilim.
Selvedges: W. shirazi brown. 2 cord.
Quality: fleshy, medium thick, coarse ribbing.
Colours: 9, *red, ivory, blue,* light blue-green, black-brown, medium brown, light brown, sand, vermilion.
Pattern: a division of the ground into quadrilateral compartments such as appears in paintings of the 15th century, filled with hooked and stepped polygons with a central star inside an octagon. Each compartment is distinguished from the other by variations in the colour combinations. To fill in the rest of the central field on the right is an additional stripe with 18 squares.

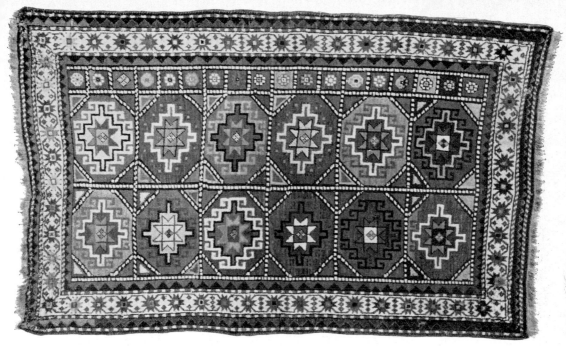

42. Gendje, 19th century. (238—242) 240×111 (108—114) cm. (below).
Warp: W. S-plied, 3 strands, twisted, undyed light, also 2 light with 1 brown.
Weft: W. S-plied, 2 strands, twisted, dyed reddish. 2—3 shoots alternating sinuous.
Pile: W. Z-spun, 2 strands, untwisted. Knots T. I: h. 28, w. 28 = 784 per sq.dm.
Upper end: a few shoots remaining of a red W. kilim.
Lower end: 1 cm. red W. kilim, warp threads looped and twisted.
Selvedges: thick W. shirazi, not original.
Quality: soft, fleshy, thick, coarse.
Colours: 11, *indigo* (surmey), *white, cochineal red,* light blue, medium blue, dark green, dughi, olive, vermilion, ochre, black-brown.
Pattern: the central field is divided up into diagonal stripes, on which are rows of multicoloured flowers in different combinations. The main border has a floral scroll broken down into hooked diamonds and opposing arrows.

43. Karabagh-Chelaberd. 19th century. 'Eagle Kazak'. 197×156 (153—159) cm.
Warp: W. S-plied, 2 strands, twisted, undyed light, also light with light brown.
Weft: W. S-plied, 2 strands, twisted, undyed black-brown. 2—4 shoots alternating sinuous.
Pile: W. Z-spun, 2 strands, untwisted. Knots T. I: h. 28, w. 28 = 784 per sq. dm.
Upper end: — Lower end: — Selvedges: W. shirazi brown not original.
Quality: fleshy, thick, firm, coarse granular.
Colours: 7, *red, dark blue, ivory,* black-brown, indigo (surmey), olive-yellow, some vermilion.
Pattern: two gigantic geometric flowers developed from Caucasian motifs of the 17th and 18th century fill the red central field almost completely. This type is called variously 'eagle', 'sword', 'sun' or 'escutcheon' Kazak because the motifs can with a little imagination be interpreted as eagle wings, swords, radiating suns or shields.

44. Shirwan, 19th century. 171 × 107 (104 × 110) cm.
Warp: S-plied, 3 strands, twisted, 1 thread light with 2 threads light brown or vice versa.
Weft: C. S-plied, 2 strands, twisted, undyed light. 2 shoots alternating sinuous.
Pile: W. Z-spun, 2—3 strands, untwisted. Knots: T. I: h. 40, w. 33 = 1320 per sq. dm.
Upper end: a few shoots remaining of a C. kilim.
Lower end: as upper end.
Selvedges: thick W. shirazi not original.
Quality: dry, thin, firm, fine granular.
Colours: 9, *surmey, red, white,* light blue, medium blue, olive-green, brown-black, light brown, dark red-brown.
Pattern: the surmey central field has two large stepped polygons on a bar ending in gigantic emblem-like geometric flowers. Geometric flowers, birds and quadrupeds as filling. In the main border a dentelated pattern of diamonds and triangles derived from a stem scroll, on a brown-black ground.

occasional slight depression of the warp and the very rare use of cotton as a white weft. They are never as large as the largest kasaks.

Their palette is a little richer; bluish cochineal or Karabagh red is more in evidence. An intense vermilion (cinnabar) red is sometimes insufficiently fixed and comes out in the first wash. The designs are in general less simple. One type of pattern continues the rows of squares with hooked stepped polygons inside octagons (fig. 39), such as are seen in paintings of the fifteenth century. The colours of pattern elements are varied to such an extent from square to square that there is no repetition.

Fakhraly, Chayly and Scamukh are numbered among the Gendje carpets. In the Gendje region just as in the Karabagh 'dast-khali-gebe' sets are produced. These are three or four carpets to fit out a room: two narrow Kenareh on either side of a broader keley of equal length. Across the top of these three pieces a keleyghi (Ghalidshe) may also be laid.

The KARABAGH area lies to the south east of Kasak Gendje. Its southern boundary is the Arax.

Karabagh (Karabakh) carpets are rich in their range of colours and designs. Cochineal red, vermilion, brown tones, golden yellow and blue-black are the most noticeable colours.

Brown or light wool is used in a twisted three-ply for the warp and two-ply for the weft, unless the latter is dyed red or consists of undyed cotton. Two weft rows after each row of knots is the rule. The warp may be depressed. The kilims are usually woven of undyed cotton. The brown or reddish wool shirazi (selvedge wrapping) covers one or two pairs of warp threads. The height of the pile is between 5 and 10 mm., the count is between 900 and 1,600 knots per square dm. Sizes vary from 2 to 20, in exceptional cases they go up to 30 square metres. The dast-khali-gebe was a speciality of the Karabagh.

IX. Shusha, Karabagh, c. 1800. (417—427) 422 × 192 (182—202) cm.
Warp: W. S-plied, 3 strands, twisted, undyed light or light with brown.
Weft: C. Z-plied, 3 strands, twisted, undyed light. 2 shoots: 1. straight, 2. sinuous.
Pile: W. Z-spun, 2 strands, untwisted. Knots T. III, (20°) h. 27, w. 32 = 1,184 per sq.dm.
Upper end: —. Lower end: —. Selvedges: W. shirazi blue 2 cord.
Quality: soft, thin, firm, faintly ribbed.
Colours: 11, *black, olive, ivory, cochineal red, celadon green,* light blue, dughi, yellow, light brown, olive-brown, medium blue.
Pattern: black central field with a close ground pattern of fourteen rows of flowered stems. Over it three large finely stepped polygons with smaller ones and one shield along a bar. The central polygon is repeated in quarters at the corners. The olive border has a row of almost square pale blue boteh.

To the Karabagh carpets belong those of the neighbouring former khanate of Nakhi-chevan and the 'Eagle' and 'Cloud band Kasak' which correspond more in structure to Kasaks (figs. 39 and 43).

The 'Eagle' on the carpets of Chelaberd are in fact gigantic geometric flowers, which have their more naturalistic forebears in the Caucasian carpets of the seventeenth and eighteenth centuries. The equally traditional pattern of cloud bands arranged round a square with a swastika over it are found in carpets of the same structure and materials; these must therefore have been knotted in the same region of the Karabagh.

SHUSHA, the former capital of the Karabagh, took the lead in styles and produced the finest and largest carpets of this area. They are often silky to the touch, medium heavy to thin, firm and smooth or slightly ribbed. Often the weft is of cotton and the warp slightly depressed (p. 121).

Black, olive-green, ivory, stone (celadon or jade) green, pink and natural cochineal red, which is also called Karabagh red since it is native, are much prized colours.

The patterns betray Persian and sometimes European influence.

Some terms derived from the patterns have been preserved: 'balyg' means fish. This refers to Karabagh carpets with the Herati motif which is also often called 'mahi-to-hos' (fishes in a pool) in Persian because of the four curved lanceolate leaves.

'Butaly' (palms) are carpets patterned all over with the boteh, which is often also rendered in rows in the border.

'Garga' (= raven) describes carpets with the unfortunate patterns in which four large birds are placed symmetrically round each medallion.

'Lampe' (= room rug) are carpets with a large medallion on a monochrome ground.

Good Sileh and Verneh or Shadda (Shadde) work also came from the Karabagh region.

The MOGAN steppe stretches parallel to the northern half of the south-east frontier of Karabagh, on the right bank of the Arax. It lies partly in Iranian territory and shares a frontier on the east with the Talish region.

Mogan carpets are mostly in Keleyghi formats up to four square metres. They are thus about twice as long as they are wide. The three-ply twisted warp wool is un-dyed and similar to that of the Kasak Gendje region.

The two- or three-ply twisted weft of wool, cotton or a mixture of both is undyed and usually light in colour. For the kilim, cotton is often used and light wool or cotton for the shirazi. The ends of the warp threads, as in the neighbouring southern Caucasus regions, are different at top from bottom. The count varies from 900 to 1,500 knots per square dm.

The designs are simpler. The principal pattern is rows of octagons; they may enclose hooked stepped polygons as a filling for the central field, as in the well-known Gendje type (fig. 41) or stars in the main band of a broad border. These sometimes dominate the pattern so much that only a narrow stripe remains as the central field.

45. Shirwan-Marasali, 19th century. Prayer rug. (129—135) 132 × 105 cm.
Warp: W. Splied, 2 strands, twisted, undyed brown, also light with brown.
Weft: W. S-plied, 2 strands, twisted, undyed light. Also 1 strand W. plied with 1 strand C. 2 shoots alternating sinuous.
Pile: W. Z-spun, 2 strands, untwisted. Knots T. I: h. 36, w. 35 = 1,260 per sq. dm. Upper end: —. Lower end: —. Selvedges: W. shirazi blue not original.
Quality: dry, thin, firm, fine granular.
Colours: 9, *indigo (surmey), ivory, red,* light blue, dark blue, medium blue, olive-yellow, pale blue-green, dark brown.
Pattern: the typical Marasali pattern of geometric boteh in border and arch band, below which the dentelated boteh of the niche continues.

46. Shirwan-Marasali, 19th century. Prayer rug. (154—160) 157×107 (104—111) cm.
Warp: W. S-plied, 3 strands, twisted, undyed dark brown or dark brown with light.
Weft: C. S-plied, 2 strands, twisted, undyed light. 2 shoots alternating sinuous.
Pile: W. Z-spun, 2 strands, untwisted. Knots T. I: h. 44, w. 34 = 1496 per sq. dm. Upper end: —. Lower
  end: —.
Selvedges: W. shirazi red, not original.
Quality: fine, thin, firm, smooth.
Colours: *white, honey, dark blue,* red-brown, black, pea-green, green, pale blue, sand, light olive-yellow,
  light blue.
Pattern: dentellated diamond diaper on a white central field, filled with stylised flowers. Over it the heavy
  dentelated band of the arch with typical Marasali geometric boteh. The pattern is made more soothing
  because the same flower form is repeated diagonally to left and right upwards from the vertical axis.
  The honey-coloured border has the fragmented stem pattern (goblet, or oak leaf) of dentelated leaves
  and calyxes.

47. Shirwan-Ssalyan, 19th century. Prayer rug. 150 × 89 (86—92) cm.

Warp: W. S-plied, 3 strands, twisted, undyed. 2 light with 1 dark brown.

Weft: C. S-plied, 3 strands, twisted, undyed white, 2 shoots alternating sinuous.

Pile: W. Z-spun, 2 strands, untwisted. Knots T. I: h. 36, w. 40 = 1,440 per sq. dm.

Upper end: warps woven into a thick kilim, then knotted into a net.

Lower end: as upper end.

Selvedges: C. shirazi blue, 2 cord.

Quality: silky, firm, medium thick, smooth.

Colours: 9, *cochineal, celadon green, surmey,* ivory, black, olive-yellow, light blue, light brown, medium brown.

Pattern: the red band of the arch cuts off the niche from the surmey central field. The niche is filled with rows of the Caucasian flowered stem, in which each flower has a different colour combination from all the rest. On the gable 2 geometric motifs.

48. Kuba Karashli, c. 1930. 130 × 83 (81—85) cm.

Warp: C. S-plied, multiple machine twisted, undyed light.

Weft: as warp.

Pile: W. Z-spun, single. Knots T. III, 60°: h. 64, w. 48 = 3,072 per sq. dm. Upper end: 2 cm. C. kilim white.

Lower end: 1 cm. C kilim white, warps looped and twisted.

Selvedges: W. shirazi blue 2 cord.

Quality: like heavy velvet, firm, thick, ribbed.

Colours: 8, *pale blue, red, surmey,* sand, olive, ivory, dark red, light brown.

Pattern: three large red flowers geometricised to rectangles stand free in the pale blue central field. The red forked leaf scrolls belonging to them are separate, since the pattern is no longer understood. An elaborate geometric scroll in the red border. 5 guard stripes.

49. North Shirwan, 19th century. 'Kuba-shirwan'. c. 224×124 cm.

Warp: W. S-plied, 3 strands, twisted, undyed light or 2 light with 1 dark brown.

Weft: C. S-plied, 2 strands, twisted, undyed light. W. ditto. 2 shoots alternating sinuous. Also 3 shoots:
  a C. and a W. shoot together, alternating with the 3rd, sinuous.

Pile: W. Z-spun, 2 strands, untwisted. Knots T. I: h. 39, w. 29 = 1131 per sq. dm.

Upper end: a few shoots remaining of a light W. kilim.

Lower end: —. Selvedges: W. shirazi white, 4 cord not original. Under it a white C. shirazi original.

Quality: fine, not quite thin, firm.

Colours: 7, *brown-red, medium blue, ivory,* sand, black-brown, light brown, dark blue.

Pattern: 10 pairs of forked leaf scrolls stand out against the blue central field so that they dominate the
  large stepped polygons. A quantity of geometric flowers and a few quadrupeds as filling. Powerful Kufi
  border on a light ground.

50. Kuba-Perepedil, 19th century. (124—128) 126×96 (94—98) cm.

Warp: W. S-plied, 3 strands, twisted, undyed light, dark brown and light with dark brown.

Weft: W. and C. S-plied, 2 strands W. plied with 1 C. undyed light brown. 2 shoots: 1. straight, 2. sinuous.

Pile: W. Z-spun, 2 strands, untwisted. Knots T. III, 30°: h. 46, w. 36 = 1,656 per sq. dm.

Upper end: 2 cm. W.-C. kilim undyed, warps knotted in net.

Lower end: as upper end.

Selvedges: C. shirazi white, 2 cord.

Quality: smooth, leather hard, thin, faintly ribbed.

Colours: 9, *surmey, ivory, olive-yellow,* medium blue, dark green, purple-brown, light brown, red, light blue.

Pattern: the typical perepedil horn-like geometric scrolls (goat horns) are arranged symmetrically over the
  central field. Between them opposed flowers geometricised to animal forms, with attached leaves.

The KUBA SHIRVAN region is where most Caucasian carpets are made. Shirvan includes the region south of the eastern outrunner of the Caucasus, Kuba the region to the north of it as far as the Caspian Sea.

The most usual formats are of one to four square metres. Sizes of ten to fifteen square metres are very rare, twenty very exceptional.

The fineness of their knotting (1,600 to 3,000, in some cases up to 3,500 knots per square dm.) and of the patterns is common to the carpets from both parts of the region. With the introduction of cotton for the weft the count has if anything been increased. Neither a very high count nor a woollen weft are any indications of great age. The repertoire of design is so rich that only a few of the most remarkable can be listed here:

a vertical row of stepped polygons (fig. 44), large star-shaped medallions (p. 131) and the double Caucasian stem scroll (fig. 47), fine lozenging with a stylised floral filling (fig. 46), endless repeat of small floral stars (p. 161) or a Persian-influenced stem pattern with prominent palmettes and forked leaves. The carpets of Kuba are more uniform in structure and on the whole, with a few exceptions, the composition of the patterns is more delicate than on the Shirvans.

SHIRVAN: the light brown or mixed brown and white wool warp is three-ply, occasionally two- or four-ply twisted. The undyed weft is of white to brownish cotton or wool. In old pieces woollen and cotton weft rows sometimes alternate or a wool thread is plyed with a cotton. Length of pile and count vary considerably. Carpets from the western part of Shirvan especially may have a longer pile and a lower count than is usual in the rest of Shirvan. They then resemble the Karabagh carpets rather more in touch. The kilim are of white cotton, more rarely of wool; the same is true of the shirazi, which goes round one or two pairs of warp threads and is sometimes dyed light or darker blue or something between red and brown. In south Shirvan the ends of the warp threads, as in the other south Caucasian regions, are left as loops at the bottom end and knotted or plaited at the top; in north Shirvan as in Kuba they are cut at both ends and similarly knotted, usually in several rows to form a net.

Marasali carpets are made in Marasa (figs. 45, 46). Characteristic are the angular

X. S. W. Shirwan, 19th century. Akstafa. c. 305 × 131 cm. (p. 131).
Warp: W. S-plied, 3 strands, twisted, undyed light and 2 light strands with one dark brown.
Weft: C. S-plied, 2—3 strands, twisted, undyed. 2 shoots alternating sinuous.
Pile: W. Z-spun, 2—3 strands, untwisted. Knots T. I: h. 41, w. 32 = 3,112 per sq. dm.
Upper end: 2 cm. W. kilim light with blue soumak stitches. Every 6—8 warp threads knotted together.
Lower end: 2 cm. remaining of a W. kilim light. Some warp threads still looped and twisted.
Selvedges: C. shirazi light blue, 2 cord.
Quality: soft, thick, heavy, rather smooth.
Colours: 13, *cherry, ivory, medium blue, black,* green, dark blue, red-brown, strawberry, yellow, light olive, salmon, cochineal, cinnamon.
Pattern: the red central field has a rising stem like a tree over which are placed four large star medallions. Winged beasts (peacocks?) are placed in the interstices, apparently derived from forked scrolls. A close scatter pattern of geometric animals and flowers.

boteh in the wide outline of the mihrab arch. These also appear as a filling for the central field and, the crests alternately facing left and right, in the border.

Akhssu among other carpets produces the Bidsho. A symmetrical rising flattened flower palmette and arabesque leaf pattern is known as a Bidshof (fig. 52).

Shirvan carpets with large stylised birds down the sides of the central field (p. 131) are called 'Akstafa' in the trade. Kasak carpets are made in the district of Akstafa.

Kerimov attributes the type known as Gabystan to the carpets from the neighbourhood of the capital of the former khanate of Shemacha (Shirvan). Strangely enough this name is used in the trade to denote all smaller and short-clipped Shirvan carpets.

The fine 'Salian' (fig. 47) is knotted in the villages of Karabaghly, Shykh-Ssalakhly and Khalach. In its colour scheme the typically Karabagh cochineal red and celadon green predominate.

KUBA: the carpets have for the most part a slightly depressed warp. The three-ply twisted warp is similar to that of the Shirvan carpets; usually it is light coloured, and for pieces of the last four decades is made of mechanically twisted cotton. The weft is usually two-ply twisted of white cotton, more rarely light coloured wool. The pile is short, from 3 to 5 mm. The touch is fine, almost thin, somewhat ribbed. The ends are as a rule done with blue kilim or rows of a blue Soumak-like stitch. The warps are knotted at both ends, almost always net fashion, and identical. The shirazi of cotton or wool round one or two pairs of warp threads is blue, rarely white. Blue is the dominant ground colour of the central field.

The best-known Kuba carpets are Perepedil, Karagashli, Chichi, Tseyva and Seichur.

The best-known Perepedil pattern is that called 'Vurma' (snakes) (fig. 50). These are symmetrically arranged geometricised stem scrolls, unusually primitive for Kuba. From the scatter motif of the filling pattern larger pairs of motifs are emphasised, which could be seen as camels or tortoises, were there not leaves attached which betray them as flowers geometricised past recognition.

Karagashli has large diamond-shaped or rectangular palmettes with four forked scrolls radiating from them. Fig. 48 shown a Soviet-produced Karagashli. The forked scrolls stand alone, the pattern is no longer understood. The thick carpet is skilfully knotted, fine and close on a machine-spun cotton warp.

Chichi border

There are three kinds of Chichi carpets. Stem scrolls in the main border geometricised to small diagonal bands are common to them all (see drawing).

Zeyva has a main motif of three or four gigantic flowers, geometricised to radiating medallions and reminiscent of the 'eagle' of Chelaberd.

51. Kuba Seykhur, 19th century. 156×124 cm.

Warp: W. S-plied, 3 strands, twisted, undyed light.

Weft: as warp. 2 shoots alternating sinuous.

Pile. W. Z-spun, 2 strands, untwisted. Knots T. I: h. 68, w. 39 = 2,652 pr. sq. dm.

Upper end: 2 cm. W. kilim light. Warps knotted together in groups of 6

Lower end: as upper end.

Selvedges: W. shirazi light, 2 cord.

Quality: fine, thin, leather hard, fine granular.

Colours: 9, *dark blue, chestnut, ivory,* light blue, brown-black, olive-yellow, light brown, green. Purple given by chessboard alternation of red and blue knots.

Pattern: large chestnut red medallions in the blue central field, with typical beam-like stems running off diagonally from them. Each pair joins its neighbour at the edges of the field in part of another medallion. A detail from half-drop rows of a large motif is thus implied.

52. Kuba Seykhur, 19th century. 144 × 103 (101—105) cm.

Warp: W. S-plied, 3 strands, twisted, light, also 2 light and 1 brown.

Weft: W. S-plied, 2 strands, twisted, undyed dark brown. 2 shoots alternating sinuous.

Pile: W. Z-spun, 2 strands, untwisted. Knots T. I: h. 40, w. 32 = 1,280 per sq.dm.

Upper end: row of blue soumak weave.

Lower end: as upper end.

Selvedges: W. shirazi blue 3 cord.

Quality: fine, almost thin, finely granular.

Colours: 9, *dark blue, white, red, dughi,* black-brown, medium blue, green-blue, light blue, olive-yellow.

Pattern: the colour scheme, the style of the running-dog motif in the light border and the blue soumak weave at the ends are characteristic of Kuba, but the Bidsof pattern filling the dark blue ground is from the neighbouring region of Shirwan. The close symmetrical rising pattern consists of geometric palmettes and scrolls.

53. Dagestan, 19th century. (262—272) 267 × 118 (115—121) cm. (detail).
Warp: W. S-plied, 3 strands, twisted, undyed dark brown.
Weft: as warp, but light and dark brown. 2 shoots: 1. straight, 2. sinuous.
Pile: W. Z-spun, 2 strands, untwisted. Knots T. II 25°: h. 32, w. 34 = 1,088 per sq.dm. Upper end: —.
  Lower end: —.
Selvedges: W. shirazi light and dark blue, not original.
Quality: dry, thin, firm.
Colours: 9, *dark blue, light olive-brown, ivory, red, mauve,* olive-yellow, light blue, black, dark brown
Pattern: olive-brown central field with half-drop rows of large stepped polygons derived from geometric
  flowers. Accurately drawn Kufi border on yellow ground. Guard stripes have rows of Caucasian carnations.

54. Derbend, 19th century (148—152) 150 cm. × 101 (97—105) cm. (p. 137 above).
Warp: W. S-plied, 3 strands, twisted, undyed light.
Weft: W. S-plied, 2 strands, twisted, undyed light. 2 shoots alternating sinuous.
Pile: W. Z-spun, 2 strands, untwisted. Knots T. I: h. 42, w. 33 = 1386 per sq.dm. Upper end: —. Lower
  end: —. Selvedges: W. shirazi dark brown, 2 cord over 3 warp threads each. Quality: soft, medium
  heavy, granular.
Colours: 9, *ivory, brown-black, red-brown, pink,* navy blue, olive-yellow, dark brown, medium blue, blue-green.
Pattern: this interesting Derbend has a light central field with heavy dragon-like scrolls arranged round
  two stepped polygons so that they suggest another similar motif and thus a fragment of a system of a
  continuous diamond diaper. Main border has a fragmented stem scroll and two figures of women.
  Running-dog band in guard stripe.

55. Caucasus. 19th century. 184 × 116 (111—121) cm. (p. 137 below).
Warp: W. S-plied, 2 strands, twisted, undyed light, brown and light with brown.
Weft: W. S-plied, 2 strands, twisted, undyed light brown. 2 shoots alternating sinuous.
Pile: W. Z-spun, 2 strands, untwisted. Knots T. I: h. 35, w. 30 = 1,050 per sq.dm. Upper end: 2 cm.
  W. kilim light blue remaining. Lower end: as upper end. Selvedges: W. shirazi light 3 cord.
Quality: soft, almost thin, coarsely granular.

Colours: 7, *red, ivory, dark blue, green,* light blue, medium blue, olive-yellow.

Pattern: this carpet cannot be closely attributed to any particular area of the northern region of the eastern Caucasus from its structure and material. The large stars with light outlines on the red ground of the central field are typical of Lesghi.

56. Dagestan, 19th century. Prayer rug. (130—134) 132 × 109 cm.

Warp: W. S-plied, 3 strands, twisted, undyed light brown, dark brown and light with dark brown.

Weft: C. S-plied, 3 strands, twisted, undyed white. 2 shoots, 1. straight, 2. sinuous.

Pile: W. Z-spun, 2 strands, untwisted. Knots T. III 50°: h. 56, w. 46 = 2576 per sq. dm.

Upper end: —. Lower end: —.

Selvedges: W. shirazi red, not original. Beneath it parts of the original shirazi W. blue, 1 cord.

Quality: fine, thin, almost board like.

Colours: 9, *ivory, red, dark blue, olive-green,* yellow, light blue, surmey, black-brown, yellow-brown.

Pattern: the light central field is covered with a toothed diamond diaper, filled with stylised flowers; over it is laid the strong toothed outline of the arch. The design composed of 160 flowers is quietened by each horizontal row only having two of the many different flower forms alternating along it, or even only one repeated. A scroll reduced to a wedge-shaped hook on the red ground of the main border.

57. Baku, 19th century. Prayer rug. (156—168) 162×112 cm.

Warp: W. S-plied, 3 strands, twisted, undyed light brown, also light with dark brown.

Weft: W. S-plied, 2 strands, twisted, undyed light brown. 2 shoots alternating sinuous.

Pile: W. Z-spun, 2 strands, untwisted. Knots: T. I: h. 34, w. 32 = 1,088 per sq.dm. Upper end: —.
  Lower end: —. Selvedges: W. shirazi, 2 cord round 3 warp threads each, brown, red-brown, yellow-brown and black-brown.

Quality: fleshy, like thick velvet.

Colours: 7, the tones typical of Baku: *brown, turquoise, black, beige,* pale blue, yellow-brown, red-brown.

Pattern: the band of the arch separates the niche from the brown central field. It is filled with 2 vertical
  rows of contiguous octagons which have an interior design of plain or hooked stepped polygons. The
  archway and spandrels filled with diamond-shaped boteh.

Characteristics of the Seiehur are the 'running dog' ornament in the border (fig. 52) and thick diagonal bands branching out from large cross-shaped medallions in the central field (fig. 51). These bands lead from the cross-shaped medallions to the arm of a similar motif protruding into the centre field from the sides. We have thus a detail of a system of half-drop rows and lozenging. The Bidshof pattern has been adopted into the Seiehur (fig. 52). In the colour scale a special blue, white and green are noteworthy.

The best Soumak carpets are made in the Kuba region.

The republic of DAGESTAN adjoins the Kuba region to the north. In structure the carpets of both regions are similar except that the Dagestans are on average more on two levels. The pile varies as in Shirvan.

The most usual patterns are prayer rugs with a light ground with rows of stylised flowers in a mihrab, usually divided into diamonds (fig. 56), and runners with diagonal stripes or flowers shaped like stepped polygons in half-drop rows (fig. 53).

Derbend (fig. 54), the former capital of Dagestan, was producing good carpets in the first half of the nineteenth century. Later it produced mostly inferior carpets.

The most northern part of the carpet-producing area of the Caucasus is Leghi. These have the structure of firmest Degestan carpets. A strong green is striking in the larger-scale patterns. A pattern with vertical repeats of large star medallions is widespread (fig. 55).

In the relatively small area round BAKU, the capital of Azerbaijan, carpet production was restricted by the progress of industrialisation. Recently attempts have been made to encourage it again.

The old carpets of this region, to which belong the peninsula of Apsheron and the western outskirts of Baku included in the former small khanate, have many structural features in common with the hand-knotting of the neighbouring region of Shirvan and Kuba. The wool for the three- or four-ply twisted warp, on one level, is usually brown or dark brown; so is the wool for the weft which is two- or three-ply twisted, though it is usually of light coloured cotton. The finishing of the ends varies, being executed either as in Shirvan or as in Kuba. The shirazi goes over one pair of warp threads, more rarely over two or three. The knotting is not as close as

XI. Kuba-Dagestan, 19th century. 137×97 (95—99) cm. (p. 141).
Warp: W. S-plied, 3 strands, twisted, undyed light.
Weft: W. and C. S-plied, 2 strands, undyed, 1 strand cotton twisted with 1 wool. 2 shoots: 1. straight, 2. sinuous.
Pile: W. Z-spun, 2 strands, untwisted. Knots T. III 60°: h. 64, w. 32 = 2,048 per sq.dm.
Upper end: stripes of soumak light blue, warp threads knotted into a net. Lower end: as upper end.
Selvedges: C shirazi light blue 1 cord. Quality: velvet-like, firm, thin, ribbed.
Colours: 11, *honey-yellow, white, red,* light blue, dark blue, dughi, black-brown, olive, dark red-brown, light yellow, orange-red.
Pattern: the honey-yellow central field is closely covered with the half-drop rows of geometric flowers. In every other row linear cross-shaped flowers are stressed. In the intervening rows flowers geometricised into octagons alternate regularly with star shaped flowers. The white main border with two main guard stripes has the alternation of birds and rosettes which is taken from Khila.

in Kuba and Shirvan and the count is rarely higher than 1,600 knots per square dm. The length of piles varies as in Shirvan.

The carpets of Baku differ from all others made in the Caucasus in their pallid and sombre colours. The majority of tones, from light blue to turquoise or dark yellow-brown to brown look faded (fig. 57).

The patterns of Baku and Ssurakhany, on the east coast of the Apsheron peninsula, have rows of boteh, lozenges and octagons.

The accurately worked carpets from Chila, west of Baku, are relatively fresher in colour and their patterns show a Persian influence. The central field of the boteh-Chila (p. 151) is patterned all over with bright coloured boteh. Large indented finely stepped polygons are laid over them, which are usually repeated in quarters as a corner filling. This stepped polygon design is also laid over the best-known ground pattern of the Afshan Chila: a flower stem, similar to one Kuba Shirvan type.

The main border almost always contains stylised birds in regular alternation with rosettes (cf. p. 141) or is divided up into narrow diagonal stripes (p. 151). For the weft the wool is also sometimes dyed blue.

The best Sileh were made in the Baku region.

TALISH is the southernmost tip of Russian territory on the Caspian Sea. The carpets are about one metre broad and have lengths from 225 to 330 cms. The narrow central field (fig. 58) is usually dark blue, more rarely yellow or cochineal red. It is covered with an all-over pattern of identical small flowers, stars or star lozenges, though quite often it is left quite plain (met-haneh). In the latter case it is given an

Talish border

extra edging with a fine band of medakhyl. The light coloured main border domin-ates the design. In it are large eight-petalled rosettes alternating regularly with four smaller ones (see drawing).

The border pattern corresponds approximately to that in fig. 57 if the thin joining stems are removed. It must therefore derive from this double stem which is peculiar to the Caucasus alone.

An original and frequent trait is a miniature motif placed in the met-haneh field.

The woollen warp is more often two-ply than three-ply, twisted and undyed. The weft is the same, and usually consists of undyed cotton. After every row of knots come two shoots of weft, as is the rule in the Caucasus apart from a few exceptions. In addition wefts are added from the sides to a width of 6 cms. These short wefts may be found in certain parts of the ground-weave in carpets of other provenances, but they are used regularly in Talish carpets. The kilims are, like the weft, usually of undyed cotton. The shirazi of wool or cotton round one to four warp threads is dyed blue or more rarely undyed white. The count varies between about 1,000 and 1,700 knots per square dm.

58. Talish, 19th century. Met-haneh. (314—324) 319 × 106 cm. (left).

Warp: W. S-plied, 3 strands, twisted, undyed light brown, dark brown or 1 strand light with 2 dark brown.

Weft: C. S-plied, 3 strands, twisted undyed light. 2 shoots alternating sinuous. Additional short double shoots at the sides. Pile: W. Z-spun, 2 and 3 strands, untwisted. Knots T. I: h. 40, w. 31 = 1,240 per sq. dm. Upper end: 1 cm. C. kilim light remaining. Lower end: as upper end. Selvedges: C shirazi light 4 cord.

Quality: fine, medium heavy, very firm, Colours: 11, *navy blue, white, red, dark green,* black, medium blue olive-yellow, red-brown, brown, light brown, dark brown.

Pattern: the narrow blue central field surrounded by a blue band of medakhyl is overpowered by the broad four-fold border. The peace of the central field is emphasised by a small octagon and a miniature losenge. Caucasian scroll as the main border (see p. 143).

59. Talish, 19th century. 'Lenko ran'. Prayer rug. (139—145) 142 × 87 cm. (p. 144 right).
Warp: W. S-plied, 3 strands, twisted, undyed light, brown and light with brown.
Weft: W. S-plied, 2 strands, twisted, undyed light. 2 shoots alternating sinuous.
Pile: W. Z-spun, 2 strands, untwisted. Knots: T. I: h. 36, w. 28, = 1,008 per sq. dm. Upper end: —.
  Lower end: —. Selvedges: W. shirazi black not original. Quality: soft, medium heavy, very firm.
  Colours: 11, *surmey, red, ivory, pea-green,* light blue, orange-red, cinnamon-red, medium blue, olive-
  yellow, dughi, black-brown.
Pattern: the red outline of the arch divides the mihrab from the indigo central field. It is dominated by an
  octagon which is enclosed by two heavy geometric scrolls and has a geometric floral motif in the centre.
  The four large octagons show a connection with Turcoman guls. A row of octagons in the main border.

60. Caucasus, 19th century. Kelim. (178—198) 188 × 154 (144—164) cm.
Warp: W. S-plied, 2 strands, twisted, undyed light. 48 threads per dm.
Weft: W. S-plied, 2 strands, twisted. 190 shoots per dm. Contours stitched.
Upper end: 8 cm. wide striped palas, then warp threads plaited into horizontal braid. Lower end: as
  upper end, palas 10 cm., then warp threads plaited into a horizontal braid.
Selvedges: thick wool shirazi blue-red round 2—3 warp threads.
Colours: 7, *surmey (indigo),* ivory, olive-yellow, green, black-brown, medium blue, dark violet brown.
Pattern: the indigo central field has diagonal rows of indented lozenges. The main border is divided into
  fields containing indented and hooked lozenges in regular alternation. 11 guard stripes.

145

61. Caucasus, 19th century. Soumak. 214×159 (156—162) cm.

Warp: W. S-plied, 3 strands, twisted, undyed light. 75 threads per dm.

Weft: W. S-plied, 2 strands, twisted, undyed dark brown, 1 shoot after every 2 or 3 pattern rows.

Pattern row weft: W. S-plied, 2 strands, twisted. At the front led over 4 warp threads obliquely upwards and then brought back in the opposite direction behind two warp threads. Diagonal direction changes after each row, so that herring-bone structure ensues (technique see p. 33/34).

Upper end: warp threads knotted into net. Lower end: as upper.

Colours: 7, *surmey,* red-brown faded to *olive,* cherry, yellow-olive, medium blue, light blue, dark brown.

Pattern: the olive central field has 3 large blue medallions placed one above the other in a row. Their ribbon outline is reminiscent of Ushak carpets of the 17th century. In the blue main border horizontal scorpion-like stem scrolls alternate with various forms of geometric flower. Reciprocal running-dog band in the outer of the four guard stripes.

62. Caucasus, 19th century. Verneh. Shadda rug. 192×131 (126—136) cm.

Warp: W. S-plied, 2 strands, twisted, dyed rust-red and blue. 80 threads per dm.

Weft: W. S-plied, 2 strands, twisted, dyed rust-red. 80 shoots per dm.

Pattern: W. S-plied, 2 strands, slightly twisted, and C. (white) S-plied, 4 strands, twisted. Technique see p. 149.

Upper end: about every 8 threads knotted.

Lower end: about every 4 loops knotted.

Selvedges: thick W. shirazi red round 4 bunched warp threads.

Colours: 7, *red, blue, white,* yellow, black, green, strong red.

Pattern: except for the two large horizontal fields at either end with geometric flowering trees all the
 fields have animals in specifically Caucasian style.

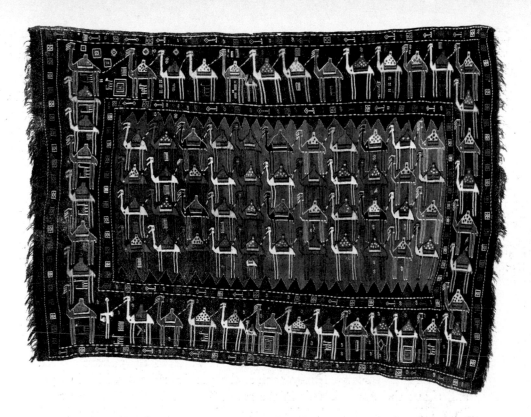

63. Caucasus, 19th century. Dyeddyim. Front and back of a bag. 104 × 44 cm. (above, p. 148).
Warp: W. S-plied, 3 strands, twisted, undyed light. 80 threads per dm.
Weft: W. S-plied, 2 strands, twisted, undyed brown. One shoot after each row of pattern weft. 60 per dm.
Pattern weft: W. S-plied, 2 strands, twisted, and C. (white) S-plied, 2 strands, twisted. All in the same
   direction, over 2 warp threads up to the left and back round 1 thread behind.
Upper end: 3 cm. W. kilim red turned back and hemmed. Lower end: red palas stripe not original.
Colours: 11, *surmey, white, orange-brown,* medium blue, dark brown, dughi, brown-red, red-brown, light
   olive, purple, light brown.
Pattern: two octagons with hooked stepped polygon, round them birds and horses (?), 2 camels and a man.

64. Caucasus, 19th century. Dyeddyim. Front of a bag. 58 × 58 cm. (p. 148 below).
Warp: W. S-plied, 3 strands, twisted, undyed light brown. 90 threads per dm.
Weft: W. Z-spun, single, red-brown. One shoot after each shoot of pattern weft. 135 shoots per dm.
Pattern weft: W. S-plied, 3 strands, twisted. All upwards round 2 warp threads in front, one behind.
Quality: thin, leather hard. Colours: 13, *surmey, green-blue, chestnut, ivory,* dark brown, red-brown, black-
   brown, olive, medium blue, light blue, light yellow, purple, sand.
Pattern: the indigo central field contains an oddly geometricised white scroll beneath a square octagon. It
   is surrounded by four octagons. Stylised animals and geometric floral motifs are scattered in as a filling.
   The green-blue main border has a regular alternation of 8-rayed stars and flattened crosses.

65. Caucasus or north Persia, 19—20th century. Double bag, Khurdyin. c. 155 × 65. (above).
Warp: C. S-plied, 6 strands, twisted, undyed light.
Weft: as warp. 2 shoots alternating sinuous. In the woven part W. Z-spun single.
Pile: W. Z-spun, 2—3 strands, untwisted. Knots T. I: h. 37, w. 27 = 999 per sq. dm.
Upper end: W. kilim with colour fields between the slits for the cord. Lower end: W. kilim blue as
   transition to the back woven on double warp. Selvedges: W. shirazi red 3 cord, sewn on to back.
Quality: fleshy, heavy, thick, coarsely granular.
Colours: 9, *dark blue, rust red, ivory,* light brown, brown, olive-green, light blue, dark red, olive-yellow.
Pattern: in both dark blue central fields a light octagon running out into a T hook above and below,
   containing a hooked stepped polygon. The pattern is Caucasian, the structure Persian in origin.

Talish carpets with a very particular pattern have acquired the name of Lenkoran, which is that of the capital of the region (fig. 59). The dominant motif is an octagon flanked by two heavy arabesque scrolls, in which lies a centipede-like geometric flower. The octagons attached to the chief motif are related to the Turcoman gul. The colour scheme is darker than on other Talish carpets.

Palas, Kelim and fine Djidjim are also produced in the Talish area.

Flat weaves

Weaving and tapestry are older in the Caucasus than hand-knotting. Since the pile carpet, unlike these ancient processes, needed shearing it is still called 'gras' in many areas today (contraction of 'migrasi' = shears, Arabic) or 'gaychi' (shears, Azerbaijani). Not only carpets are hand-knotted, but many kinds of bags for heavy wear: khurdjin, kheyb, choval and the mafrash, a large box-like bag with side walls. Hangings, blankets, pouches, the back of paniers and whole bags too are woven and worked.

PALAS is the simplest form of weaving called in English tabby, plain or taffeta weave and in the USA cloth weave. It is used throughout the whole world: the weft thread is carried at right angles to the warp threads, alternately passing above and below them, and then beaten firmly against the previous shoot which has passed below and above the warp threads in the reverse order. In the Caucasus two-ply twisted wool is generally used. This weave only permits of horizontal striped patterns.

Palas weaving is used for simple pouches, wrapping cloths, the backs of bags and for covering tents. It is thus most widespread among the nomads in the Mogan and south-eastern Karabagh regions.

In the KELIM (p. 34) the yarn (in the Caucasus usually twisted two-ply) of one colour is woven to and fro in the appropriate part of the pattern until the neighbouring part is begun in another colour. This technique dictates patterns with straight, stepped or indented contours (fig. 60). Kelim is woven for blankets, curtains or to decorate tents and rooms for weddings. It is woven in many countries.

XII. Khila, 19th century. 'Boteh-khila'. 375 × 208 (205—211) cm.
Warp: W. S-plied, 3 strands, twisted, undyed. 2 light strands with one dark brown.
Weft: W. S-plied, 3 strands, twisted, dyed light blue. 2 shoots alternating sinuous.
Pile: W. Z-spun, 2 strands, untwisted. Knots T. I: h. 36, w. 38 = 1,368 per sq.dm. Upper end: —.
  Lower end: —. Selvedges: shirazi dark blue not original. Quality: now soft, thin.
Colours: 9, *dark blue, red, pale blue-green,* ivory, medium blue, olive-yellow, dark green, medium brown, fawn.
Pattern: the central field of dark blue is surrounded by a band of medakhyl and covered with rows of boteh. The boteh change the direction of their crests in each row, and each one has two further boteh inscribed concentrically within it. Three dentellated stepped polygons lie over the ground pattern and corresponding corner fillings. The main border has diagonal stripes ('barber's pole pattern') and there are five guard stripes.

To make the pattern finer with diagonal outlines and without the slits created by the Kelim weave, the Verneh and Shadda (shedde) technique was evolved (fig. 62). The basis is a palas. After a few shoots, however, pattern threads are introduced at every required position. Thus each separate detail of the pattern is begun across the whole breadth of the work: each pattern thread is carried over two or more warp threads and then taken to the back; there it hangs down during the passing of the next shoot. After this line of weft the pattern is continued at each place by one thread, before the next weft is shot. As the pattern threads can be shifted one warp thread to one side at the back each time, very fine diagonal outlines can be achieved. By beating the weft lines close together the pattern threads are pressed forwards and create a slight relief effect. Now and again the patterns are completed by embroidering. For white elements in the pattern cotton is sometimes used. Very rarely the patterns are worked in silk.

These products being primarily woven by cattle-raising peoples, there are frequently representations of animals in them. Curtains, blankets, horse-, camel- and tent-bags for all conceivable objects of daily use are produced in this technique, which is most widespread in the Kasak, Karabagh and Karadagh regions.

SOUMAK weave is illustrated on p. 33. It allows the executing of knotted carpet designs. There is a striking similarity with an early Ushak design in a standard pattern (fig. 61) of vertical rows of large lozenge-shaped medallions whose outlines form crosses pointing inwards. In old pieces the palette is light: white, yellow and red make a bright effect. Later darker tones characterise the colour scheme. The wool for warp and ground weft is mainly three-ply, for the pattern yarn two-ply twisted. In spite of its name, the Caucasian home of the Soumak, which was earlier widespread in Karabagh, Shirvan and Kurdistan as well, is Dagestan.

SILEH is technically speaking a special kind of Soumak. This is described on p. 34. The warp consists of two- or three-ply twisted wool, the ground weft of two-ply twisted wool or cotton. The pattern yarn is two-ply twisted wool and cotton for white elements of the design. The Sileh was worked in the Karabagh, Nakhichevan and Kasak regions and later in Baku as well. Baku Sileh are distinguished for their specially high quality.

DJIDJIM covers several kinds of weaving: first simple palas weave but with the warp and not the weft forming the pattern; second the refined Soumak in which the pattern yarn is only carried obliquely over two warp threads and a ground weft is introduced after each pattern shoot; third, this same type of Soumak but when the warp is depressed at ninety degrees, and the pattern weft is only seen in front as single humps. In general Djidjim usually means the technique described on p. 35. The material for warp and pattern weft is as in Sileh. For the ground weft single untwisted woollen yarns are often chosen because of the fineness of the work.

66. Caucasus, 19th century. Sileh. (275—285) 280 × 203 (197—209) cm. Two strips sewn together.

Warp: left strip: W. S-plied, 3 strands, twisted, undyed light. Right strip: W. S-plied, 2 strands, twisted, undyed light with dark brown. 80 warp threads per dm.

Weft: C. S-plied, 2 strands, twisted. One shoot straight after each row of pattern. 60 shoots per dm.

Pattern weft: W. S-plied, 2 strands, twisted, and C. S-plied, in the left strip 3 strands, in the right 2 strands, twisted, white. All in the same direction over 4 warp threads in the front obliquely upwards and back behind two.

Upper end: left strip: about every 15 warp threads plaited together. Right strip: warp threads looped and twisted, light plaits added. Lower end: reverse of upper end.

Colours: 13, *red-brown, white, wine-red, surmey, (indigo), celadon-green, light blue,* vermilion, blue-green, black, dughi, olive, sand, honey-yellow.

Pattern: the heavy S-shaped ornament repeated in four rows on a red-brown ground is shown by earlier Sileh to be the ultimate geometricisation of a floral motif. The spaces have geometric flowers.

154

Persian (Iranian) carpets

Geography and history

Iran has approximately the form of a triangle 1650,000 square km. in area. Its base is formed by the Zagros that stretch from the Armenian highlands to the Indian Ocean. Their peaks rise up to 5,000 m., and cut off the high Iranian plateau from Mesopotamia, while the Kurud mountains run parallel to them with heights reaching to 4,000 m. The northern side towards the Caspian Sea and western Turkestan is formed by the Elburg mountains (the Damavand peak is over 5,000 m.) and its continuation, the Kopet Dagh, and the eastern side towards Afghanistan and Pakistan by the Qayan mountains. The broad plateau lying at between 1,000 and 2,000 m. above sea level is undrained, apart from a few rivers from the peripheral mountains, that run into the Persian Gulf and the Caspian Sea. Its climate is characterised by extremes of temperature. Winter and early spring are the period of precipitation. The mountain regions have a milder summer and very cold winters. The western slopes have more precipitation and are wooded in parts, and some poor crops can be harvested. Only the narrow coastal region round the Caspian with its sub-tropical climate and patches of primaeval woodland is more richly endowed by nature. The climate of the low plain by the Persian Gulf round the oil-bearing region of Abadan is extremely humid and hot. A large part of the interior is covered by the uninhabitable salt deserts of Dasht e Kavir and Dasht e Lut. The most important towns developed in the watered oases surrounded by the endless terrain of steppe and bare hills. For centuries man has been in conflict with nature to wrest a living from the soil. Only artificial irrigation can ensure a minimum of food for the population. From an aeroplane the view is of a sand sea crossed by gigantic rocky massifs in which the tiny green segments and squares of the oases are threatened with extinction. The shaft holes of the underground canals (ghanats) are strung out like a string of beads from the mountains to the oases. Since nearly all the natural water courses dry out in summer the water tables are tapped at the foot of the mountains, and the water is carried down the natural inclines in tunnels to the watering oases in the plain with their better soil. It takes endless labour to keep the ghanats clean. They often run 30–50 m. below the surface and the numerous entrance shafts are there for this purpose. The oases produce cereals, vegetables, tobacco, sugar cane, melons, tropical fruits and olives, and raisin grapes and dates are important export goods along with petroleum, cotton, silk and carpets. The flowering garden has always been the symbol of Paradise for the inhabitants of the steppes. This Iranian word for garden has even entered our own religious vocabulary.

The topography and climate of Iran made it a natural home for the development of hand-knotting: the wool of the unimaginably contented herds of sheep that roam the steppes can be worked into the ideal insulation against cold both for the nomads and semi-nomads (still today comprising a fifth of the twenty-million-strong population), for the peasants, and for the town dwellers who at present form a third of the total population. The nomads are mostly semi-nomadic. In winter they seek out the milder zones with their great flocks of sheep, and in summer they go up to the higher pastures while some sections of the tribes stay behind in the cultivated regions. A very few railways were built between 1927 and 1938 and a few roads also cross the tremendous distances, but it will be many long years before the camel, horse and donkey become redundant over the breadth of the land.

The inhabitants of Persia are predominantly Iranians, descendants of the Indo-Aryan tribes. In the north-west provinces Kurds, Turks and Armenians (these latter also round Isfahan) form a large share of the population. Turcomans in the north east, Arabs in the south and Jews round Hamadan are other ethnic groups. The Lours and Kurds in the west and north-west and the Bakhtiars in the province of Isfahan speak Persian, the Gashgai in the province of Fars, the Afshars further north-east and the Turcomans in Khorassan speak Turkish dialects.

Iran is the great land bridge from Central Asia to the Middle East. Lying athwart the cross roads of the routes from south Russia, western Turkestan and Mesopotamia to India, and on the old caravan routes from the Far East to the Mediterranean, it became both the reloading point for traders and the centre of cultural exchange between East and West — and also the catchment basin for the waves of peoples flooding out of the northern steppes.

Archaeology has shown that by the fifth millenium BC a neolithic culture of agri-cultural nomads had arisen. In the middle of the second millenium 'Annubanini, the mighty king of the Lullu', like other rulers of the third, second and first millenia, had his portrait engraved in the rock walls flanking the road that leads from the lowland plain up through the Zagros mountains and Kermanshah to Hamadan. Caravans have been treading this road for 5,000 years, and for centuries the Kurds have followed it every spring, driving their flocks up to the mountain pastures, and every autumn when they bring them down again to the Gemsir (= warm land) plain. Since the foundation of Islam the pilgrims journey along it to Mecca or from the west to Kum and Meshed. The armies of Alexander the Great, Seleucos, Antio-chus and the Arabs tramped up it to conquer Iran, Baktria and India, and the troops of the Achaemenids, Parthians, Abbasids, Seljuks and Mongols marched down it to subjugate the lowland.

From the north the first great wave of Aryan peoples (after 1800 BC) who gave their name to the country was followed six hundred years later by the second: Amadai (Medes) and Persua (Persians) who settled in the west of Persia. While the Persians later spread southwards into 'Persis' (Fars) the Medes founded their empire with its capital of Ekbatana (Hamadan) at the end of the eighth century, clearly in conjunction with the Cimmerians who began to press in from the Caucasus about 800 BC. (A section of this Indo-European people had turned westwards and destroy-ed the Phrygian empire of King Midas in Asia Minor).

The Scyths following the path of the Cimmerians overran the Middle East to the frontiers of Egypt and for a quarter of a century, from about 650 BC, held the suzerainty of Iran. Once they had been driven back beyond the Caucasus by the

Medes, the Assyrian empire defeated and the Persians made dependent on the Median Great King, the Median Empire attained the zenith of its power.

In 552 Cyrus proclaimed himself ruler and founded the dynasty of the Achaemenids. In a few years the first Persian Empire arose, with its principal cities at Susa, Ekbantana and Babylon. Asia Minor (King Croesus) together with the Ionian Greek cities were overthrown; the conquest of Babylon released the Jews from the Babylonian captivity and allowed them to return to their native land. The residence of Pasargardai was built. Cyrus's son Cambyses conquered Egypt and mounted the throne of the Pharaohs. Darius I (521–486) the Great King and most important of the Achaemenids brought Thrace and Macedonia into the empire. In Persepolis rose up the palatial mansions of the winter residence and nearby in Nagsh e Rustam the imposing royal tombs.

Artists and craftsmen from every province of the vast empire were summoned to build the mighty edifice with reliefs glorifying the power of the Great King. The new style is compounded of countless elements. In the carvings the spirit of the Greeks is attempting to animate the pomp of Assyria with feeling, to permeate the monumental Persian development of animal style with a deeper sense of rhythmic peace, equilibrium, solemnity and confidence. The Iranian animal style is rooted in a tradition from a distant past: from the animal art of the nomads and early Iranian ceramics to the Luristan bronzes of the ninth and eighth centuries. These are one more illustration of the mystical association of the horse with death, being buried in graves just as real horses were buried by other peoples, as grave goods.

Calm, assurance and ornamental effect by repetition are equally outstanding features of the design on the Pazyryk carpet (p. 16), the oldest surviving hand-knotted carpet, which dates from about this time. Like everything in Persepolis the curtains and carpets were, according to tradition, of colossal proportions.

The Achaemenids allowed the twenty-eight tributary nations their cultural and religious autonomy. Iran is a land of many religious foundations: the monotheistic religion of Zarathustra superceded the older polytheism. The cult of Mithra which originated in Persia later travelled as far as the Rhine and across to Britain with the Roman legionaries. The teaching of Mani, Manichaeism, which at one time had a follower in St Augustine, finds its echoes in the Albigensian uprisings in southern France in the Middle Ages.

Henceforward the kings are depicted under the winged solar disc, the symbol of the highest deity Ahuramazda, the pure spirit. In the third century Zoroastrianism is proclaimed the sole state religion. At the present day some 20,000 devotees of this ancient Persian religion, the Parsees ('Serdoshti'), are still living in Iran.

Intelligently organised administration, impartial justice, uniform coinage, regular taxation, splendid imperial roadways and irrigation systems consolidate the empire and its prosperity. Persepolis, Pasargardai, Ekbatana and Susa are the capitals.

Darius and his son Xerxes, whose despotism already foreshadows the decline of the dynasty, conducted ultimately unsuccessful wars against Greece. Where weapons failed on the western frontiers of the empire throughout a century and a half of fighting, Persian gold succeeded.

Darius III, the last Achaemenid king, was overthrown by Alexander the Great in 331 BC. As a reprisal for the destruction of Athens Persepolis went up in flames. Thousands of camel-loads of gold and other treasure were carried away by the victors.

Greeks and Iranians lived side by side in the cities. New ideas and forms of art flooded the land. Western influences were fused with the indigenous, which in the long run proved the stronger.

The early death of Alexander in 323 ended his dream of integrating two continents and cultures. Persia fell to Seleucos, one of Alexander's generals. The dynasty ruled from Seleukia, later Ctesiphon, over the whole Persian empire. In 250 BC the Parthians, a horse-riding people from the lands east of the Caspian, rose up and took power. After defeating the Seleucids and the Romans whom the wealth of Iran had made covetous, the Parthians again made it the centre of an empire which the Sasanids, who took control five centuries later, extended from the Mediterranean to the Indus. The capital was still Ctesiphon on the Tigris.

The Parthians made the horse acceptable to art. Under the Sasanids the king is forever glorified on stone reliefs, gold and silver dishes, in the stuccos decorating the palace halls and in costly stuffs; he is always on horseback, receiving his insignia of power from the highest deity who is himself also on horseback, bringing down rich quarry at the hunt, or surrounded by dancers and jugglers, symbolising the lavish feasts. The landscape is no more than linear ornament, showing a leaning towards endless patterns. Through trade relations and by itinerant artists, Parthian-Sasanid art radiated out to Coptic, Byzantine, early Romanesque and Chinese art. From it stem the origins of the horsemen in the mediaeval textiles of the West. The Eurasian stem scroll style, the wave scroll probably formulated by the Minoan-Mycenaean culture — symbolising the phenomenon of eternally flowing movement — appears in Europe and Asia in many variants and later becomes the dominant element in the designs of carpets. In Islam, for which the Arab armies pouring across the land won Iran in AD 634, the arabesque style develops.

Iran was ruled by the Umayyad caliphs from Damascus and then by the Abbasids who resided in Baghdad. Under their rule, which soon became no more than nominal, native and Turkish dynasties rose to power. Nishapur, Rages (Rayy) Sultanabad and Shiraz were now the most important cities of Iran.

In 1050 Isfahan became the capital of the Seljuks. By intelligent methodical government they tried to unite the quarrelling followers of Islam; they took over the protection of the Caliphate of Baghdad.

The next flood to break over the land was the hordes of Genghis Khan, whose horsemen brought Iran in 1256 into the Mongol empire that stretched from China to the Mediterranean. At first the ruthless government of the non-Muslim Mongols — the last Caliph of Baghdad was executed — filled the world of Islam with fear and horror. But Iran, which had crumbled after the end of the Seljuks into a welter of rival princedoms, was now united. Art and learning were encouraged at the court of Tabriz. Fifty years later fragmentation again threatened; but Timur, the wise conqueror of the line of Genghis Khan, prevented it. The government of his successors lasted until the fifteenth century and brought an uncommon flowering of learning, science and art to the courts of Tabriz and Herat. At this time Far-Eastern symbols like the cloud band and the dragon were adopted more freely into the art of Iran from which Islam with all its abhorrence of images had never quite expelled all representation of men and animals.

Soon after the death of Timur, southern Iran, Kurdistan and upper Mesopotamia again became independent. Dynastic struggles prepared the way for the rule of the Saffavids (1501–1721) who became the creators of the new Persian empire. Ismail, the founder of the dynasty, united a band of soldiers at the age of fourteen and led them to defeat the troops of the prince of Shirvan. He took over the region west of the Caspian and in a few years had conquered an empire which reached from the Euphrates to Khorassan. Shi'ism became the state religion.

The glorious reign of Shah Abbas the Great (1587–1628) began with misfortunes: besides Georgia, Azerbaijan and Armenia he lost the regions of Herat and Meshed. The capital was moved from Kasvin to Isfahan. After a decade all the lost provinces had been recovered and the frontiers pushed back to the Euphrates, the Persian Gulf and the Amu Darya. The city of Isfahan arose spacious and splendid. European visitors dwell in raptures on the fairy tale delights of this city, the facades, domes and towers with their tiles glistening and gleaming in the sun. The court displayed enormous luxury. Trade and art flourished.

The textiles of this time, the silks, brocades and satins have some themes in their decoration corresponding to painting; in carpet designs the influence of miniature painting is dominant: hunting scenes, landscapes and gardens. The 'Polish' carpets characteristic of the period of Shah Abbas subordinate considerations of taste to the need for ostentation with gold and silver brocading. The refined late style is the beginning of the decline.

The Turcoman Nadir Shah (1688–1747) destroyed the fifteen-year-old reign of terror instituted by the Afghans in 1722, fought off Turcomans and others and attacked the empire of the Great Mughal. His booty included the peacock throne. Nadir Shah extended his frontiers from the Euphrates to the Indus; all Asia trembled at his power. After his assassination Ahmed Shah founded an independent Afghan empire in the east of Iran.

In Iran Agha Muhammad, the leader of a Turcoman tribe, founded the Kadshar dynasty which ruled from Teheran after 1786. His successor lost Georgia, Azerbaijan and Armenia to Russia, and the frontier became as it is today. In 1907 a revolution forced the adoption of a constitution and the deposition of the Kadshar ruler. The country was divided into Russian and British spheres of interest. In 1925 Parliament elected the Prime Minister and Chief Military Commander Reza Khan to be Shah. Under him and his son Muhammad Reza Pahlavi Persia has been evolving gradually from a feudal to a modern state. In 1925 it adopted the name of Iran.

Persian (Iranian) carpets to the end of the eighteenth century

No carpets have been preserved in Persia from before the end of the fifteenth century. Until the Persian origin of the Pazyryk carpet and the Basadar fragments are confirmed, the large carpets and fragments from the first half of the sixteenth century are the earliest known and tangible examples. Their highly developed technique and size presupposes a long tradition in the craft and in manufactories. The tradition must have developed here too from nomad and peasant knotting on smaller formats for their own use, through the family concerns producing for sale and the larger urban workshops, to the large manufactories linked to the court with all technical means at their disposal. Persian miniatures of the thirteenth, fourteenth and fifteenth centuries show carpets with squares and half-drop rows of two equally important motifs in a continuous pattern. Star, rosette and cross motifs, often more finely elaborated, give a more rigid tile-like effect. The enrichment of technique tended to entail a rather bloodless rendering of the traditional patterns, which stands in contrast to the rich stem and scroll decoration on the walls in some of the same miniatures. Miniatures of the period round 1500 and the carpets of the first half of the sixteenth century show a radically different approach to design: instead of the small-scale division of geometric elements into rows there is a sudden incursion of medallions stressing the centre of the carpet, and fine branching and curling tendrils with flowers and arabesque leaves. This was a revolution in the design of carpets, they could no longer be knotted without the most exactly recorded models. Having seen from the documentation of the miniatures how conservative were the knotters, rigidly following the old geometric patterns, we turn to the book illuminators as the probable originators of the new designs. Medallion and scroll ornament is character-

XIII. Shirwan, 19th century. 310×117 (115—119) cm. (p. 161).
Warp: W. S-plied, 3 strands, twisted, undyed dark brown or one light strand with 2 dark brown.
Weft: W. Z-spun single and C. S-plied, twisted, undyed light. 2—3 shoots: 1. straight, 2. sinuous, or 2. straight, 1. and 3. sinuous.
Pile: W. Z-spun, 2 strands, untwisted. Knots T. III up to 40°: h. 48, w. 50 = 2,400 per sq.dm.
Upper end: some shoots remain of a W/C. kilim white.
Lower end: as upper end. Selvedges: C. shirazi white 2 cord.
Quality: fine, firm, thin, smooth.
Colours: 11, *dark blue, ivory, red,* light blue, black-brown, dark green, olive-yellow, cochineal-red, black, dark red-brown, sand.
Pattern: the dark blue central field is patterned over with diagonal rows of floral stars of uniform shape. Their colours are richly varied, but in every other row every second star is light, making the continuous pattern more clearly articulated. Between the stars is a scatter of miniature geometric flower heads and two birds.

istic of the book illustrations of the time. The idea of the endless continuation of the pattern, of a random choice of a portion of the constant flow of infinity enclosed within the frame of the border is now only adumbrated by repeating parts of the medallion or similar sections in the corners, and the cutting off the patterns with the borders. The compositions are centripetally arranged, seemingly finite against their rich stem patterning, and rising in one direction. The whole repertoire of forms from miniature painting, animals and animal combat, clouds and cloud bands, trees, garlands and — mostly imaginary — flowers, scenes of paradise and the hunt and even calligraphy all find an entrée into the carpet designs, which consist of an artful combination of several different planes.

The colour range is extended to between fifteen and twenty-four shades and is enhanced by silk and gold and silver thread. Cotton is used to improve the firmness and regularity of the ground-weave. With silk for both ground-weave and pile the count may be as much as 14,000 knots per square dm.

The introduction of silk and of gold and silver into the pile of the luxury carpets is a questionable improvement. The irridescent lustre of the silk tends to make the pattern hazy and the shining metal disrupts it. Metal thread cannot be used for the pile. The warp is depressed at ninety degrees and it is woven in (p. 33) round the upper threads of the warp, sometimes floating over several warp threads. This brocading is entirely contrary to the style of the knotted carpet, only considerations of luxury and display could give rise to it. The small saving on knotting time is counterbalanced by the cost of the metal and the difficulty and hence the cost of making the threads. The brocade threads in fact have a core of silk which is wrapped round with a band of gold or silver leaf about a millimetre thick. The metal must previously have been beaten into foil, a very tedious process which is described in Exodus 39.ii: 'And they did beat the gold into thin plates, and cut it into wires, to work it in the blue, and in the purple and in the scarlet, and in the fine linen, with cunning work.' The cheaper, softer but less durable 'false gold wire' which lacks the true lustre of gold, made of animal membranes covered with gold foil, seems not to have been used.

The excessive use of this inappropriate material, especially in the 'Polish carpets' for the sake of primitive effect, practised during the heyday of the Saffavid dynasty under Shah Abbas, illustrates the danger into which the carpet could fall when over-refined by the near-fantastical virtuosity of designers, dyers and knotters. Its real force declined. Inappropriately elegant designs, in which influences from other branches of art were dominant, were threatened with degeneration each time the wave of creativity reached a trough. Degeneration set in once Persia had over-stepped the crest of her political and economic success. Many of the manufactory carpets of the late eighteenth century were no more than the paltry progeny of their sixteenth- and seventeenth-century forebears.

Working from tradition, geographical conditions, patterns, colours and material we can trace the historical carpets of the sixteenth, seventeenth and eighteenth centuries to four great centres: north-western Persia with its centre at Tabriz, central Persia with Kashan and from the end of the sixteenth century Isfahan, southern Persia with Kirman and eastern Persia presumably with Herat. The clearest analysis is given by K. Erdmann in his book *Oriental Carpets*.

TABRIZ was chosen by Ismail I (1506—26), the first Saffavid, as his residence. It was lost to the Ottomans in 1514 and during the following decades constantly changed hands. It is an astonishing fact that during these restless years truly great carpets were produced, among them the two discovered in the Mosque of Ardebil where Shah Ismail lies buried. Their inscription reads, 'Beyond thy threshold I am without refuge here in the world. Outside these gates there is no trusty place for my head. Finished by the servant of the threshold Maqsud Kashani in the year 946.' It thus gives a secure dating to the year 1539—40. From the better-preserved parts of both carpets, which have a knot count of over 5,000 knots per square dm., the world-famous specimen in the Victoria and Albert Museum, with dimensions of 1,152 × 534 cm., was put together (fig. 68).

Knot count, colours, design and material of the early north-west Persian carpets show that there were several large workshops in this region. The most important schemes of design are either a system of stems, Paradise or garden ground pattern overlaid by a large medallion, or the filling of the central field with a net of small medallions composed of shields or rows of small shield and quatrefoil medallions. This second scheme recalls the earlier purely geometric division of the field.

67. Persia, 17th century. 910 × 245 cm. (detail). (p. 165 above.)
Warp: C. S-plied, 3 strands, twisted, undyed light.
Weft: C. undyed brownish. 3 shoots: 1. and 3. straight, 2. sinuous.
Pile: W. Z-spun, 2 strands, untwisted. Knots P. II: h. 44, w. 41 = 1,704 per sq. dm. Upper end: —.
Lower end: —. Selvedges: W. shiraziired.
Colours: 10, *dark blue, red, ivory,* light blue, yellow, green, dark brown, red-brown, brown, dughi.
Pattern: the dark blue ground of the central field contains a fragment from a continuous system of soft, straight, partly lozenge-shaped flower scrolls with large palmettes. The position and shape of the palmettes in the central and outer vertical rows stress the vertical axis, while those in the rows between them stress the diagonal. The pointed oval rosettes set obliquely with four forked leaf attachments were taken over in many Caucasian carpets and became the chief motif of the Karagashli. The main border has a palmette stem on a red ground.

68. North-west Persia (Tabriz) 1539—40. 1152 × 534 cm. (detail).
Knotted carpet from the Mosque of Ardebil. 5,200 knots per sq. dm.
The dark blue central field is covered with a dense flowered stem pattern. The sixteen-lobed central medallion with sixteen pointed oval attachments and a lamp hanging at either end along the vertical axis is composed into the ground pattern, as is the repetition of almost a quarter of it in each corner. This medallion is patterned with a delicate arabesque dominated by forked scrolls surrounding a central eight-lobed flower. The main border has a band of cartouches and eight-lobed flowers over a fine flowery scrolled ground. Symmetrical bands of cloud are dominant in the cartouches, arabesque crosses in the rosettes. These is a cloud band scroll on the inner guard stripe, on the outer an arabesque scroll with palmettes. A panel bears the inscription, 'Other than thy threshold I have no refuge in this world. My head has no protection other than this porch. The work of the servant of the threshold Maqsud Kashani in the year 946'.

164

The large medallion is usually compact, and the designers are never at a loss for a new variant. It may have shield, cartouche or lamp attachments in the direction of the length and a quarter of it be repeated in each corner. The corner filling is also done with other linear designs. In the main borders are usually cartouches alternating with eight-petal rosettes or strap-like arabesque scrolls. Great attention is paid to felicitous use of the corner. Deep red, full blue and in some specimens white are the main colours. Wool, cotton and silk are all used in the ground weave. The knotting material is always wool, never silk. Silver and gold brocading occasionally occurs in small parts of the pattern. The count reaches from 4,000 to 9,000 knots per square dm.

A second group, which entirely eschews the use of silk and brocading, with a count of from 2,500 to 3,000 knots per square dm., abandons the representation of trees, garlands, animals and men. Its ground patterns are often more angular, arabesque, as later in Heris, and their medallions massively drawn.

KASHAN, centre of the silk industry, made the most splendid carpets, of which the most famous is the Vienna hunting carpet of the imperial house of Hapsburg (fig. 69). Silk and brocading are used to an extent hitherto unprecedented, and the count at times reaches more than 10,000 knots per square dm. for the delicate designs. Hunting and animal combat motifs are preferred, in patterns unsymmetrical and even at times quite unorganised. The boundary between painting and knotting seems to have been eliminated.

In the early seventeenth century ISFAHAN continues the exaggerated use of silk and brocading practised in Kashan, usually with a less dense count.

Many patterns borrow from the forms of older or even from contemporary styles of other regions. Sometimes even the principle of unity in the central field is given

69. **Kashan, 16th century. Hunting carpet.** c. 685 × 325 cm. (detail). (p. 167 above). Silk carpet with metal brocading.
Weft, Pile: silk. Knots P. II, 85°: h. 116, w. 112 = 12,992 per sq.dm. Upper end: —. Lower end: remains of a silk kilim, raspberry-red. Selvedges: —. Quality: like thin velvet.
Colours: 14, *wine red, pistachio green*, green, navy blue, pale blue, surmey, brown-black, yellow, olive-yellow, sand, ivory, olive-brown, gold-silver.
Pattern: medallion and corner pieces. The central field is filled unsymmetrically with innumerable hunting motifs. Winged jinns are seated in the main border against a soft rich pattern of flowering stems.

70. **Isfahan or Kashan, 17th century. So-called Polish carpet.** 200 × 138 cm. (p. 167 below).
Warp: silk, S-plied, 2 strands, twisted, dyed, yellow.
Weft: silk, single, dyed reddish. 3 shoots: 1. and 3. straight, 2. sinuous. Brocading: silk, S-plied, 2 strands, twisted, yellow wrapped with metal foil. Technique (see p. 34): the brocading floats over 4—5 warp threads, then behind an upper thread of the strongly depressed warp and again over 4—5 threads etc. The brocading is invisible on the back. Pile: silk, 2—4 strands, untwisted. Knots P. III, 80°: h. 104, w. 84 = 8,744 per sq.dm.
Upper end: silk kilim yellow/black/red. Lower end: remains of a silk kilim red and yellow mixed.
Selvedges: 3 cms. without knotting, no special strengthening.
Quality: extremely thin, smooth. Colours: 18, *cream, red, light blue, blue-black*, light yellow-green, Prophet's green, dark olive, light olive, purple, olive-yellow, dughi, pale blue, green-blue, dark blue, medium yellow-brown, black-brown, metallic gold and silver now oxidised. The colours, now pale, were originally very bright.

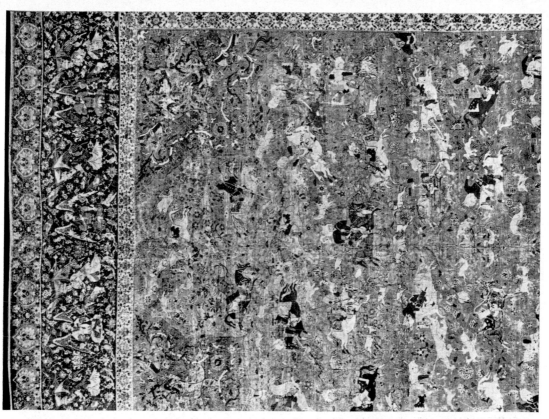

up, and the parts of the background remaining free because of the pattern are kept in different colours. In the late style, which as yet hardly affects the provinces — Kirman, Tabriz and Herat — it is impossible not to notice the signs of a degeneration of artistic responsibility and conscience. Other pieces are carefully and lovingly worked, like the very small garden carpet entirely of silk in the Archaeological Museum in Teheran, which has a count of more than 14,000 knots per square dm. and the signature: 'Nematola Djoshegani in the year 1082 (1671 AD)'.

Djoshegan (Djoushagan), situated to the north-west of Isfahan in the mountains, had a highly productive manufactory.

The resettled Julfer Armenians clearly exercised a strong influence on the production of the Isfahan manufactories, but it cannot be distinguished in detail in the patterns. The volume of production and export, as in Kashan, was very large. In Kashan it is recorded that King Sigismund III of Poland sent an emissary to supervise the fabrication of the carpets commissioned by him. The numerous carpets found in Poland with the royal arms interrupting the run of the pattern have given their name to the whole category of brocaded carpets. The decadent pallor of their colours is the patina of age. The colour scheme was originally extremely strong, but it was difficult to make the dyes take on the silk.

The mihrab arch of the little-known prayer carpets, richly decorated with flowers and calligraphy, approximates in form to a large curved horseshoe.

The Saffavid court maintained a warehouse in Isfahan for its carpets, as did the Ottoman court in Istanbul.

In the south Persian centre round KIRMAN the carpets are large and noticeably narrow, and the patterns are not arranged round the centre of the carpet. The borders are modest both as regards size and pattern. The vertical floral pattern with or without a vase, the lozenges and half-drop rows, and the large-scale divisions by gigantic curved arabesque stems all emphasise the vertical axis. The lozenges formed by large lanceolate leaves show a connection with the Caucasian 'dragon carpets'. Luxuriance is coupled with strictness in the plant patterns. The colours are rich and strong. Strictness of composition and renunciation of silk and brocading in the pile, in a count of hardly more than 4,000 Persian knots per square dm. enabled this region to maintain its tradition with a continuity which proved to be of importance for Persia until well into the nineteenth century.

The early carpets from the east Persian region round HERAT have no medallions but they stress the centre of the inner field to some extent inasmuch as the spiral stem system of the ground pattern is mirrored round the vertical and horizontal axes. This background scheme is not always easily seen at first sight behind the prominent palmettes and cloud bands. The chief colours are deep wine red, moss green and yellow. Brocading is rare. During the seventeenth century curved lanceolate leaves gradually turn into gigantic sickles while the pattern diminishes in scale and the basic divisions are thus enhanced. Four curved lancet leaves, with four palmettes arranged symmetrically round a lozenge-shaped mesh of stems, form the great Herati motif. Later in west and north Persia the Herati motif was perpetuated in a smaller form as the most important element of an endless repeat.

 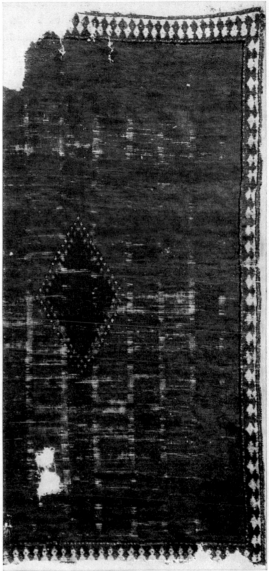

71. a. b. Doruye = druya = two — faced carpet. Caucasus-Persian frontier region, 19th century.
c. 193 × 132 cm.

Warp: C. S-plied 5 strands, twisted, undyed.

Weft: C. Z-spun 4 strands, untwisted undyed. 2—3 shoots alternating sinuous after each 2 rows of knots.

Pile: W. Z-spun, 2 strands untwisted. Knots P. II, 70°: After each row of knots on the front follows a row of knots on the back on the same pairs of warp threads, and only then the weft shoots. h. 40, w. 34 = 1,360 per sq. dm. (both sides together).

Upper end: remains of a C. kilim bright blue (C. S-plied, 6 strands), remains of 4 rows horizontal plaits.

Lower end: remains of a 2 cm. wide C. kilim bright blue, filling up the warp loops.

Selvedges: remains of a W. shirazi red round 4 bunches of warp threads.

Quality: soft, very heavy. Colours: 7, *red, blue, yellow,* ivory, blue-green, some black-brown and light olive.

Pattern: front: a blue diamond in the red central field. Back: broad blue and green vertical stripes with yellow edges. Medakhyl border on both sides.

In the eighteenth century this area was the first to be exposed to the Afghan invasion; after the restless reign of Nadir Shah, Herat was lost to the Persian empire.

The tendency towards emphatic enrichment of surface pattern, partly by borrowing designs from other areas, can be seen frequently from the end of the seventeenth century. In other carpets on the other hand there is the attempt to cling to tradition, even though the old patterns are impoverished and stiff. The political and economic decline dragged down many large manufactories at the same time as the workshops attached to the court collapsed.

Persian (Iranian) carpets of the nineteenth and twentieth centuries

The last unmistakable innovations of north-west Persia were the garden and tree carpets of the eighteenth century. In the garden carpets an earlier pattern is readopted: decorative canals enclose quadrilateral beds filled with flowering trees, shrubs and birds, and eight lobed round or oval medallions. In the eighteenth century the canals are seen in birds' eye view, and have become straight and broad, the water is in ornamental waves and the fishes are angular. Trees and bushes are angular, the medallions geometricised to cartouches. In the tree carpets there are rows of cartouches — a horizontal row of large asymmetrical cartouches alternates with a row of smaller symmetrical ones — and in between them are placed thick curved tree trunks that dominate the design, and look bare because the leaves are scanty on thin flowered branches.

TABRIZ in the nineteenth century continues the tradition of the medallion carpets and stylised floral patterns, adding to it patterns and forms from all the larger Persian manufactories, including the hunting carpets. Since it was also the trade and export centre for east and central Persian carpets — a considerable part of the south Persian exports found their way through Arabia to Cairo — Tabriz had the perfect opportunity to examine every pattern and copy it. Being the Persian city nearest to Europe it ran far ahead of every other Iranian carpet centre.

XIV. Meshgin. North-west Persia, 19th—20th century. Kenareh. (379—389) 384×91 (88—94) cm. (detail). (p. 171).
Warp: C. S-plied, 2 strands, twisted, undyed.
Weft: as warp: 2—3 shoots alternating sinuous.
Pile: W. Z-spun, 2 strands, untwisted. Knots T. I: h. 25, w. 24 = 600 per sq.dm. Upper end: 2 cm. C. kilim. Threads knotted in threes. Lower end: —. Selvedges: W. shirazi brown 2 cord round 3 threads.
Quality: soft, heavy, firm, coarse.
Colours: 9, *medium brown, brown-black, sand, medium blue,* red, light blue, light red-brown, olive-yellow, light blue-green.
Pattern: the brown-black central field has a thin straight stem running along its vertical axis. At the bottom three geometricised branches turn out at their side and run up the central field in zig-zags, forming twelve hexagons. These hexagons and the spaces outside them are occupied by naive representations of nomads and all their animals (horses, camels, cows, goats, dogs and poultry). Border of diagonal stripes.

The wool of north-west Persia is heavy and matt; only the fine wool from the flocks bred by the Sheik of Maku in the northernmost region of the Perso-Turkish frontier lend a little more lustre to the dyes. H. Jacoby reports that he had hanks of the same wool dyed with the same madder in Tabriz and in Sultanabad; while the wool dyed in Tabriz showed the usual tired matt tone, Sultanabad achieved a fuller and more radiant, slightly bluish red. As so often therefore it is the chemical content of the water that is the deciding factor. Tabriz was equally well situated for importing as for exports, and chemical dyes from Europe arrived here first. Because of the tendency of the first chemical dyes to fade, and because of the American desire for thicker carpets, they began to abandon the traditional low pile and thus spoilt the effect of the fine-drawn patterns. As has already been mentioned, the Petag Persische Teppich-Gesellschaft AG (Persian Carpet Company) installed itself in Tabriz in 1911 and is to be credited with the preservation of the old methods of dyeing and knotting. Good models were chosen — the designs for the patterns had to be prepared mostly in museums and private collections, since there was nothing distinguished left in industry in the way of design — and hand-knotting was carried on with several different counts using natural dyes on highest quality wool, and good patterns.

In Tabriz the Turkish knot is the most widely used. The right half of the knot is made with the Tabriz knotting hook on the end of the knife as it is in several other regions in Persia where Turkish knots are the rule. This method, not employed for the Persian and djufti knots, makes the work faster. The djufti knot is done over four warp threads, and unfortunately is creeping in in a number of manufactories which use the Persian knot, or the Turkish knot without the Tabriz hook. The parts of the carpet knotted in this djufti knot contain only half the number of knots to the number of pairs of warp threads. They are more quickly produced, but their pile is only half as close as when the normal Persian or Turkish knots are used. The knotting hook makes the Tabriz knotters the speediest in all Persia.

The ground-weave is cotton. Silk and wool in the ground-weave are very rare. The quality is very varied in craftsmanship, pattern and material. Good clearly defined and finely knotted designs are the exception nowadays. The count is on the whole medium fine to fine. In recent years however small pieces have been produced, both of the worst commercial wares with only 200 knots to the square dm., and of the finest work with over 8,000 knots per square dm. The large manufactories are able to produce very large as well as medium-sized formats. The largest carpets yet ventured (Petag) measured close on 200 square metres. The warp had to be set up in a tower. Since wood was not capable of bearing such a load over such a span the warp and cloth beams were made of iron T girders. Pushtis, corresponding to the Turkish yastiks, are also made in Tabriz. They are small pieces of carpet for the upper side of cushion covers.

Besides good and average quality wools much inferior wool called tabachi is sometimes used, taken from dead animals in the large slaughter houses. Dyeing with synthetic colours has been well mastered.

If it is still difficult to recognise a Tabriz with its characteristic lotus palmette because of the colour schemes and the large repertoire of patterns, then the matt wool and the rather irregular look of the back, showing spreading and contracting wefts. are the best distinguishing marks.

A good Tabriz species is Sarand; Sharabian is like Heris, hard as a board but unsatisfactory in colouring; Choy is medium fine.

In the nineteenth century very good carpets came from Marand, north-west of Tabriz. Tabriz has produced many famous knotters, such as Haji Yalil Marandaila (= from Marand). Carpets from the area between Lake Urmia and Heris were formerly called Bagshaish (Bakhshis). These were good, usually large keleys in lustrous wool both with Ferahan-(boteh) and Yoraghan-like patterns.

HERIS about 100 km. east of Tabriz has remained by and large true to its well-known strongly geometric designs, but for a few slight modifications (fig. 73). The carpets used formerly to be called Iris as well as Heris. The large-scale angular stem medallions and corner pieces are drawn in soft clear colours against a red or more rarely a blue or ivory coloured ground. This design is admirably suited to modern

72. Tabriz, mid-20th century. 191 × 137 cm. (p. 175 above).
Warp: C. S-plied, 5 strands, twisted, undyed.
Weft: One thick cotton, undyed, straight.; one thin, sinuous. C. Z-spun, 2 strands, untwisted, undyed.
Pile: W. Z-spun, 2 strands, untwisted. Knots T. III: h. 48, w. 44 = 2112 per sq. dm. Upper end: fringe.
  Lower end: as upper end. Selvedges: W. shirazi round 5 bunched warp threads.
Quality: dull, medium thick, medium granular.
Colours: 9, *dark blue, brick red, light olive, white,* dark olive, yellow-olive, dark red-brown, light blue, pink.
Pattern: a sixteen-lobed medallion in the dark blue central field, with four other sixteen-and eight-lobed
  flowers inside it concentrically. A vertically and horizontally symmetrical ground pattern of curved leaf
  stems with palmettes, composite flowers and birds. In the main border an arabesque stem with palmettes.

73. Heris, 20th century. 374 × 260 cm. (p. 175 below).
Warp: C. S-plied, 6 strands, twisted, undyed.
Weft: C. 1 thick straight; 1 thin sinuous, S-plied, 4 strands slightly twisted, undyed or undyed with dyed
  blue. Alternately one single shoot straight and one shoot straight with one shoot sinuous.
Pile: W. Z-spun, 2 strands, untwisted. Knots T. II 20°: h. 36, w. 26 = 936 per sq. dm. Upper end: —.
  Lower end: remains of a C. kilim light blue. Selvedges: W. shirazi olive-brown round 2 left-twisted
  pairs of warp threads. Quality: dry, firm, medium heavy, coarsely ribbed.
Colours: 11, *brick red, dark blue, ivory,* medium blue, green, light blue, brown-red, light olive, dughi, black-
  brown, yellow-olive.
Pattern: the characteristic Heris pattern: the red central field contains a large angular arabesque medallion
  with geometric floral filling round the central motif and palmette attachments on the vertical axis. The
  large light corner fillings only leave a portion of the edge of the central field free along the sides. For the
  main border a double angular thin stem with palmettes enclosed in arabesque leaves.

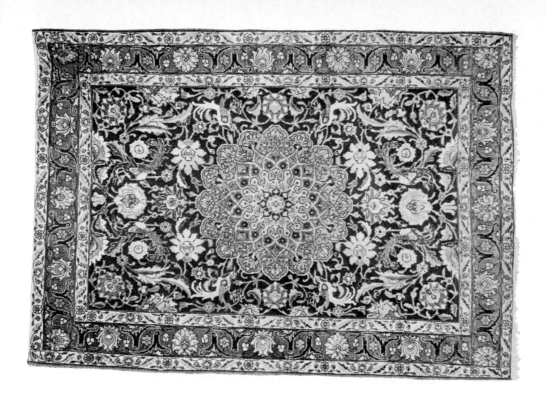

long piles and the medium-fine knotting in Turkish knots on a strong cotton warp. The weft is usually of cotton and often has a characteristic peculiarity. It alternates a single, thick and straight shoot as in Hamadan weave with a similar shoot accompanied by a second thinner sinuous weft. The count is medium fine, in older pieces sometimes fine, and in silk pieces exceptionally fine. These latter usually have rounded medallions with attachments.

The formats reach from the rare Namaseh and Sejadeh to carpets of 800 × 500 cm. The poorer Heris quality is called Yoraghan (Geravan), the finest with softer wool 'peshm-i-Meshed' (pashmi-e-Mashad — wool from Meshed). This fine quality of wool comes from Maku.

The Ahar, called after the village once famous for its carpets, is knotted in a manner similar to the Heris, but the medallion is more oval and the detail more naturalistic. At present its carpets, predominantly dyed with natural colours, are the best from the Heris region.

Mehravan used to produce acceptable carpets but has sunk to the lowest Bakhshi quality.

ARDEBIL, south of the Russian border and the Talish district provides carpets of quality in sizes up to 300 by 200 cm., with rigid Caucasian Shirvan-like patterns. They are also similar to the Caucasian carpets technically, and difficult to distinguish from the latest Caucasian products. In Tabriz trade parlance 'Ardebil runners' includes all stair carpets from the mountainous region west of Ardebil. These are mostly thick and rustic, all wool and coarsely worked; they are especially the Meshgins from the region of Meshginshar and the Sarabs from the area of that name, together with those of Veramin, among the best products of modern Persian nomad and cottage industry.

The MESHGIN is darker in tone. The picture on p. 167 shows part of a particularly original example.

The SARAB, likewise in Turkish knots and very firmly knotted, often looks like an old Hamadan runner. The wool is outstandingly good. Recently some of the colours have been produced with chemical dyes and occasionally carpets of room size have been made.

KARADJA (fig. 71) are made in the Karadagh (= black mountain), the frontier region between Russia and Iran. They too are entirely of wool (recently cotton warps also) and their designs are reminiscent of the Caucasus. The formats are kenareh and sejadeh. Keleys are less usual, because the pattern looks restless on such an area. The very rare reversible carpet (doruye, druya) with the pile on both sides (illustrated in fig. 66), probably comes from the north-western frontier region of Armenia. For the rows of knots on alternate sides the Persian knot used here was evidently better suited, but otherwise the colours, materials and structure all conform to those of the carpets of this region. Beautiful untufted Sileh and Verneh were also produced in large quantities in the Karadagh.

Mianeh, on the road and railway from Tabriz to Kasvin (Gasvin) produced thick medium-fine hand-knotted keleys until the end of the nineteenth century. The small floral patterns show a remarkable bluish red. Now runners similar to Hamadans

74. Karadagh. North-west Persian and Russian frontier region. 19th century. 'Karadya'. (172—178)
175 × 135 (133—137) cm.

Warp: W. S-plied, 3 strands, twisted, undyed light to dark brown.

Weft: W. S-plied, 2 strands, twisted, undyed brown. 2 shoots alternating sinuous or single and double shoots alternating sinuous. Additional shoots from the sides to up to 25 cm. in depth.

Pile: W. Z-spun, 2 strands, untwisted. Knots T. I: h. 33, w. 27 = 891 per sq. dm. Upper end: —. Lower end: —. Selvedges: W. shirazi dark brown 2 cord. Quality: smooth, fleshy, coarsely granular.

Colours: 9, *surmey, rust red, ivory, light green-blue,* light blue, black brown, light olive, light olive-yellow, light brown.

Pattern: the indigo central field contains a large hooked lozenge and two large stems geometricised to rectangles with leaf attachments resembling little flags. Within the lozenge is a finely stepped polygon containing an octagon decorated with a stem cross and four rosettes. An almost symmetrical scatter pattern of rosettes, lozenge, quadrupeds and birds. In the main border lozenges in regular alternation with a pair of small quatrefoil flower heads.

come from there, and are hardly to be distinguished from those of Sendshan (Tsanyan, Zenjan, 140 km. south-east of Mianeh) with their disagreeable red. The 'Sendshan Mossul' have a pretty exact measurement of 200 × 100 cm.

From the region between Mianeh and the Caspian Sea come the Kelardasht. They resemble the 'Kurd Kasaks' from the frontier region towards Kasak in their sombre colouring and dark brown woollen underweave.

Kasvin (Gasvin), with the remains of its old rammed earth town walls, lies picturesquely in an oasis where the great roads fork, from Teheran to Reshd on the Caspian and from Hamadan to Tabriz. It was formerly an important collecting centre for carpets.

TEHERAN never succeeded in developing a tradition of design. The carpets are worked in Persian knots, fine or very fine in gauge on a cotton ground-weave (fig. 96), but they have no individuality. Delicate floral designs, some with medallions, gardens and paradise patterns, mostly on a light ground, are the most popular. The formats reach from sarenim to carpets of forty square metres and more.

Carpets from VERAMIN (40 km. south-east of Teheran) are to be classified into two fundamentally different types — the manufactory and the nomad or peasant pieces:

75. Feramin, mid 20th century. Manufactory carpet. 203 × 105 cm.
Warp: C. S-plied, 3 strands, twisted, undyed white.
Weft: C. 1. thick straight, undyed. 2. thin sinuous, Z-spun, 2 strands, untwisted, dyed light blue.
Pile: W. Z-spun, 2 strands, untwisted. Knots T. III, 80°: h. 48, w. 68 = 3,264 per sq.dm.
Upper end: 3 cm. C. kilim white, then warp threads knotted together in tens. Lower end: as upper end.
Selvedges: W. shirazi dark blue round 6 bunched warp threads.
Quality: dry, medium thick, fine granular.
Colours: 9 *blue, white, red,* olive-brown, dark brown, light blue, black, some pink and light green.
Pattern: the blue central field is covered with the mina-khani pattern. In the main border a white stem scroll with lotus flower. The spaces made by the scrolls are alternately red and blue; thus the principle of the unity of the ground of the border has been abandoned.

76. Bidjar, 19th century. 155 × 126 (124—128) cm. (p. 179 below).
Warp: W. S-plied, 3 strands, twisted, undyed light brownish.
Weft: W. S-plied, 2 strands, slightly twisted, undyed dark brown. 2 shoots (Bidyar weave see p. 30).
    1. extremely thick, straight, 2. thin, sinuous.
Pile: W. Z-spun, 2—3 strands, untwisted. Knots T. II, 80°: h. 36, w. 40 = 1,440 per sq.dm. Upper end:
    row of herringbone, W. 4 strands; then warp threads knotted in fours. Lower end: as upper end, but
    without knotting of warp threads.
Selvedges: W. shirazi light brown round 4 warp threads.
Quality: fleshy, very thick and firm, coarse ribbing.
Colours: 13, *brown, light brown, light red,* sand, dark blue, medium blue, green, dark red-brown, ivory,
    olive-yellow, black-brown, some dughi and purple.
Pattern: the central field contains a fragment of the continuous half-drop repeat of ten or twelve lobed
    rosettes and geometric flower crosses. The main border began as a cloud band scroll with cartouches, and
    was then continued narrower as a double stem with flower rosettes.

178

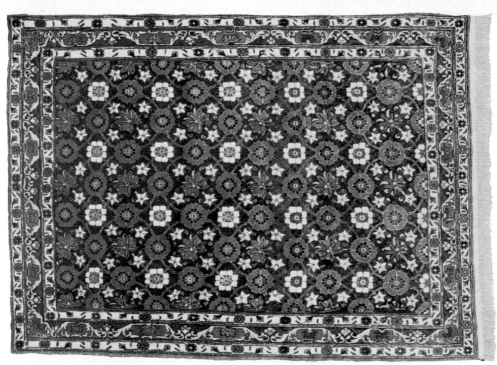

the manufactory carpets have a medium-long pile and are extremely well made in Turkish knots on cotton warps. The thicker straight weft is usually undyed, the thinner, sinuous one is light blue. The formats are usually narrow and do not generally go above twelve square metres. The most usual pattern (fig. 75) is a mina-khani in an airy three-colour scheme of blue, white and red.

77. Veramin. 19/20th century. Torba = Small bag, c. 46 × 33 cm.
Warp: W. Z-spun, 2 strands S-plied undyed dark and Cotton Z-spun 3 strands S-plied undyed.
Weft: W. Z-spun single dyed red. One weft sinuous.
Pile: W. Z-spun 2–3 strands. Knots: T. I: h. 36, w. 32 = 1.152 knots per dm². Work begun at the narrow part.
Upper end: W. kilim rust red, turned over and sewn.
Lower end: W. kilim red-brown as a transition to the back wall palas, which is woven on pairs of warp threads.
Touch: fleshy, thick, coarse granular.
Colours: 9, *surmey, ivory, rust red,* light brown, navy blue, light olive, green, olive-yellow, black.
Pattern: a primitive Harati motif on surmey central field. In the narrow part rosettes and animals which stand on their heads (following the direction of the work).

The simple kenareh, keleys and small pieces of nomad and cottage industry are worked entirely in wool, unless cotton is used for the warp. The colours are good, somewhat sombre, the patterns uncomplicated, the pile is long. On this page is illustrated one of the original bags from this region, used in the household to store pulses and other food.

From SEMNAN, 200 km. east of Teheran in an oasis on the edge of the great salt desert, come good carpets in sizes of sedjadah up to 600 × 400 cm., without any individuality in design. They are naturalistic and similar to those of Isfahan.

BIDJAR (Bijar, Bidshar) lies about half way between Sendshan and Sehna (Sanan-day). Carpets from Bidjar and the forty or so villages round about are the thickest

XV. Ferrahan, 19th century. c. 203 × 133 cm. (p. 181).
Warp: C. S-plied, 6 strands, twisted, undyed.
Weft: C. S-plied, lightly twisted, undyed. 2 shoots: 1. straight, 2. sinuous.
Pile: W. Z-spun, 2—4 strands, untwisted. Knots P. II; 20°: h. 40, w. 35 = 1,400 per sq. dm. Upper end: 2 cm. remaining of a C. kilim undyed light, ribbed.
Lower end: 3 cm. C. kilim of douple shoots undyed light. The last shoot plaited with warp thread loops.
Selvedges: W. shirazi surmey round 3 warp threads.
Quality: dry, thin, leather hard.
Colours: 13, *surmey, terracotta, celadon-green,* ivory, light blue, medium blue, blue-green, purple, brown-black, dughi, olive-brown, dark violet-brown, light olive-yellow.
Pattern: the relatively narrow indigo central field (borders: central field = 73 : 60) contains the Herati pattern, also called mahi-to-hos (fish in pool). Ferrahan border on a red ground, with four guard stripes containing carnation stems on corroded celadon-green (ab-i-sangar).

and most hardwearing of any. They have a long pile and an extremely thick packing weft which is invisible from the outside (drawing on p. 30). They are nearly all worked in Turkish knots and medium fine to fine, and they range in format from sejadeh to 600 × 400 cm., in exceptional cases up to forty square metres.

The ground-weave is wool in smaller formats, cotton in larger. They have a variety of patterns: herati, stylised medallions with corner fillings — often on a monochrome ground — palmette stems, geometric angular medallions with small-scale filling elements, stylisations of early Isfahan patterns or the simple do-guleh (cf. fig. 76) which is also characteristic of the simpler carpets from the surrounding Gerus region. The rare Sauchbulagh (the Kurdish word sawjy-bulag means cold spring) is very good Kurd work from the region south of Lake Urmia; it is like the Bidjar, and may reach large formats. It is worked in lustrous wool in Turkish knots, generally on a woollen ground-weave. It usually shows a medallion in muted colours with a wonderful green, on a blue background.

KURD is the name for the nomad and peasant carpets worked in west Iran, east Anatolia and northern Iraq by the Kurds. They use lustrous wool and Turkish knots for coarsely knotted long-piled namaseh, sarenim and kenareh formats. The colours are dark and the patterns simple and geometric. The long woollen pile tends to curl over.

These simple carpets are not the only work done by Kurds; Iran Bidjar and Sehna carpets are mostly made by Kurds.

SEHNA (Sinah, Senna, now Sanandaj) in the centre of Kurdistan produces on average the finest Iranian carpets. The patterns are worked in Turkish knots — why exactly the Persian knot is called after the town of Sehna, where it is never used, is inexplicable — on a cotton or silk warp and they require a short pile. The silk warp is striped in several colours. The Sehna carpet is recognisable at first sight and touch. No other carpet is as granular. The fine weft is shot straight through the thin warp. The rows of knots are densely packed and the warp is alternately raised and depressed by the straight weft, so the knots are turned right and left row by row ('salt and pepper'). The count can be anything up to 8,000 knots per square dm. The narrow formats occasionally reach twenty square metres. The most usual patterns are boteh, ranging from small to very large, the tops all bending in the same direction in half rows (fig. 78), fine diagonal stems which carry alternately vertical and horizontal small boteh, and the Herati pattern with a rhombic medallion. At the turn of the century there appeared a naturalistic flower posy and a geometric palmette pattern. The tender colouring is dominated by ivory, red and pistachio or celadon green.

Sehna is also known for the finest Kelims. They are woven so finely on a wool or silk warp that only the smallest slits occur at the joins between one colour and the next. The main pattern is the herati, often with a light-coloured diamond-shaped medallion. They are only made in small sejadeh sizes (fig. 79).

In HAMADAN and its extensive region stand more than ten thousand looms. Knotting is done in Turkish knots on cotton warps; it is usually coarse, more rarely medium fine. The pile, in answer to the climate, is long. The weft is unmistakable to sight and touch at the back, being straight, thick and almost always of cotton. The formats used to be kenareh and keley; room-size carpets were rare. Now sejadeh sizes, kenareh and carpets of 300 × 200 to 600 × 400 cm. are quite usual, some are even larger. They have abandoned the lovely old patterns with large zig-zagged diamond medallions, often on a ground of two tones of natural camel colour, or with a small-scale boteh background (fig. 81) and the broad camel-coloured edging round the border. However it is still possible to find a good number of beautiful older small formats, produced for home use. The floral pattern now preferred is unsuitable since the knotting is not fine enough and the pile too long. The chemical dyes in general use look very stark and require a harsh bleaching wash. The best modern representative of Hamadan is Ekbatan. Under its old name of Ekbatana, Hamadan, standing on the edge of a plain 1,800 m. above sea level on the northern slopes of the Alvand (3,571 m.), was the capital of the empire of the Medes and the summer residence of the Achaemenids.

To the Hamadan carpets belong Injelas, Koltuk (Goltuk), Tafrish, Karagös, Bordshaln, Malayer, Saveh and Kkamseh. Their formats are all dosaer and sejadeh. The most usual design of the Injelas, medium fine knotted in lustrous wool, is a stylised herati on a red ground with a dark border. They are among the most beautiful of modern Hamadans.

78. Sehna, 19th—20th century. Front of choval or pushti. 100 × 54 cm. (p. 185 above).
Warp: C. S-plied, 4 strands, twisted, undyed.
Weft: C. S-plied, 3 strands, twisted. 1 shoot straight.
Pile: W. Z-spun, 2 strands, untwisted. Knots T. I: h. 60, w. 60 = 3,600 per sq.dm. Upper end: —.
 Lower end: —.
Selvedges: W. shirazi brown round 10 bunched warp threads.
Quality: dry, almost thin, hard, strong fine granulation.
Colours: 8, *ivory, red, green, black,* light blue, yellow-olive, some wine-red and dughi.
Pattern: one of the characteristic Sehna patterns: large boteh in three half-drop rows between stylised floral stems on an ivory central field. All crests turned to the right and rich interior floral ornamentation.

79. Sehna, 19th—20th century. Kelim. (156—160) 158 × 130 (128—132) cm. (p. 185 below).
Warp: W. S-plied, 2 strands, twisted, undyed light. 68 warp threads per dm. Pattern weft: W. slight S-ply, 2 strands. c. 280 shoots. (kelim technique, see p. 34).
Upper end: warp threads plaited in horizontal braid, then knotted in two rows of net. Lower end: as upper.
Quality: hard, granular, firm.
Colours: 7, *black, raspberry-red, olive-yellow,* ivory, light blue, coral, dark red-brown.
Pattern: the black central field is covered with the Herati pattern. The middle of the three border stripes has diagonal stripes. The other two have a wave band on an ivory ground. The ground colour of the outer stripe is continued in blue after the first third.

184

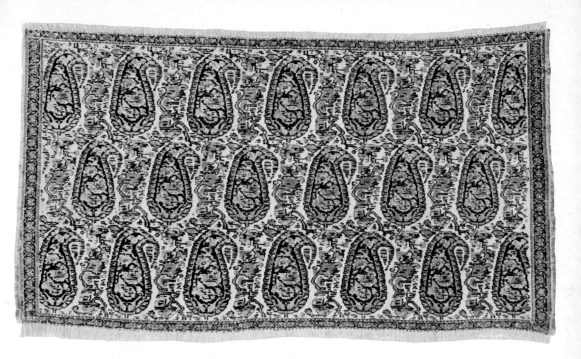

The Koltuk (Goltuk, fig. 80), hand-knotted by nomads, usually shows a geometric medallion with a small-scale filling or the Herati design of the Ferahan. The design and weight of the carpet sometimes lead to confusion with Bidjar.

The Tafrish (Tafresh, south-west of Saveh) is usually patterned with a medallion on a monochrome ground.

The Karaghös of the Karaghösli (black-eyed) nomads in the region round Hamadan generally has a primitive Ferahan pattern or a simple medallion with corners. Yellow often stands out from among the dark colours.

The Bordshalu has crude floral medallions and a narrow border.

The Malayer (fig. 82) is often excellently knotted and used to have very beautiful independent patterns and colours. At present although the patterns, colours and knotting are becoming increasingly stereotyped, it is still good.

The Saveh is among the best of the new Hamadan styles. The Maslagan (Maslavan) from this region has found many admirers. It sometimes uses the Persian knot and has wool or hair for the weft. The formats are sejadeh and kenareh, rarely sarenim. The typical pattern (fig. 84) is a large medallion spreading broadly into the narrow ends with a large zig-zag edge over vertical chains of little flowers on a blue or red ground. Another good-quality modern Hamadan type is the Shasevan. The worst is the Khamseh.

80. Koltuk, region of Hamadan, 19th—20th century. (191—199) 195 × 145 (140—150) cm. (p. 187 above).
Warp: C. S-plied, 5 strands, twisted, undyed.
Weft: C. S-plied, 5 strands, lightly twisted, undyed thick. 1 shoot straight, at a short distance also double shoots in the same shed. (Hamadan weave, see p. 30).
Pile: W. Z-spun, 2 strands, untwisted. Knots T. III: h. 29, w. 38 = 1,102 per sq.dm. Upper and lower end: —. Selvedges: W. shirazi black-brown round 3 warp threads. Quality: silky, board hard, thick, slightly granular.
Colours: 7, *camel* (in several shades), *red, surmey,* medium blue, dark brown, green-blue, olive-yellow.
Pattern: the soft (camel) wool of the originally red central field has lost colour completely, leaving only the upper sixth, which is knotted in different wool. The indigo hexagonal medallion with a lozenge-diapered hooked hexagon superimposed on it is, like the central field, closely strewn with geometric motifs, birds, horses and human figures. The border has a tile effect produced by four birds symmetrically arranged round a cross-shaped geometric stem motif.

81. Hamadan, 19th—20th century. 280 × 156 (154—158) cm. (187 below).
Warp: C. S-plied, 4 strands, twisted, undyed.
Weft: C. S-plied, 4 strands, slightly twisted, undyed. One shoot straight (Hamadan weave). Isolated double shoots from the sides up to 25 cm. deep.
Pile: W. Z-spun, 2 strands, untwisted. Knots T. I: h. 29, w. 27 = 783 per sq.dm.
Upper end: —. Lower end: —. Selvedges: W. shirazi 2 cord round 4 twisted warp threads.
Quality: soft, very heavy, firm, coarsely granular.
Colours: 11, *red, camel-brown, olive-yellow,* black, olive-green, vermilion, light blue, white, black-brown, dughi, yellow-brown.
Pattern: red central field with continuous half-drop rows of two kinds of boteh: small symmetrical boteh on a little foot flanked by two green boteh leaves alternating regularly with large floral boteh, with crests curving alternately left and right. Round the borders the broad camel-coloured (shuturi) edge typical of older Hamadans.

82. Malayer, region of Hamadan, late 19th century. Kenareh. 530 × 115 (113—117) cm. (detail). (above)
Warp: W. S-plied, 3 strands, twisted, undyed light brown.
Weft: W. S-plied, 4 strands, slightly twisted, undyed light brown. 1 shoot straight.
Pile: W. Z-spun, 2 strands untwisted. Knots T. II, 20°: h. 30, w. 33 = 990 per sq. dm. Upper end: 2 cm.
 W. kilim light brown, fringes. Lower end: —. Selvedges: W. shirazi single cord in various colours.
Quality: soft, medium heavy, slightly granular.
Colours: 8, *rust-red, orange, olive-yellow, ivory,* surmey, navy blue, dark brown, some olive.
Pattern: 6 large small stepped hexagons are aligned with 7 chequered diamonds along a bar over a striped
 ground.

83. Saruk, 19th century. Rupalani = saddle cover. 99 × 96 (93—99) cm. (p. 189 above).
Warp: C. S-plied, 4 strands, twisted, undyed.
Weft: C. S-plied, 4 strands, lightly twisted, undyed, thick, and C. S-plied, 2 strands, lightly twisted, dyed
 blue, thin. 2 shoots: 1. thick, straight, 2. thin, sinuous.
Pile: W. Z-spun, 2 strands, untwisted. Knots P. II 85°: h. 74, w. 72 = 5,328 per sq. dm. Upper and Lower
 ends: —. Selvedges: W. shirazi red single cord. Quality: dry, leather hard, thin, finely granular.
Colours: 9, *surmey, vermilion,* sand, some light blue, brown-red, black, crimson, olive-green and olive-
 yellow.
Pattern: bright red central field with herati pattern, the seat plain surmey with only two flower vases and
 four flower heads. Shekiri border.

84. Maslagan (Maslavan), mid-20th century. 194 × 132 cm. (p. 189 below).
Warp: C. S-plied, 6 strands, twisted, undyed.
Weft: C. S-plied, multiple, slightly twisted, undyed and dyed blue grey. One shoot straight.
Pile: W. Z-spun, 2 strands, untwisted. Knots T. I: h. 36, w. 32 = 1,152 per sq. dm. Upper end: fringe.
 Lower end: 2 cm. C. kilim, white. Warp loops filled with thick shoots.
Selvedges: W. Shirazi black brown round 6 bunched warp threads.
Quality: rather smooth, thick, horizontal ribbing.
Colours: 10, *terracotta, surmey, white,* light blue, dark red-brown, olive, pale olive-yellow, grass-green,
 olive-brown, pink.
Pattern: the standard Maslagan pattern: a large serrated medallion over the surmey-coloured central field
 with its flower chains.

KERMANSHAH (Kirmanshah) has recently developed into a modern city and possesses an oil refinery. Earlier it was primarily a market for Kurd carpets produced in the region. The modern manufactory carpets are coarse to medium fine in Turkish knots on a cotton warp. They may reach formats of more than 20 square dms. The floral patterns borrow from the large central Persian manufactories and do not turn out very satisfactorily, since the knotting is not fine enough. Kermanshah is also a trading centre for Turkoman prayer rugs with a similar pattern to the Yomud (fig. 116).

The carpets from the FERAHAN (Feraghan) area in the triangle formed by Arak (Sultanabad), Kum and Kashan are soothing and calm in effect. The Herati or Ferahan patterns are well drawn on a blue or more rarely a dark red or light coloured background (p. 181). The design, developed in earlier centuries in Herat, looks different according to the distance from which it is seen: close to, the single Herati motif is dominant, while from further away, first a diagonal and then a squared pattern emerges. The main border shows the herati border pattern with the celadon green (ab-i-sangaer) characteristic of Ferahan. It is produced in old pieces from isperek and copper vitriol and the dye has corroded the wool. The celadon green parts of the design therefore lie lower than the pattern of other colours, and these seem to stand out in relief. Old Ferahans are worked on a cotton warp in Persian knots with a medium-fine count. The pile is short, and feels firm. The normal formats are sejadeh and keley up to 420 × 200, rarely 700 × 350 cm. SARUK (Saruq) came from the village of that name in the region lying to the west of Ferahan, to the north of Arak (Sultanabad). The old Saruk is often very finely knotted on a cotton warp in either Turkish or Persian knots. It is clipped very short, is dry, leather hard and finely granular in feel and almost indestructible. It is usually found in sejadeh format. The free delicate design of a medallion and corner fillings usually leaves only a small part of the central field background visible. Rust red, ivory and blue-black are the dominant tones (fig. 83, 86). In the twentieth century Saruk has become the term for the best quality carpets from Arak and the regions of Mahallat, Kezzaz and Khansaer to the south. The floral patterns of these thick carpets are very distinctive.

XVI. Kirman, 19th century. Kirman-lawer. 76 × 64 cm. (p. 191).
Warp: C. S-plied, 6 strands, twisted, undyed.
Weft: C. S-plied, 4 strands, slightly twisted, undyed. 3 shoots: 1. and 3. (thick) straight, 2. (thin) sinuous.
Pile: W. Z-spun, 2 strands, untwisted. Knots P. II 70°: h. 78, w. 70 = 5,460 per sq.dm. Upper end: 4 shoots C. kilim undyed light, fringes. Lower end: as upper end, but warp threads looped and twisted.
Selvedges: W. shirazi not original. Quality: like velvet, thin, hard, fine-ribbed.
Colours: 13, *cream, olive, wine red,* pink, brown-black, light green-blue, light blue, pale blue, white, medium brown, orange-brown, olive-green, olive-yellow.
Pattern: typical court scene taken from miniature painting: the king sits on his throne at the entrance to his tent, leaning on a large cushion. Flanked by two attendants, he watches the scene in the park: two men who apparently are laying a dispute before him. Inscription in the cartouche: 'This is the picture of Tamerlane'.

MAHAL (fig. 87) is the collective term for the coarse, at most medium-fine carpets from Sultanabad (now Arak) and the very extensive region surrounding it to the north, west and south. The manufactory carpets from Sultanabad were the cheapest and least durable made in Iran even before the First World War, because of the softness of their lustrous wool. Mushkabad, which had made good carpets, had to lend its name to the poorest, very coarse quality.

The Persian knot is nearly always employed. The ground-weave is cotton. There is no particular Mahal pattern. They will knot anything for which they think there is a market, from Ferahan to large-scale flower and medallion design. They use strong colours and often include tabachi. European influence sometimes penetrates. The most recent Mahals show an improvement in quality, especially the 'Saruk-Mahal' (fig. 85) from the manufactories of Sultanabad which belongs to the class of good commercial wares; the same can be said for the Viss, which usually has a geometric medallion with massive pendants and hooked outline on a monochrome ground, or the Ferahan pattern.

At the end of the nineteenth century the English firms of Hotz and Son and Ziegler and Co. founded their own manufactories in Sultanabad. They produced carpets of good quality, the Ziegler carpets notably in pastel shades.

After the First World War production became entirely dependent on the American market. The region had produced no important designers and later all too readily seized on non-Persian designs. The economic crisis and the need to respond to the constantly changing fashions in the USA enforced a versatility not at all in keeping with traditional Persian ways, and uniform changes of design. The descendants of the Armenians deported by Shah Abbas to the district of Kemereh which belongs to this region knot the Lilian (Lilihan) corresponding in structure to the new Hamadans. These Armenian villages, like a few Turkish ones, use the Turkish knot which is not otherwise customary in this area.

The SERABEND from the fertile highland region of the same name west of Burujerd (140 km. south of Hamadan) has only one pattern: small boteh in half-drop rows on a red, blue or rarely ivory ground. The crest usually changes sides from row to row. The border is chiefly ornamented with an angular wave scroll, containing a boteh in each curve. The smaller bands also often have this boteh scroll very delicately drawn ('shekiri' = sugary border). The Turkish knot is general. The ground-weave is cotton, the count medium fine, the pile short. The formats go from namaseh to keley and up to carpets of about 550 × 400 cm. The quality is very varied. There is both a coarse quality with bad chemical dyes and a very good one in natural dyed wool. The finest of the older Serabend carpets with rows of small boteh (jokingly called the flea pattern) and unlike other Serabends, with a lustrous and rather longer pile, is the Mir. It is in sejadeh, keley or kenareh format (cf. fig. 85).

KUM (Ghom, Qum) 140 km. south of Teheran with the tombs of Fatima and of Shah Abbas and one of the most important Shi'ite pilgrimage centres, has been producing very good carpets for some time past. The ground-weave is cotton, the knots Persian, in dry wool, the colours are mostly light. The count is fine to very fine, the pile short. The main designs are rows of vases or boteh (fig. 88). They also make

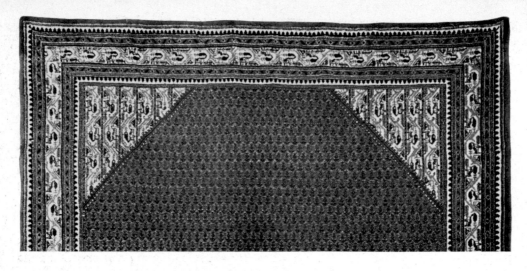

85. Saruk-Mahal, mid-20th century. Saruk-Mir. 323 × 219 cm. (detail).
Warp: C. S-plied, 12 strands, twisted, undyed.
Weft: C. S-plied, slightly twisted, dyed blue. 2 shoots: 1. thick, straight, 2. thin, sinuous.
Pile: W. Z-spun, 2 strands, untwisted. Knots P. II: h. 40, w. 46 = 1,840 per sq. dm. Upper end: 2 cm. C.
  kilim white with thick light blue shoots. c. 20 warp threads knotted together.
Lower end: every 8 warp threads pulled into a knot by a 3-strand shoot.
Selvedges: W. shirazi red round 7 bunched warp threads.
Quality: soft, thick, coarse granular.
Colours: 8, *red, ivory, navy blue,* light blue, black-blue, pink, light green, yellow.
Pattern: this good quality modern carpet shows the classic Mir pattern: miniature boteh in rows on a red
  ground, changing the direction of their crests at each row. In the corner fillings, as in the main border, a
  boteh wave stem on ivory ground. 8 guard stripes.

86. Saruk, early 20th century. 153 × 104 cm.
Warp: C. S-plied, 12 strands, twisted, undyed.
Weft: C. S-plied, multiple, slightly twisted, undyed. 2 shoots: 1. thick, straight, 2. thin, sinuous.
Pile: W. Z-spun, 2 strands, untwisted. Knots T. III, 70°: h. 62, w. 60 = 3,720 per sq. dm. Upper end:
  1 cm. C. kilim light with double shoots. Row of red-green oblique stitching, fringe.
Lower end: Warp loops filled with double shoots to a 2 cm. kilim. Row of red/dark-blue oblique stitching.
Selvedges: W. shirazi red single cord round 4 warp threads.
Quality: dry, almost thin, very firm, fine ribbing.
Colours: 10, *rust-to-brick-red, blue-black, ivory,* pale blue, dark blue, medium blue, light red-brown, yellow-
  brown, blue-green, olive-yellow.
Pattern: rust-red central field with a blue-black oval medallion with palmette attachments along the
  vertical axis and light 24-lobed central star. Medallion, central field and pale blue corner fillings are covered
  with flower sprays. The wide main border has only two narrow guard stripes.

87. Mahal, mid-20th century. 200 × 134 cm.
Warp: C. S-plied, 4 strands, twisted, undyed white.
Weft: 2 shoots: 1. thick C. dyed blue, straight. 2. thin C. Z-spun, 2 strands; untwisted, dyed blue, sinuous.
Pile: W. Z-spun, 2 strands, untwisted. Knots P. II, 70°: h. 36, w. 30 = 1,080 per sq. dm. Upper end: —.
Lower end: 2 cm. C. kilim light brown, then warp loops plaited into a horizontal braid.
Selvedges: W. shirazi dark blue round 3 bunched warp threads.
Quality: soft, thick, coarse granular.
Colours: 14, *black-blue, light yellow-green, pink, red,* white, medium blue, light blue, grass-green, brown,
  black, yellow, dark olive-brown, light olive, wine.
Pattern: the confused palmette stem composition leaves only part of the central field free; it is filled round
  a small medallion with 8 large boteh-shaped flowering sprays. The rather taste less pattern is not helped by
  the scarcely medium-fine knotting.

195

hunting carpets on the classical pattern and animal carpets. Production is considerable. The basic colours are ivory, red or blue.

The KASHAN (Keshan) is the most conservative of all Iranian carpets. Kashan, like the carpet centres of Kum and Nain, situated on the western edge of the great salt desert of Dasht-i-Kavir, was one of the great mediaeval carpet centres of Iran. After the end of the Saffavid dynasty production declined until 1890.

The Kashan is either very fine or exceptionally fine, worked in Persian knots with the best wool. The ground-weave is cotton, in the silk Kashan almost always silk. The fine blue weft thread can hardly be seen at the back. The pile is very short on older pieces, but has been left longer in the past twenty years. Specimens that have been carelessly worked, with the weft showing irregular and clear at the back and the pattern not so clear, are called 'Harun' and cost considerably less. Since the patterns have been preserved virtually unaltered the careful use of chemical dyes soon met with success. The chief tones in the very wide range of colours are red, blue and cream. Green as a ground colour is extremely rare.

88. Kum (Ghom, Qum), mid-20th century. 354 × 230 cm.
Warp: C. Z-plied, twisted from 3 right plied threads, undyed white.
Weft: 2 shoots: 1. thick, straight: C. undyed white. 2. thin, sinuous: C. S-spun, 4 strands, slightly twisted, undyed white.
Pile: W. Z-spun, 2 strands, untwisted. Knots P. II 80°: h. 40, w. 56 = 2,240 per sq. dm. Upper end: green-red row of stitches, 2 cm. C. kilim white, fringe.
Lower end: as upper end, but warp loops plaited into horizontal braid.
Selvedges: W. shirazi red single cord. Quality, dry, medium thick, almost smooth.
Colours: 12, *white, light blue, light olive,* red, green, dark blue, black, pink, yellow-brown, olive-yellow, brown-red, brown.
Pattern: the boteh pattern in this good quality manufactory carpet is a standard ornament in Kum, along with vases and a small-scale star pattern. Boteh in the central field. Boteh in the main border. Boteh in both guard stripes: not over-much imagination in this rather cool coloured pattern.

89. Kashan, 2nd quarter 20th century. 200 × 130 cm.
Warp: C. Z-plied, twisted from 2 right-plied yarns, undyed.
Weft: 2 shoots: 1. thicker, straight, C. unplied, dyed blue grey. 2. thinner, sinuous, C. S-plied, 2 strands, slightly twisted, dyed blue.
Pile: W. Z-spun, 2 strands, untwisted. Knots P. II 80°: h. 60, w. 64 = 3,840 per sq. dm.
Upper end: blue-red row of stitches, 1 cm. C. kilim with double shoots, fringe. Lower end: as upper end, but 2 cm. C. kilim, then warp threads looped and twisted. Selvedges: W. shirazi dark blue single cord.
Quality: soft, medium thick, board like, smooth.
Colours: 11, *surmey, brownish red, ivory, light blue,* pink, black, olive, light olive, olive-yellow, pale raspberry-red, medium blue.
Pattern: the characteristic Kashan pattern: on an indigo ground a curving red medaillion with shield attachments along the vertical axis. Central fields, medallion and medallion-coloured corner fillings richly ornamented with curved flowered stems. The wide border has delicate stems with rosettes and obliquely set palmettes. Carnation and wave stem in the very narrow guard stripes.

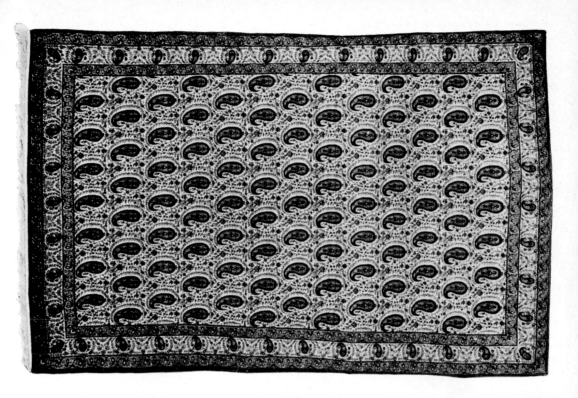

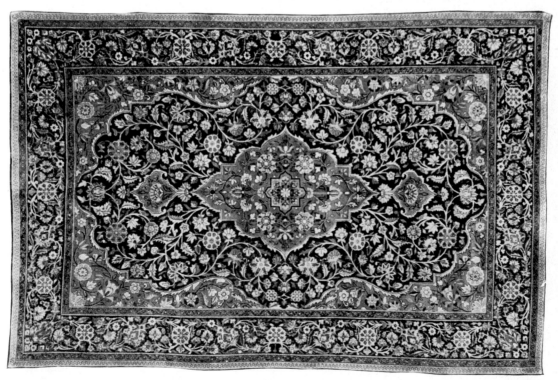

197

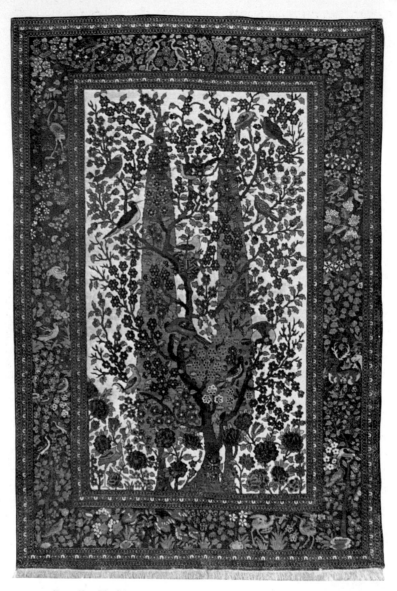

90. **Kashan, c. 1900. Paradise Kashan.** 208 × 138 cm.

Warp: C. Z-plied from 2 right-plied yarns, undyed.

Weft: 2 shoots: 1. thick, straight, C. S-plied, 2 strands, twisted, undyed. 2. thinner, sinuous. C. S-plied, 3 strands, twisted, dyed light blue.

Pile: W. T-spun, 2 strands, untwisted. Knots P. II 90°: h. 68, w. 70 = 4,760 per sq. dm. Upper end: grey-green/orange oblique stitching, 1 cm. C. kilim, fringe.

Lower end: as upper end, but without kilim.

Selvedges: W. shirazi red single cord round 4 bunched warp threads.

Quality: velvet like, medium heavy, smooth.

Colours: 13, *ivory, wine, green,* medium blue, light blue, dughi, black, grey, dark olive, medium brown, mauve, dark brown, olive-yellow.

Pattern: paradise motif influenced by painting. A flowering tree with gay birds and peonies in front of two green cypresses. The asymmetrical pattern of the main border has many different birds and a deer in flowering trees, branches and bushes.

198

91. Isfahan, mid-20th century. 154 × 103 cm.

W a r p : C. S-plied, 3 strands, twisted, undyed.

W e f t : 2 shoots: 1. thick, straight C. undyed. 2. thin, sinuous. C. Z-spun, single, undyed.

P i l e : W. S-plied, 4 strands, slightly twisted. Knots P. II 85°: h. 88, w. 100 = 8,800 per sq. dm. U p p e r e n d :
2 cm. C. kilim of double shoots, 20 warp threads knotted off together.

L o w e r e n d : as upper end, but warp threads knotted in 10s.

S e l v e d g e s : W. shirazi red single cord round 4 bunched warp threads.

Q u a l i t y : silky fine, almost thin, smooth.

C o l o u r s : 10, *ivory, red, surmey,* medium blue, light blue, light olive, olive-yellow, light red-brown, grey,
pale green.

P a t t e r n : the ivory-coloured central field is covered symmetrically with stressed curved stems with palmettes,
composite flowers and acanthus leaves. The 8-rayed medallion with central arabesque star and the surmey
corner pieces have a gentle floral pattern. In the broad main border a palmette is enclosed by alternate
pairs of acanthus leaf and narcissus on a stem.

The standard design, composed in several planes, consists of a richly curved medallion, almost always with vertical pendants along the vertical axis, and corner pieces which almost completely occupy the edges of the central field, on a background covered with symmetrical naturalistic palmette stems (fig. 89). Rows of vases and a stem rising from vases, without a medallion, are less frequent. On the other hand the tradition of the hunting and paradise Kashan (fig. 90) is continued. The broad main border has lotus palmette stems, the two very narrow guard stripes are patterned with a thin carnation wave scroll. The dimensions go from 180 × 100 to 600 × 400 cm.

ISFAHAN (Ispahan) was the capital of Iran under the Saffavid dynasty and had the court manufactory. It did not survive the Afghan invasion. For nearly 200 years its production of carpets was insignificant. Both the cottage and factory carpets are excellently worked. The underside is granular and irregular in aspect. The white weft thread varies in thickness and shows periodic little knots. The cotton ground-weave, the very fine to exceptionally fine count and the short pile give it a dry, leather-hard feel. In older examples the extensive use of the Turkish knot is noteworthy. Some parts of the pattern or its outlines are sometimes of silk. Isfahans entirely of silk are rare; on the other hand silks — recently mercerised cotton with a silky sheen — are customary for the ground-weave of the exceptionally fine pieces. The chief background colours are ivory, cream and blue. The colour range is the richest of all Iranian carpets.

The designs with and without medallion are very finely articulated. The outlines of the different elements of the patterns — leaves, palmettes and composite flowers — are feathered. The illustration (fig. 91) shows a modern Isfahan with more than 8,000 knots to the square dm. In fig. 93 can be seen a Nain with more than 9,000. The manufactory of Nain (140 km. east of Isfahan) produces the finest of Isfahan-style carpets. Their colour scheme is cool.

Djoushegan (Joshagan), which had an outstanding manufactory in the Saffavid period, was still known in the first half of the nineteenth century for very good

XVII. Kirman, 19th century. Kirman-Laver. Saddle cover = rupalani. c. 113 × 101 cm.
Warp: C. S-plied, 2 strands, twisted, undyed.
Weft: C. S-plied, 3 strands, slightly twisted, dyed light blue and undyed light. 3 shoots: 1. and 3. (thick, light) straight, 2. (thin, blue) sinuous.
Pile: W. Z-spun, 3 strands, untwisted. Knots P. II, 70°: h. 52, w. 52 = 2,704 per sq. dm. Upper end: —. Lower end: 2 shoots C. kilim. Warp threads looped and twisted. Selvedges: W shirazi single cord round 4 warp threads, dark blue. The two knotted triangles sewn on. Quality: silky, firm, medium heavy, fine ribbing.
Colours: 11, *surmey, red, light olive-brown, yellow-brown,* medium red-brown, light blue, light green-blue, ivory, olive-green, light olive-green, rust-red.
Pattern: the blue-black ground holds a flowering shrub, whose richly curving branches spread over the whole surface. A sickle-shaped section without pile left for the saddle strap.

carpets. Very fine examples made entirely of lustrous wool in Turkish knots often have a red weft. The Djoushegan on p. 204 is probably 150 years old. The count of the modern Djoushegan is medium fine. The warp, and usually the weft as well, is of cotton. It has a strict design of a medallion or a half-drop arrangement of trees and shrubs on a blue or red ground. The formats go from 200 × 120 to 400 × 230 cm., rarely 730 × 400 cm.

The Murdshakhar (Murdchehort, 50 km. north of Isfahan) has a finer count than the Djoushegan, with similar patterns, though it is more angular and stricter and the medallion is less frequent.

The tribe of the Baktiars living in the extensive region south-west of Isfahan only makes a proportion of what are called Baktiari carpets, in formats from sedshaden to 500 × 350 cm. These carpets vary widely in quality (tabachi is even used some-times). They have had an exceptionally wide distribution in recent decades and are made in hundreds of villages in the region. The gauge varies from coarse (c. 600 knots per dm.^{2}) to fine (over 2,000 knots per square dm.). The best kinds are called Bibibaff after the princess Bibi-Hanum to whom the Bakhtiars owe the development of their carpet industry. The ground-weave is cotton. The warp ends are usually left without kilim or knots. Where the main design is not a medallion, strictly drawn in conformity with the density of the knots, square or lozenge compartments pre-dominate as the decoration of the central field; the compartments are filled with stylised and geometric flower sprays, flower stems or flowering trees. Very harsh white and a brown-tinged red predominate (fig. 94).

The Lours living in this region produce the 'Louri Baktiar', mostly in keley format.

From YESD (Yazd, Yezd), about 20 km. east of Isfahan on the edge of the Lut desert, come carpets almost always of large format which are often only to be distinguished from the older Kirmans by their blue weft. They are worked with fine lustrous wool in Persian knots with very fine counts on a cotton warp. The weft is wool or cotton. The population of Yesd is a by-word for reliability. 'Wares from Yesd' is a term of quality understood all over Iran. The long format and rather sombre co-louring have not made the carpets very popular for export. The carpets made there for the home market with a cotton pile and a small-scale geometric pattern in blue and white look like the cheapest of factory articles after long wear. They are very useful however for use in the open air — part of the forecourt of a mosque for exam-ple is laid with them.

KIRMAN (Kerman) is one of the great ancient Iranian carpet centres. Until the second half of the nineteenth century its unassuming carpet industry continued the old patterns in simplified designs. It seems that Ravar, north of Kirman on the edge of the Lut desert on the old caravan route to Meshed, rather than the town itself has carried on production. Its older carpets bear the name of Laver, which is the garbled dialectal form of the word Ravar. A bluish red and a particular green are note-worthy in its colour range. In feel the underside is ridged, because the very fine weft yarn adapts to the curve of the warp threads. On p. 201 we illustrate a beautiful saddle cover, and on p. 191 a carpet with a very delicately drawn court scene.

Kirman owes the prosperity of its workshops from the end of the last century to

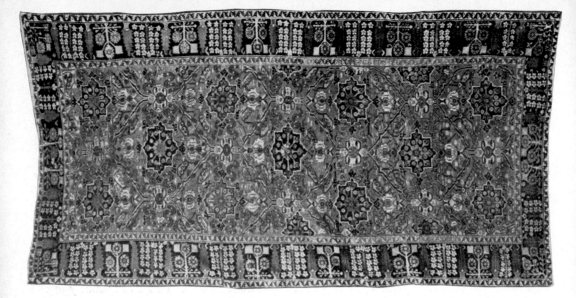

92. Djoushegan, c. 1800. c. 270 × 140 cm.

Warp: W. S-plied, 2 strands, twisted, undyed light.

Weft: W. Z-spun, 1 or 2 strands, untwisted, dyed red. 2 shoots alternating sinuous.

Pile: W. Z-spun, 2 strands, untwisted. Knots T. I: h. 52, w. 50 = 2600 per sq. dm. Upper end: —. Lower end: —. Selvedges: —.

Quality: silky, thin, soft, smooth.

Colours: 11, *geranium-red, dark blue, yellow, ivory,* green, dughi, red, medium blue, light blue, black-brown, medium brown.

Pattern: the red central field is latticed with yellow stems forming lozenges, which enclose eight rayed medallions surrounded by cloud bands. (This motif appears geometricised in the 'Cloud-band Kasak' fig. 39). The simple static border is in striking contrast to the flowing design of the central field.

93. Nain, mid-20th century. 229 × 156 cm.

Warp: Mercerised cotton. Z-plied, twisted from 2 right-plied strands, undyed.

Weft: 2 shoots: 1. straight, C. undyed light. 2. sinuous, C. Z-spun, 2 strands, untwisted, light blue.

Pile: W. Z-spun, single. Knots P. II, 85°: h. 104, w. 88 = 9,152 per sq. dm.

Upper end: C. kilim white: c. 5 cm. wide, single shoots, red-green row of stitching, then 5 double shoots, fringe.

Lower end: C. kilim white, double shoots, red-green row of stitching, warp loops twisted.

Selvedges: W. shirazi red single cord round 4 bunched warp threads.

Quality: velvet-like, almost thin, very firm, smooth.

Colours: 12, *ivory, dark blue, wine,* light brown, dark brown, medium brown, light blue, green, light green, olive, grey, brown-yellow.

Pattern: this carpet justifies the reputation of Nain to knot the finest carpets. In the main border two complex palmette-arabesque systems overlap.

94. Bakhtiari, mid-20th century. 256 × 156 cm.

Warp: C. Z-plied, twisted from 2 right-plied 3-strand threads, undyed.

Weft: 2 shoots: C. grey brown: 1. thick, straight, 2. thinner, sinuous.

Pile: W. Z-spun, 2 strands, untwisted. Knots T. I: h. 28, w. 22 = 616 per sq. dm.

Upper end: fringe. Lower end: fringe.

Selvedges: extremely thick W. shirazi black-brown single cord round 15 bunched warp threads.

Quality: soft, very thick, coarse.

Colours: 12, *dark blue, grass-green, white, pink, purple, red,* blue-black, dark brown, grey, yellow, orange.

Pattern: this Bakhtiari in over-strong colours belongs with commercial wares. The primitive pattern however is suited to the coarse knotting. It illustrates the transition from stylisation to geometricisation.

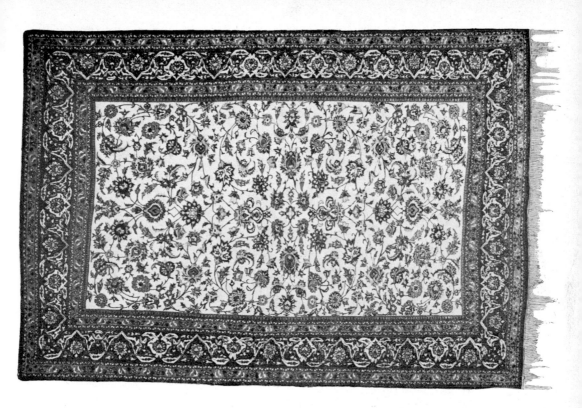

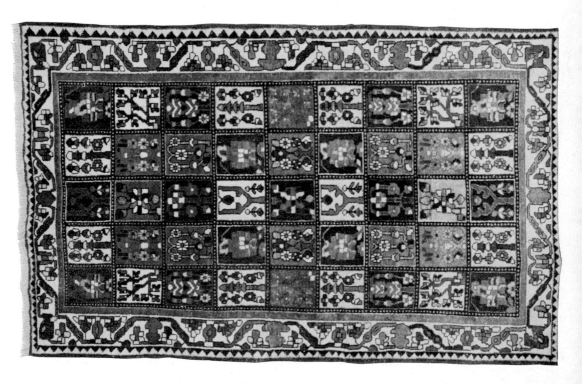

95. Kirman, mid-20th century. 348 × 251 cm.

Warp: C. S-plied, 5 strands, twisted, undyed white.

Weft: C. S-spun, 3 strands, slightly twisted, undyed. 3 shoots: 1. and 3. straight, 2. sinuous.

Pile: W. Z-spun, 2 strands, untwisted. Knots P. III 85°: h. 80, w. 64 = 5,120 per sq. dm. Upper end:
1 cm. C. kilim white, then warp threads knotted in sixes. Lower end: as upper end, but warp threads looped and twisted.

Selvedges: W shirazi bright green single cord round 4 warp threads.

Quality: soft, thick, fine granular.

Colours: 17, *pistachio-green, pale blue, sand,* medium blue, dark blue, pink, wine, brown-red, ivory, cream, green, brown-orange, light brown, dark brown, some grey, dark purple and purple.

Pattern: this modern Kirman, of excellent quality, with a green ground shows strong French influence in the pattern (Louis Philippe). The medallion has a rocaillerie frame; the broad European border is dominant. Roses predominate in the naturalistic pattern.

the popularity of its carpets in Europe and America. They are knotted in very good lustrous wool in light shades. Foreign businesses entered production at that time; as they developed, the traditional patterns and short pile went by the board. The very skilful native designers evolved numerous new patterns to suit the count of 2000 to 4000 knots per square dm. and a medium-long pile. The beautiful wool and rich palette of light pastel shades contributed to their success. They have the largest repertoire of designs, along with Tabriz: medallions with emphasised outlines, rows of naturalistic flowering trees and cypresses, finely branched curving flowering trees

96. Mesched, 19th century. Carpet with mihrab. 220 × 140 cm.

Warp: C. S-plied, 10 strands, twisted, undyed.

Weft: C. S-plied, 3 strands, twisted, undyed. Some dyed blue. 2 shoots: 1. straight, 2. sinuous.

Pile: W. Z-spun, 2 strands, untwisted. Knots P. III 80°: h. 52, w. 60 = 3,120 per sq.dm. Upper end: 2 cm. C. kilim, undyed. Lower end: 1 cm. C. kilim undyed, some warp threads still looped and twisted.

Selvedges: W. shirazi dark blue round 5 twisted threads.

Quality: smooth, very firm, medium heavy, fine granular.

Colours: 15, *sand, dark red-brown, wine-red, light blue,* dughi, red, light green, light olive-green, medium blue, dark blue, olive, black, white, light olive, pale green.

Pattern: the upper corners of the central field are filled with a stem pattern which gives rise to a decorative mihrab. On its sand-coloured ground two flowering trees flank a large vase from which rise flowering shrubs. In the branches are birds, below are leopards attacking fawns and threatened by snakes. In the main border a scroll pattern of composite flowers with dominant boteh leaves.

97. Meshed, first half 20th century. 193 × 127 cm.

Warp: C. S-plied, 9 strands, twisted, undyed white.

Weft: 2 shoots: 1. thick, straight: C. undyed light. 2. thin sinuous: C. Z-spun, 2 strands, untwisted, dyed light blue. Irregular light straight double shoots typical of Khorassan, without the sinuous blue shoot.

Pile: W. Z-spun, 2—4 strands, untwisted. Knots P. II, 85°: h. 68, w. 60 = 4,080 per sq. dm. Upper and lower end: —. Selvedges: W. shirazi blue single cord round 4 bunched warp threads. Quality: silky, medium heavy, stiff, smooth.

Colours: 12, *wine, black, white, light brown, yellow-brown, blue,* green, olive, dughi, bright green, yellow-olive, brick-red.

Pattern: wine-red central field with a round 16-lobed medallion with long palmettes attached in the vertical axis. Four more 16-lobed figures concentrically inside the medallion. The corner fillings, on a blue ground, almost frame the whole central field. Main border has a fine flowered stem with palmettes framed by pairs of acanthus leaves. 6 guard stripes.

98. Senna. 19/20th century. Saddle cover. c. 76 × 153 cm. (p. 209 above).

Material and structure as in No 78, but 3,120 knots T. II per dm². Edges, sides and slit thickly whipped with silk, green, purple. Touch: dry, thin, leathery, very granular.

Colours: 10, *yellow, red, black,* light blue, pale blue, orange-red, violet, pale mauve, pale blue-green, ivory.

The yellow ground is closely covered with horizontal rows of small boteh all changing the direction of their crests from row to row. Between them gentle diagonal stems set with flower rosettes. A few very small birds scattered. Angular wave band for narrow border.

99. Gashgai. Shiraz region, 19th century. Saddle cover. now 106 × 87 (82–92) cm. (p. 209 below).

Warp: W. Z-spun, two strands S-plied, undyed light.

Weft: W. Z-spun, two strands dyed red. 2 wefts alternating sinuous.

Pile: W. Z-spun, 2 strands. Knots T. I: h. 44, w. 48 = 2112 per dm².

Colours: 9, *brown-yellow, black, red,* surmey, light blue, red-brown, ivory, dark brown-red, dark green.

A border with two guard stripes surrounds the central field, black except for two spandrels scattered with stems and blossoms. The black is divided into lozenges, in each is a small boteh. The red saddle-slit ends in two goblets with a flower. In the yellow main border alternating opposed geometric flowers.

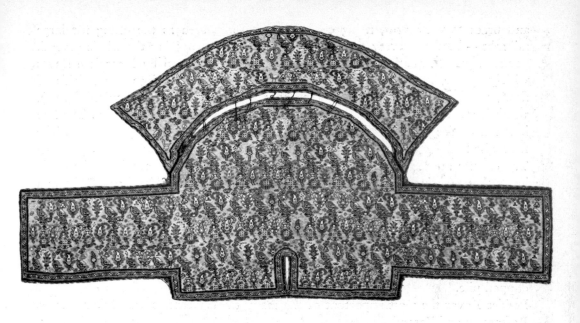

209

and branches with birds, rising out of vases — also used as the filling for large mihrabs — botehs of every size interlaced and densely covering the whole ground, portrait, garden, hunting and animal types, lozenges formed by lanceolate leaves with palmette, flower, animal and herati filling, quartering into small fields of flowers and many more, including the one, now by far the most popular (fig. 95), which is more in keeping with a Paris Savonnerie carpet than a Kirman. The line between border and central field is lost, and its original meaning forgotten. The favourite background colour for this pattern is a light green.

The carpets are technically well made, with Persian knots, apart from the djufti knots that are often smuggled in. Cheaper kinds contain tabachi. The weft shows a peculiarity: instead of the usual practice with a strongly depressed warp where there is one thick straight weft thread and a second thinner sinuous one, the Kirman has two straight weft threads, between which there is a third thinner sinuous one.

All sizes are made from namaseh up to 500 × 350 cm., also almost square formats. Kirman-Laver or Kirman Ravar was the name for the finest quality with close-clipped pile.

Besides Ravar the most important of the many smaller centres are Mahan, Jupar, Rafsanyan and Zarand.

KHORASSAN, the north-eastern province of Iran, was probably the country of origin of the early 'Herat' carpets. The lack of any knotting tradition in Herat leads one to conclude that the erstwhile capital city of east Persia, Herat, only lent its name to the many Khorassan carpets that it needed and procured from the neighbourhood to the north.

North Khorassan is one of the most important wool-producing areas of Iran. The short-fibred softer wool of the autumn shearing was generally used for the pile because it was easier to prepare with the customary primitive methods. This lustrous soft wool makes the older carpets less durable. Prejudice against new methods prevented the dyers from achieving the results of their more go-ahead colleagues at the other end of the great desert in Kirman. Their rather bright colour range was dominated by blue-red, light to dark brown and white.

The most important knotting centres of the province are Meshed, Birchend, Kain, Sabzevar and Kashmar (Turshis).

XVIII. **Gashgai, Shiraz region, 19th century.** (178—182) 180 × 104 (101—107) cm.
Warp: W. S-plied, 2 strands, twisted, undyed light and light brown, also one thread light with one brown.
Weft: W. S-plied, 2 strands, untwisted, dyed red. 2 shoots alternating sinuous.
Pile: W. Z-spun, 2 strands, untwisted. Knots P. Ib: h. 40, w. 29 = 1,160 per sq. dm.
Upper end: —. Lower end: —.
Selvedges: thick W. shirazi black-white, not original. Beneath it the remains of the typical Shiraz multi-coloured W. shirazi round 4 warp threads.
Quality: smooth, rather thin, slightly ribbed.
Colours: 9, *brick-red, white, medium blue,* vermilion, olive yellow, black brown, dark blue-green, light brown, surmey.
Pattern: except for the corner pieces decorated with stylised cocks the red central field is finely striped. On the stripes the first quarter has a stem, then rows of miniature boteh with crests to the left. In the main border a double stem with S-shaped leaves.

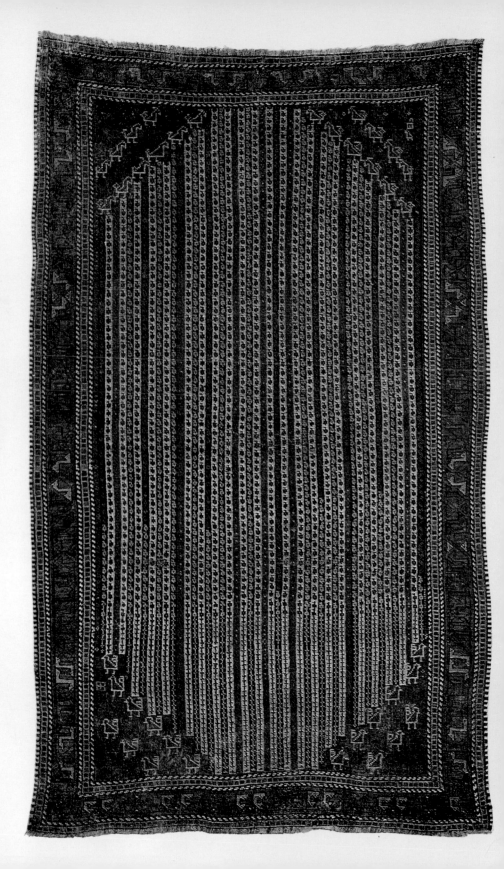

MESHED (Mashad), the holy city, is the capital of the province. The sanctuary of the town is the tomb of the Imam Reza. According to tradition he was poisoned there in the year 818 by the son of the Caliph Harun ar Rashid, who nine years previously had also died there on a campaign. It is the most important pilgrimage centre of the Shi'ites and attracts hundreds of thousands of pilgrims e v e r y year. Mongol and Afghan invasions and Turcoman raids brought dire disturbances and sometimes the city was lost to the Persian state. Nadir Shah made it his capital.

In Meshed both Persian (Farsibaff) and Turkish (Turkbaff) knots are used, on a cotton warp. The djufti knot is native here, and is often used sporadically even in older pieces. The back of the carpet then looks as though it had been darned in innumerable places. The term for the quality of a carpet with the correct (tai) knots is Taibaff. Another peculiarity of the ground-weave of the Khorassan carpet is the weft: the thick straight weft is covered by the thin sinuous weft threads accompanying it. At regular or irregular intervals however it is taken alone across the whole breadth, and is then visible as a broad line. The count reaches from 2,000 to 4,000 knots per square dm. Smaller formats are rare, the sizes range between 300 × 200 cm. and 600 × 400 cm.

The most usual pattern is a medallion approximating to a circle with (sometimes enormous) pendants on a monochrome or richly flowered ground (fig. 96). In older pieces Herati and boteh are often found as the chief pattern with a Herati border. The borders of almost all east Persian carpets are broader and have more guard stripes than the average.

Kain (Ghain) in the hilly land of Kainat south of Meshed towards Birdshend used to be famous for short-clipped, very fine Khorassan carpets, mostly in keley format. Today the extent of production is small. It is also small in Gonabad half way between Meshed and Kain.

Birdshend (Biryand) has also been producing hand-knotted carpets for a long time. The colours are rather stronger. The wool is harder. The finest carpet of this region is the Mud. It has become the term for best quality Khorassans.

From the hills of the same name north-east of Birdshend comes the exceptionally carefully worked Dorush. It very often appears in unusual dimensions.

The Asghand (Azghand) is an average Birchend quality.

The Sabzevar, from the town lying 160 km. west of Meshed, corresponds to a good Birchend.

Turshis (now Kashmar) was once an important trading centre, 160 km. south-west of Meshed. It was known for the worst kind of Khorassan carpets in djufti knots; it has improved the quality of its carpets.

The Turkbaff, i. e. a Khorassan carpet made with Turkish knots, has a darker blue-red colour scheme.

Meshed is both the trading centre for the manufactory carpets already described, and for the wares knotted by the nomadic Baluchi who will be discussed in the next chapter.

East of the mouth of the Atrek lies a corner of western Turkestan in Persian territory. The good Turcoman work of the tribes who have long lived there, the Atabai and Yafarbai, together with that of the Tekke who transferred from Russia a few decades ago, is assembled in Gorgan and Gombad-i-Rabus. Unfortunately the Yomuds there have largely abandoned the Dyrnak gul (p. 237) on their large carpets, in favour of an imitation of the Tekke pattern.

From Moussabad in east Khorassan comes a not very pleasing Turcoman-type carpet in light red and white. The pieces are from 120 × 70 cm. to 220 × 110 cm. and knotted sparsely on a cotton warp. The weft is also cotton, rarely wool or goat hair. The woollen pile, recently also of artificial silk, contains white knots in cotton.

The AFSHARI live as nomads and semi-nomads in the broad regions of Persia south and west of Kirman to the south-east of Lake Niri, which were granted to them under the Saffavid dynasty. Tradition has it that Shah Tahmasp, son of the founder of the dynasty Ismail I, was unable to master the rebellious Turkish tribes in Azerbaijan except by deporting sections of them to south Persia.

Afshar carpets are made in the tents and settlements of the nomads and also in the Persian villages of the area. The Turkish nomads sometimes added naturalistic patterns borrowed from the villagers to their own geometric or strongly stylised motifs, like the well-known alternating rows of bunches of roses.

100. **Gashgai. Shiraz region. 19th/20th century. Small bag = Tantye,** carried on a belt or hung on a strap over the shoulder. 34 × 32 cm.
The central field is contained in a simple border and has two pairs of opposed birds in typical Gashgai style surrounded by small birds and flower heads. C. 1,200 knots P. II (60°) per dm².

Older Afshars (fig. 101) are still worked entirely in wool; the more modern have a cotton warp and sometimes use tabachi instead of the good pile wool. Since the Persian knotters cling to the Persian knot while the Turkish is the traditional knot of the Afshari, Afshar carpets may be in either. The count varies between about 800 and 1,500 knots per square dm. The formats range from namaseh up to carpets of 400 × 300 cm. Dominant colours are blue-red, blue and ivory. The patterns are various: large concentric lozenges, boteh with or without a beaded edge and dots in half-drop rows, angular medallions with pendants on a monochrome or stylised floral ground. Cocks or dogs are often interspersed.

The chief place of assemblage of the Afshar carpets traded in Kirman is Saidabad (now Sirdyan), which is also the name of the finest kind. Other good qualities come from Niris (Neyriz) and Estabanat.

101. Afshar, c. 1900. Saidabad. (150—156) 153 × 122 cm.

Warp: W. S-plied, 2 strands, twisted, undyed light and light with light brown.

Weft: W. Z-spun, 2 strands, untwisted, dyed brownish to red. 2 shoots: 1. straight, 2. sinuous.

Pile: W. Z-spun, 2 strands, untwisted. Knots T. II 80°: h. 36, w. 36 = 1,296 per sq. dm. Upper end: —.
 Lower end: —. Selvedges: W. shirazi in colours 3 cord, warps twisted.

Quality: silky, medium firm, almost thin, coarse ribbed.

Colours: 9, *surmey, red, white,* celadon, dark green, bright blue, medium blue, yellow-brown, dark brown.

Pattern: surmey central field with half-drop rows of large symmetrical palmettes with dotted outlines and
 little flower flags at the points. This leaf form is foreshadowed in the carpet of another Turkish people,
 the Seljuks, 600 years earlier (cf. drawing p. 21 left). In the white main border hexagonal leaves and
 carnations in pairs alternate on a thin straight stem. 5 guard stripes.

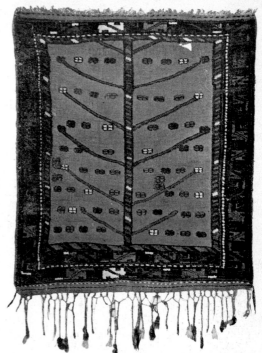

102. Gashgai, region of Shiraz, early 20th century.
(196—202) 198 × 154 cm.
Warp: Goat hair S-plied, 2 strands, twisted, undyed
black brown with light.
Weft: W. Z-spun, 2 strands, untwisted, undyed black-
brown. 2 shoots: 1. straight, 2. sinuous.
Pile: W. Z-spun, 2 strands, untwisted, Knots P. III,
70°: h. 38, w. 40 = 1520 per sq. dm.
Upper end: 1 cm. W. kilim black-brown, red-green oblique stitching, fringe. Lower end: as upper end.
Selvedges: W. shirazi red green round 7 bunched warp threads.
Quality: soft, medium thick, hard, ribbed.
Colours: 9, surmey, ivory, brown, medium brown, orange-brown, orange-yellow, green, dark green,
light brown.
Pattern: Four hooked lozenges along a bar, over a vertically orientated geometric pattern of small motifs;
among these more than 500 animals.

103. Lur, early 20th century. 231 × 158 (154—162) cm.
Warp: W. S-plied, 2 strands, twisted, undyed light and light with black-brown.
Weft: W. Z-spun, 1—2 strands, untwisted, dyed reddish. 2—5 shoots alternating sinuous.
Pile: W. Z-spun, 2 strands, untwisted. Knots T. I: h. 32, w. 20:640 per sq. dm. Upper end: —. Lower
end: —. Selvedges: W. Shirazi red-green single cord round 4 bunched warp threads.
Quality: soft, heavy, firm, coarse granular. Colours: 7, *brilliant red, dark blue, orange,* ivory, black-brown,
pale blue, light olive green. Pattern: the life-size tiger, bleeding at the neck, and destroying the pattern
by its disproportionate size, is intended to avert unknown, fearsome dangers from the tent.

104. Gashgai, region of Shiraz, 19th—20th century. Technique: nimbaff = half knots. 119 × 109 cm.
Warp: W. S-plied, 2 strands, twisted, dyed gold yellow.
Weft: W. S-plied, 3 strands, slightly twisted, dyed gold brown. Plain weave, coarsely ribbed because of the
thick warp threads. In the knotted parts only every second pair of shoots continues alternating sinuous,
while the other turns round before the knotting.
Pile: W. Z-spun, 2 strands, untwisted. Knots T. I: h. 26, w. 18 = 468 per sq. dm.
Upper end: 3 cm. continuation of the ground-weave, thick red-blue row of stitching. Lower end:
red-white oblique stitching, 5 cm. ground-weave with red-blue stitching, then warp threads plaited into
a net, ending in coloured tassles.
Selvedges: thick W. Shirazi red-gold brown single cord round 4 bunched warp threads.
Colours: 9, *gold brown, dark blue,* dark red, white, brown, green, light blue, vermilion, black-brown.
Pattern: the technique, called golbaryasteh (projecting flowers) because of its plastic effect, is not suited
for floor carpets, but for hangings, blankets and the like.

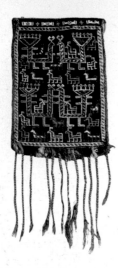

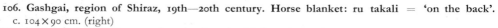

105. **Gashgai, region of Shiraz, 19th—20th century. Gailanden = pipe bag (dyeddyim technique).** 38 × 27 cm.
Warp: W. S-plied, 2 strands, twisted, dyed blue. 120 threads per dm.
Weft, ground weft: as warp, but only slightly twisted. 72 shoots per dm.
Pattern weft: W. slight S-twist, 2 strands; C. (white) S-plied, 3 strands, twisted. 9 colours. Ground colour dark blue.

106. **Gashgai, region of Shiraz, 19th—20th century. Horse blanket: ru takali = 'on the back'.** c. 104 × 90 cm. (right)
Warp: Goat hair S-plied, 2 strands, twisted, undyed light with dark brown.
Weft: W. spun, 2 strands, untwisted, undyed brownish. 2 shoots: 1. straight, 2. sinuous.
Pile: W. Z-spun, 2 strands, untwisted. Knots P. II, 50°: h. 50, w. 40 = 2,000 per sq.dm. Upper end, lower end: W. kilim undyed.
Selvedges: W. shirazi green-red round 6 warp threads.
Quality: fine, thin, hard, fine granular.
Colours: 7, *ivory, blue-black,* orange-red, medium blue, green, dark brown, brown-red. The blanket is worked in one piece. The inner band of the border has a row of small boteh.

107. **Gashgai, region of Shiraz, 19th—20th century. Horse blanket. Dyeddyim with embroidery.** c. 167 × 172 cm. (two strips sewn together). (p. 219 above).
Warp: W. S-plied, 2 strands, twisted, dyed dark blue, 120 threads per dm.
Weft: ground weft: W. slight S-twist, 2 strands, dark blue, straight, so that in the woven dark blue part a panama-like weave is made. 80 shoots per dm.
Pattern weft: W. S-plied, 2 strands, and C. (white) S-plied, 3 strands, twisted. The patterned parts in Dyeddyim technique.
Upper end: warp threads plaited into 3 rows of horizontal braid, then twisted together in dozens and ending in tassels. Lower end: warp threads looped and twisted. Selvedges: coloured shirazi W. with tassels and braids ending in tassels worked in.
Colours: 9, *dark blue, red, white, light olive-yellow,* light blue, light green, black, brown-red, orange-yellow.
Pattern: the close pattern of rows of animals is arranged in the rectangular field in rows facing in four directions. A double medakhyl band as a frame for the patterned field. In the olive-yellow main border a geometric stem. The motifs standing isolated in the dark blue field are embroidered.

108. **Gashgai, 19th—20th century. Ornamental breast band = sineban, for horse or donkey.** 6 × 76 cm., woven (Pyeddyim). (p. 219 kelow).

SHIRAZ is the picturesque capital of the south Persian province of Fars which was the central province of the Achaemenid empire with its residences at Persepolis and Pasargardai. It is one of the oldest cities of Iran. Relatively untouched by the historical catastrophes which beset Persia until the Afghan invasion, Shiraz prospered culturally and economically. Two of the greatest Persian poets, Saadi (1184—1282) and Hafez (Hafis, 1320—89), were born and buried here. The city suffered under the Afghan domination, but Karim Khan Zand, who was for a time the absolute ruler of Persia though he only called himself Vakil (governor), repaired the damage. Some of the largest buildings in the town, including the bazaar — still a worth-while find place for collectors of old and small nomad textiles, knotted or woven — were erected by him. Good irrigation schemes made fertile fields in the surrounding narrow valleys.

No carpets are made in Shiraz, but it is the trading centre for the work of the nomads and semi-nomads and for the villages of the province. In the summer the nomads all seek out the mountain regions with their flocks of sheep and herds of camel, horses and mules, and in winter they wander in the plains. The richest are the Turkish GASHGAI. Their work expresses the sense of beauty, the craftsmanship and the admirable perseverance of the Gashgai women. Their carpets, all of wool unless dark goat hair is used in the under-weave, are the most beautiful in the province, but represent only a small proportion of the carpets sold in Shiraz. Dealers have invented the name Mecca Shiraz for the best. The wool is soft and lustrous, though less durable than harder wools. The Turkish knot is the most usual. The count is medium fine to fine; in one small decorative ship even more than 4,000 knots per square dm. were counted. The formats range from pushtis, through namaseh and sejadeh (these often quite wide) to carpets of 300 × 200 cm., sometimes even larger. Dark blue, brownish red and ivory are the dominant colours. The designs are numerous: geometric or strongly stylised floral patterns, among them the boteh in half-drop rows, vertical stripes or diamond compartments in the central field, small stepped rhombic medallions along a stem. The small-scale filling motifs often include cocks and quadrupeds (dogs?). The borders of older pieces often contain the Ashkali pattern. Even more than some of the main patterns there are several border designs, such as oblique stripes and the 'oakleaf' pattern, which show a striking connection with Caucasian borders; presumably

XIX. **Turcoman, 17th—18th century.** c. 190 × 110 cm. (detail).
Warp: goat hair S-plied, 2 strands, twisted, undyed brown.
Weft: goat hair, Z-spun, single, undyed brown, 2 shoots alternating sinuous.
Pile: W. Z-spun, 2 strands, untwisted. Knots P. Ib: h. 38, w. 29 = 1,102 per sq.dm. Upper end: —.
Lower end: —. Selvedges: —. Quality: silky, now thin, slightly granular.
Colours: 7, *dark vermilion, sand, dark blue, light blue,* dark blue-green, medium brown, ivory.
Pattern: the red central field holds three vertical rows of octagons almost touching, with angular contours. They are divided into four by two diagonally corresponding colours. A trefoil motif in each quarter, which is divided from the next by a double hook motif. The ground-coloured central lozenge holds a star. In the spaces between the octagons occurs a regular alternation of a dotted and a quartered lozenge, the latter's points run out into double hooks. The border, enlarged at the sides, consists of a little band with geometric flowers and a band divided into fields with small geometric trees all the way round.

109. Gashgai, region of Shiraz, 19th century. (321—331) 326×156 (153—159) cm. (detail).

Warp: wand goat hair, S-plied, 2 strands, twisted, undyed dark brown, light or light with dark brown.
Weft: W. Z-spun, 2 strands, untwisted, dyed red. 2 shoots alternating sinuous.
Pile: W. Z-spun, 2 strands, untwisted. Knots P. Ia: h. 34, w. 26 = 884 per sq.dm. Upper end: 1 cm. remaining of a W. kilim red brown. Lower end: 5 cm. of a W. kilim red-brown, rust-red, dark blue with simple patterns woven in. Selvedges: W. shirazi multicoloured 2 cord round three twisted warp threads. Quality: soft, now thin and flabby.
Colours: 11, *dark blue, red-brown, red,* light blue, blue green, olive yellow, light olive green, brown, black-brown, dughi, medium blue.
Pattern: the dark blue central field is enclosed by small stepped half lozenges. 3 straight vertical stems with geometric flowers and leaves. In the interstices geometric floral motifs and star octagons. At the start of the upper third 4 broadened geometric double stems with little heads, such as are found on the Y ornament of the Turcoman Engsi. Diagonal stripes on the left for the main border, on the right they only occur on four of the 6 guard stripes.

a section of the Turkish nomadic tribes from the Caucasus migrated southwards. Tribal groups of the Gashgais and other Turkish tribes are: Shash-Buluchi, Kash Guli, Darishuli, Bolli, Hebatlu, Kuhi, Namadi, Turki, Safishani, Bollvari, Farsimardan. They speak Turkish dialects and inhabit the area north of Shiraz towards the province of Isfahan, in which live other, Arabic-speaking tribes as well, such as the Arabi, and the pure Persian Lours. The majority of the LOURS however lead a nomadic life in the District of Luristan in western Persia, south of Kurdistan. Their beautiful carpets come onto the market through Hamadan and Kermanshah. They are in large sejedeh to keley formats with clear blue, red and orange-yellow (fig. 103 shows one of their striking and original designs).

All these tribes, including the Ainalu and Baharlu who are settled south of Niris, knot on horizontal looms, as do all the Persian nomads and semi-nomads (p. 25). The quality is very variable. The Gashgai carpet is the foremost; its ends are often carefully embroidered and the colours are outstanding. The different patterns no longer typify different tribes. Most Shiraz carpets come from villages and are called Dehaj (village) Shiraz. The carpets produced in Abadeh (a place half way between Isfahan and Shiraz) have a Gashgai character and with only minor variations show bunches of flowers in an endless repeat.

Latterly a new carpet from Fars has found favour with many buyers: this is the costly gabeh. The word means unclipped.

The modern thick gabeh looks unclipped in comparison with the Shiraz carpets made until now. It is coarse, but very firmly worked in Turkish knots. Its wool is of good quality and is undyed, and it still keeps the smell of the sheep and its high fat content. The natural colour scheme, ivory to very dark brown, is reminiscent of some carpets from North Africa. Simple geometric designs, usually a diamond-shaped medallion, are either placed dark against a monochrome light ground, or vice versa.

Turcoman carpets

Geography and history

The homeland of the Turcoman carpet is west or Russian Turkestan, that is to say the lowland stretching from the Caspian Sea for more than 1,500 kms. eastwards, bordered on the south and east by mountains. Those on the south partly belong to Afghanistan. Their peaks reach to 4,000, some to nearly 8,000 metres.

The greater part of the lowland is included in the two hilly deserts of Kara Kum, west of the Amu Darya, and Kysyl Kum, between the Amu Darya and the Syr Darya. A dry continental climate prevails with strong variations of temperature. Precipitation throughout the year only amounts to 120 to 130 mm. Of the streams rising in the mountains only the Atrek reaches the Caspian Sea. The Amu Darya (Oxus) and the Syr Darya (Jaxartes) flow into the land-locked Sea of Aral, a lake with an area larger than that of the whole of Wales or Switzerland. All the other water courses seep away and are dried up in the desert. At the southern edge of the great bush deserts, grass steppes stretch to a height of 3,000 metres. Only parts of the high mountains are wooded with deciduous and evergreen trees. Large settlements could on occasion arise at those places on the water courses where oasis economy was possible. Irrigation is carried out by means of Karis, which correspond to the Persian ghanats, being underground ducts for the water. The water is tapped at its table at the foot of the mountains, and brought to the fields lower down. These fields when irrigated can produce cereals, pulses, rice, fruit, vegetables and cotton.

Grazing fodder on the desert steppe land is only 30 to 50 per cent as abundant as on the steppes in the European part of Russia. To feed a fat-tailed sheep takes about six hectares. Since even the modest standard of living of a nomad family requires a herd of several hundred sheep and thirty to forty camels and horses, the steppe, in spite of its vast spaces, does not ensure the existence of an unlimited number of nomads. Their history until the second half of the nineteenth century is a series of battles over water rights and pasture lands. Until about a hundred years ago the population of native Turkish tribes, Turcomans, Kasakh Kirghis, Kara Kirghis, Kara Kalpaks, Uzbeks, Sarts, Tajiks, Arabs, Tartars and immigrant Russians can hardly have exceeded one and a half million. The 30—50-metre deep wells, dug in early centuries into the steppe, are anything up to fifty kilometres apart and contain at most some brackish water to which in time the cattle became accustomed, but which is unsuited to human needs. In the rainy season the water is collected in hollows and led into the wells where it settles above the heavier salty water and can be enjoyed in adequate quantities by humans as well as cattle for a time.

Some nomads went over to semi-nomadism at an early period: wherever the water situation made it at all possible agriculture was practised while the herds were grazing — in the rainy season even melons were raised round the steppe wells. In winter the temperature falls quickly to twenty to twentyfive degrees centigrade of frost, and snow storms cause great devastation among the herds. Lack of fuel forced even the inhabitants of the little villages (aul) which had grown up in the agricultural areas to move out into the steppe with their tents (kibitki). In course of time the steppe was bared of any growth suitable for burning for a radius of over 100 km. round every aul.

The barter of the full nomads developed rather with the inhabitants of the great oases like Bokhara, Merv and Khiva than with the semi-nomads who themselves raised sheep on the borders of the built-up areas and in the steppe, and were primarily concerned to acquire fuel. The oasis cities on the other hand took all the products of the nomad economy: skins, meat, wool carpets, camels and horses bred in the steppe, in exchange for cereals, tea, sugar, weapons and tools. Every autumn long caravans laden with nomad products streamed across the steppes in the direction of the oasis cities, returning with the goods acquired by barter. Despite armed escorts they were often attacked by bandits. Not only goods and beasts were lost; their owners and drivers might well end up in slavery.

Climate and nomad economy provided all the incentive necessary to the development of knotting. Bukhara and Khiva were the most important markets for the wares of the Turcoman steppes and auls.

Division of labour hardly existed among the Turcomans. There were no professional craftsmen. Within the family there was a division of labour by sex. The men prepared the leather and skins, made shoes of camel hide, caps of lamb skin, and harness, saddles etc. Work with wool fell to the women: spinning, plying, weaving, sewing and embroidery were learnt by the girls as well as felting and knotting. To prepare felt the wool is stretched out on a rush mat in several layers, damped and then rolled up in the mat. This roll is firmly tied up and frequently soused with water until after some time the mass has felted together. After it is taken out of the mat the wool is once more rolled up for an hour or two. Felts are used to cover the wood framework of the tent and, often in patterns, to lay on the floor.

Knotting is done primarily for home use. Only a third of the women questioned at the end of the last century said they made carpets for barter trading.

The history of western Turkestan, the region that forms the link between eastern and western Asia, is only known in the broadest outlines. It has always been coveted and disputed by the great Asiatic empires.

In antiquity Sogdiana between the Oxus and Jaxartes (Amu Darya and Syr Darya) was the Achaemenid province that projected furthest into Central Asia. The Scyths beyond Samarkand were among the twenty-eight peoples paying tribute to the Achaemenid rulers. The Sogdian capital of Murakanda (Samarkand) was occupied by Alexander the Great. Scyth and Greek rulers alternated. Parthians and Sasanids brought back the territory into the Persian sphere. The silk route, the great caravan trail from China to the Mediterranean since the early centuries of this era, made Samarkand and Tashkent develop into important trading centres. In the seventh century the territory fell to the Arab conquerors. Samarkand became one of the intellectual centres of Islam. When the Seljuks broke through from the east they occupied Merv (the ancient Margiane) in 1036 and it became a flourishing city until laid waste by the Mongols in the thirteenth century. In the fourteenth century Timur made Samarkand his residence after his great conquests were completed. He himself lived in a gigantic and splendid tent, described in every detail by Ruy Gonzales de Clavigo in his report on his embassy to the court of Samarkand, but many monumental buildings were erected at his orders, including his mausoleum. He assembled builders, furnishers and decorators from far and wide. Sheikh Mohammed from Tabriz, for example, set up the mosaic facings on the buildings. In Timur's brocade manufactories worked weavers from both China and Damascus. The demand for gold-embroidered silks was enormous, for besides robes, cloaks, quilts and cushions the construction of the gorgeous tents absorbed vast quantities of this valuable material. The mediaeval 'Pearl of the East' was the city of a powerful oriental magnate. In the first half of the fifteenth century Ulug Beg, the famous astronomer grandson of Timur, continued this building furore. His observatory is to this day the finest in the world. Later Samarkand fell to the Khanate of Bokhara which had formed like the Khanate of Khiva under Uzbek rulers. In the fourteenth and fifteenth centuries a re-grouping of the Turcoman tribes there seems to have occurred. From the sixteenth century onwards Teke, Yomuts and other tribes appear at every turn of events. The Turcomans appeared on the Syr Darya in the sixth century, arriving apparently from the north-east. In the tenth century they moved onto the left bank of the Amu Darya and into the district of Merv. Since most of the tribes had no written language their historical tradition exists in the form of mythology. The most important sources until the mid-nineteenth century are Khivan and Iranian chronicles: in the 'Shejerey i terakime' or tribal tree of the Turcomans, drawn up in the mid-seventeenth century by the Khan of Khiva Abul-Ghazi-Bogadur, the Tekke, Yomuts, Saryks and Ersari in the time of Sufyan-Khan (1525—35) are entered together with the Khorassanian Salors under the common name of 'Stone Salors'. Of their ancestry Abu Ghazi writes: 'With Salor was a certain Toi-Tutmas, the Tekke and Saryk are his descendants.'

The Salors are mentioned in the eleventh century by Makhmud of Kashgaria as one of the twenty-four tribes of the Ogus. They appear again in the fourteenth century with Rashid ad Din. This author also reports that the six branches of the Ogus tribes had each a particular protective totem animal, 'and it is their custom that whatever is the ongon of any tribe, they will not attack or fight it nor eat its flesh, because they have adopted it as a propicious omen ...'. The totemic animal names of camel, dog, wolf, sheep, fox, stag, hen etc. are also found in practically all the Turcoman tribes as the names of their various divisions. Astral totemic names also appear repeatedly — the six sons of Ogus Khan have names meaning Sun, Moon, Star, Heaven, Mountain and Sea. There are also contrasting pairs of Black (iara) and White (ak) which illustrate the splitting of many tribes into two (W. König: *Die Achal-Teke*). Tribes divided into two halves and put up territorial frontiers against each other, forming separate entities in war and for expeditions and conquests, and opposing each other both in armed combat and in peaceful contests. As the different names for the units are the same in different tribes it can be concluded that in the fourteenth and fifteenth centuries when the old tribal bands fell apart, other units voluntarily attached themselves to the obviously strong leaders of certain groups;

others were then subjugated. To strengthen the new unity they made up a tribal tree which showed all the sub-groups (in the Tekke for example there are forty-nine) as descended from a common ancestor.

Either fighting or in alliance with the khans of Khiva and Bokhara, the Turcomans had no rest for centuries. In these great expanses the economic and kinship cohesion of the large tribes was very loose. Attacks on the small village-like nomad communities (obas) forced them to combine into tribal sub-divisions (tire) which would only leave their firmly defined territory when driven out by stronger neighbours, when they lost their flocks etc. There are traditions too of payment of tribute by small tribes to the powerful Tekke so as to enjoy their protection.

Shah Abbas pushed back the frontier of the Saffavid empire to the Amu Darya. Nadir Shad had to undertake several campaigns against the Turcomans in the eighteenth century in order to put down risings of Tekke, Yomuds, Imreli, Ali-Eli and Sarlu, and prevent attacks on his garrisons. He drove tribes of Tekke and Yomuds to migrate towards Khorassan and western Iran. Both in north-east Iran and in the region of Kermanshah the knotted work of the descendants of these deportees is preserved in Turcoman designs. During this enforced sojourn in north-east Persia Ogurchik set off with a thousand kibitki round the Caspian Sea through Shemakha and the Crimea into the Urals, but he had to return once more to the southern region of the eastern shore of the Caspian. After the death of Nadir Shah (1747) the Khans of Bokhara conquered Merv, laid it waste and carried back the population into the khanate. In the seventeenth and eighteenth centuries also Khiva and Iran were repeatedly fighting the Turcomans who were also constantly at war among themselves. These latter, incited by the risings of Iranian governors, extended their plundering raid as far as Meshed and were often a vexation to the Khivans, who kept trying to put them down with punitive expeditions. In the nineteenth century too the Turcomans plundered and robbed in the territory of Khiva, Bokhara and Persia in their quest for new pastures. In the middle of the century the Khivan Khans invoked the help of the Tekke against the Yomuds and Chaudors, who were exerting strong pressure on the khanate. Thereupon Russia, who at this time was gradually gaining a stronger footing in western Turkestan, at last succeeded in pacifying the region by subjugating the strongest tribe, the Tekke (1885). According to the calculations of the Russian ethnologists the population at the end of the previous century, which is when the best carpets were made, consisted of seventy per cent Turcomans. The remaining percentage was of Turcomanised tribes of Arab stock (Shik, Syd, Makhtums, Kotcha etc.), 'Turkish' tribes who were the descendants of the inhabitants of the land before the tenth century, and Kirghiz. Except for the Kirghiz and Kotcha the non-Turcoman tribes did no hand-knotting. Plain weaves on the other hand were made by many, and especially good ones by some Arab tribes. Production at the beginning of this century was smaller than is usually thought. Bogolubow speaks of an annual average of 1,000 palas for the Russian Transcaspian, 60,000 koshmas (felts), 1,500 carpets and altogether 7,000 chovals, torbas, khurchins, kapunnuks etc. Adding the production of the rest of western Turkestan and of the Afghan region there still remains only a small surplus for the trade with Europe.

To the main tribes of Salors, Tekke, Yomud, Ersari and Saryks which formed in the Middle Ages belong an increasing number of both larger and very small sub-tribes. Sub-divisions of the Yomuds are i.a. Goklans, Ikdyr, Ogurjali, Chaudor; to the Ersari belong the Bashyr, Unish, Otli Telpe, Ulma Bedast, Daly, Kisil Ayak, Kanich. The Kanich alone claim fourteen different sub-groups. The most important of the forty-nine sub-divisions of the Tekke are the Otamysh, Tokhtamysh, Bakhshi, Sychmas, Bek, Fekil. A minority of the Turcomans are described as pure blooded (Igen): Mongol in type with a broad face, short nose and sparse beard; the majority as resembling the Aryan (Kul), with a strong beard growth.

The main dwelling areas of the non-urban population, which can only be roughly established because of their mobility as nomads, are given as follows: Tekke with about 36,800 kibitki in the oasis area of Akhal Tekke between Kysyl Arvat and Geok tepe, in the area eastwards from there in the Ashkabad district, and in the north of the districts of Tedshen and Merv.

Saryks with 7,290 kibitki in the oases of Sholatan and Pendeh.

Salors with c. 3,000 kibitki in the oases of Seraks in the district of Tedshen.

Ersari in the western part of the district of Merv, on the Amu Darya, in the Bokhara-Afghan border regions and in the khanate of Khiva.

Yomuds with c. 4,600 kibitki along the rivers Sumbar and Atrek and in the east and south of the Khiva khanate. Goklan along the Atrek and Sumbar and in Khiva. Ikdyr and Abdal on the Caspian and in the khanate of Khiva, Ogurjali on the Caspian and on the islands of Cheleken, Dolgi and Ogurchinsk.

In the Khiva khanate there were also Kirghiz who comprised the main population of the Russian steppe as far as the Caspian and on the north and east of the deserts of Kara Kum and Kysyl Kum. Arabatchi, Chaudor, Ersari and Busachli along the Amu Darya, Osbeg, Turcomanised Turks, Karakalpak etc. in the delta of the Amu Darya.

In general the Yomuds, Ersaris and some of the Tekke and Saryks of the districts of Merv and Ashkabad led a purely nomadic life. Most of the Turcomans of the districts of Merv and Ashakbad, the population of the Tetchen district and the Goklan were semi-nomadic. The Ogurtchali and all the 'Turkish' tribes lived in solid huts.

During the conquest of western Turkestan the Russians had begun the construction of the central Asian railway from the Caspian Sea through Ashkabad, Merv, Beshir, Bokhara and Samarkand to Tashkent and Andishan. This new means of transport was utilised by the carpet buyers and the sellers of aniline dyes to get into the auls. Russia so much prized Turcoman carpets, as yet little known in Europe, that according to travellers' reports there was sometimes not a carpet to be found in the aul. Russian customs policy cut off the Turcomans from the countries that supplied their beautiful natural dyes — Persia and India. This explains why aniline dyes were used even on the best wool and on superlatively knotted Turcoman carpets at the turn of the century.

Tremendous changes have come over western Turkestan in the last decades. The capital of the Soviet Republic of Turkmenistan, Ashkabad, is today itself the most important production centre for Turcoman carpets and it has succeeded Bokhara and Khiva as the trading centre. Both in Turkmenistan and in Uzbekistan — the border regions of western Turkestan also belong to the republics of Tadjikstan, Kasakhstan and Kirghizstan — collective farms, the construction of great canals and the attractions of the urban life have not left the life of the steppes unaffected. Bokhara, Khiva, Samarkand and Tashkent, names that conjure up the glamour and mystery of the East, are today large modern cities, centres of industry and culture.

Tashkent, the 'June' of Chinese chronicles of the second and first centuries BC, is the capital of Uzbekistan and has about a million inhabitants. It is the focus of Russian cotton production, and supports i.a. a textile combine, dredger, textile and agricultural machinery factories, sixteen technical colleges and a stadium with seats for 53,000. The life of Samarkand, the city designed by Timur, is dominated by factories for clothing, knitwear, locomotive components, jams, artificial fertilisers and cinema apparatus, silk spinning, a university, schools of technology and advanced study, and theatres and clubs. Khiva and Bokhara are similar. In Khiva, the late feudal capital of the Uzbek khanate, the narrow winding lanes have had to give way to modern traffic. But the grandiose townscape, mainly erected around 1800, has been preserved. Bokhara 'i-sherif' (the noble) with its mighty rammed earth fortifications is a visual history of central Asian architecture from the Sogdian buildings of the pre-Islamic period to the palace of the last emir. The most famous of the mausolea are those of the Sheikh Seifeddin Bokharsi (thirteenth to fourteenth century), Chashm-Ayub (1380) and that of the Khan Buyan Kuli, with its facing of blue-glazed tiles. The ancient citadel of 'Ark', centre of the city since the sixth century and fortress of the prince Shiri-Kish, remained a strong-point until the fall of the emirate in 1920. The extensive bazaar and the madrasah of Miri-Arab (c. 1535) are two more architectural splendours, all overtopped by the Kalyan minaret.

In the decoration of the mediaeval buildings of these towns we see many ornaments which have been faithfully preserved into the twentieth century as elements of Turcoman carpet decoration, especially in the borders.

XX. Turcoman, 19th century. Engsi = tent entrance curtain, hachlu. 142 × 120 (117—123) cm.
Warp: W. S-plied, 2 strands, twisted, undyed light.
Weft: W. Z-spun, 2 strands, untwisted, undyed brown. 2 shoots, 1. straight, 2. sinuous.
Pile: W. Z-spun, 2 or 3 strands, untwisted. Knots P. III, 60°: h. 80, w. 46 = 3,680 per sq. dm. Upper end: —. Lower end: —.
Selvedges: W. shirazi, blue not original. Quality: velvety, thin, leather hard, smooth.
Colours: 8, *morello-cherry red, surmey, ivory*, rust-red, cherry-red, vermilion, medium blue, dark brown.
Pattern: the characteristic hachlu design for the engsi: the central field is quartered by the cross. In the quarters vertical rows of Y-forked stems. Geometric stem pattern in the main border, which goes round the panel with the mihrab above the central field. Below a wide border with half-drop rows of small rosette lozenges aligned on bands. Every detail of the composite design is unmistakably Turcoman.

Turcoman carpets to the end of the eighteenth century

Good Turcoman carpets are difficult to date precisely because of their conscious adherence to tradition and the continued use of the same guls for their main pattern. Carpets from this remote region hardly ever reached the West in early times and it was not customary to knot the dates (every case of an early date on old Turcoman carpets which has been investigated has turned out to be a fake). This being so, perhaps colour schemes can help us.

On page 221 is a detail from an old Turcoman carpet which appeared in Cairo a short time ago together with a second piece almost exactly similar. Its colours, especially the light blue, show such striking differences from what has previously been looked upon as typical Turcoman that this may provide a clue to dating. Preservation of two pieces from the seventeenth to eighteenth century is probably exceptional. The taste of the West at this time is more likely than distance to have prevented the early carpets of this region from reaching Europe. The articles knotted for home needs and for barter were used up in the tents and houses of Turkmenia. General Bogolubow, Russian governor of Transcaspia in 1900, was the first connoisseur to make a large collection of Turcoman carpets and smaller knotted pieces. He presented the forty best of his 139 pieces, together with sixty-two water colour illustrations of other carpets, to the Leningrad museum. He thought it possible that the different ornaments, the guls particular to each tribe, might help to overcome the lack of ethnographic information and throw light on the origin of the different Turcoman peoples (khalk).

Turcoman carpets are unmistakable in style. They differ at first glance from those of any other provenance. There is an exceptionally harmonious repetition, peaceful yet rhythmical, of the same geometric motifs on grounds that are delicately graded from mahogany, playing over a brownish to a bluish red. This has won them the title of 'gentlemen's carpets', while the blue shimmer on many pieces, all of them knotted in the finest quality wool and perfectly clipped, has caused them to be named 'Blue Bokhara'. Infrequently the ground is kept white or the border given a different background colour from the central field. Exceptions in pattern are made by curtains for the tent entrance (engsi, p. 231 and fig. 112), prayer mats (namazlik, p. 251) and the ornamental strips for kibitki (tents) (fig. 120); also the work knotted by the Bashyr and Baluchi nomads.

For no other people has knotted work played such an important part in daily life as for the Turcomans. It is no luxury for other nomadic and semi-nomadic peoples, it is true, and indeed is still an essential requirement, but it is the Turcoman women who are outstanding for the finesse and colour sense of their work, hand-knotted with endless and loving care for the use of their families. From child-hood the girls were taught this genuine folk art, and the carpets in a dowry, always of an established number, brought the highest honour to the bride, and to her mother who taught her the craft. As the wedding caravan approached the tent of the bridegroom the leading camel wore the khalyk round its chest, with the tassels reaching to its hoofs. After the wedding it was used to frame the tent opening. Later it was developed into a special entrance decoration, the kapunnuk of the Saryk (fig. 12). Knotted or embroidered cloths and decorative strips for the neck and head of the camel (fig. 120) were matched in colour with the five-cornered osmolduks for the flanks (fig. 113). The bundles of tent poles (uk) were carried in handsome carpet bags (ukuki). The khurdjin (fig. 126) was a bag for carrying small luggage attached to the back of the saddle. The bride had knotted carpets in quantity: the tent was entered over the small 'germech'; inside, the family and visitors squatted round the fire-place on 'ojakbashi' and 'dip-khali' which lay on thick, often patterned felts (koshma). All the utensils, provisions and possessions of the household were kept in bags, torba (fig. 122) and larger choval (fig. 117), hanging from the wooden tent frame, there being no furniture. The dis-torba held the salt; the chenche torba the spoons, another the mirror (aina-kap). Long woven braids (yolami and bou, fig. 120) whose knotted patterns allowed the greatest scope to the imagination of the knotter, decorated the tent walls; the engsi (p. 221, fig. 119) closed the entrance. The greatest care, a token of her love, had been lavished by the bride on knotting the saddle cover, cherlik, and the horse rug, tainakcha (p. 241). The woven provender bags were embroidered.

Life for the Turcomans was unthinkable without carpets: the children took their first steps on the children's salachak, daily prayers (nama) were performed on the namazlik, and the dead were carried on their last journey on the funereal ayatlyk.

W. G. Moschkowa has recently done a thorough investigation of the motifs and designs on Turcoman carpets. In her study, on which we here inevitably base all our

110. **Tekke. Bukhara, Turcoman, early 20th century.** 242 × 212 cm. (detail).
Warp: W. S-plied, 2 strands, twisted, undyed light.
Weft: W. and goat hair Z-spun, single, undyed brown. One shoot sinuous.
Pile: W. Z-spun, 2 strands, untwisted. Knots P. Ib: h. 74, w. 42 = 3108 per sq. dm. Upper end: 2 cm. W. kilim undyed light, then warp threads knotted in sixes. Lower end: 3 cm. W. kilim undyed light, then long warp loops twisted.
Selvedges: W. shirazi surmey colour round 4 bunched warp threads.
Quality: velvety, almost thin, low granulation.
Colours: 5, *brown-red, white, surmey,* orange-brown, dark brown. Pattern: the eight bands of the border separate the central field from the brown-red ground. It is covered with the fine rectangular lattice characteristic of Tekke, in which vertical rows of Tekke guls alternate at a half drop with horizontally elongated stars. The main border is divided into fields with star-filled octagons by bands of geometric flower heads. (Compare the raylike sword-shaped geometric ornament in the guls with the 'swords' of the eagle kasak, fig. 43.)

111. **Yomud, Turcoman, dated 1356 = AD 1937** 331 × 206 (204—208) cm.
Warp: W. S-plied, 2 strands, twisted, undyed light.
Weft: W Z-spun, 2 strands, untwisted, undyed light and dark brown. 2 shoots alternating sinuous.
Pile: W. Z-spun, 2 strands, untwisted. Knots P. Ia: h. 68, w. 28 = 904 per sq. dm. and last row of knots T. 1.
Upper end and lower end: 8 cm. W. kilim chestnut brown/ivory with red-blue stitching. Selvedges: W. shirazi blue/brown-red 4 cord. Quality: like velvet, medium heavy, smooth.
Colours: 9, *chestnut-brown, ivory,* dark blue, cherry-red, rust-red, pale brick-red, black-brown, surmey, red-brown.
Pattern: the Yomud Dyrnak gul is in half-drop rows on the chestnut central field. In the main border an Ashik band filled with leaves geometricised to indented lozenges with inscribed stalk. In the additional borders at the ends, geometric trees or plants like flying eagles.

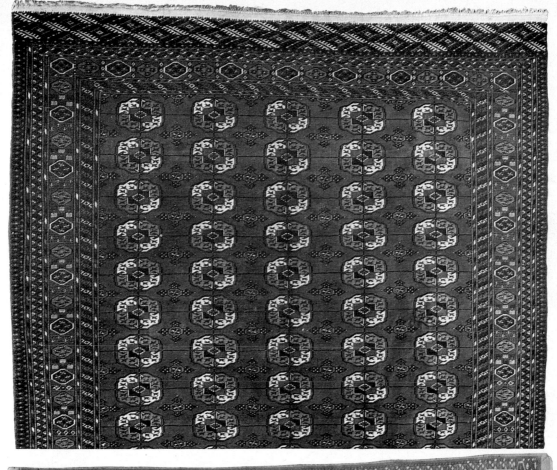

Gulaidi

Dagdan

Saryk gul

Mihrab

Salor gul

Ertmen of the Chodors

Tekke gul

Tauk Nuska
of the Arabatch

Dyrnak gul of the Yomud

Ersar gul
(Gülli gul)

Tauk gul
of the Chodors

Ersar gul
(Temirchin gul)

Kepse gul, Yomud

Yomud gul

information, she agrees with Bogolubow's suggestion that the Turcoman women as guardians of tradition in the carpet patterns are handing on all the higher feelings and values of the tribe, and of the people as a whole. In the gul she sees the pattern, ornament or emblem, for want of a better word, particular to one tribe. (Etymologically gul is probably a dialectal alteration of gül, flower.) While the small 'hallowed' motifs of magico-religious import such as the güleidi and dagdan are used universally as amulets for decorating the border, the use of the gul seems to have been strictly prescribed. The names Tekke gul, Salor gul, Ersar gul, Saryk gul etc. indicate an emblem belonging to a tribe, which until a few decades ago was only to be met in the ornament of the central field of larger carpets.

The origin of the gul, like the patterns on the engsi — e.g. the use of the mihrab, even sometimes in rows, as an amulet as in fig. 112 — poses a number of unsolved problems. Despite the tribal distinctions in the patterns, Turcoman carpets have many elements in common. Bogolubow saw these as proof of the common ancestry of groups of tribes which today are separate and independent, or as traces of the inclusion of alien groups. Tekke, Yomud, Ersari and Saryk are of common origin, according to the historical sources. The tribal differences in the carpet patterns are strongest in those places where they best succeeded in preserving their tribal cohesion and hence their traditions. The mixing of tribal patterns with alien foreign elements occurs most frequently where the confines of the tribal organisation became blurred, as among the Ersari, after centuries of cohabitation with the Bokharans under the Bokharan khans, or among the Chaudor who married into other tribes. Otherwise mixed marriages were extremely rare until recent times.

The chief pattern of the Chaudor, the ertmen, which still survives on small pieces, soon only remained in rudimentary form. The Chaudor adopted the patterns of neighbouring tribes such as the Arabatch, and elaborated them. Thus arose the rather widespread octagon with the H-shaped elements inside it. The names of adopted patterns show that their origin is still known. The Yomud call the ornament borrowed from the Tekke 'tekke nakysh'. The pattern taken over from the Saryk and Salor of Merv is called Mar gul by the Kisil Yak tribal group.

The adoption and integration of foreign designs is particularly easy to recognise in the smaller knotted pieces, for which the knotter was freer in her choice of patterns. The Salor gul lost its significance as a tribal emblem when the Salor, who considered themselves the most noble and aristocratic of the Turcoman tribes and the fathers of Turcoman carpet craft, were completely vanquished by the Tekke and the Saryk in the nineteenth century. The gul of the defeated tribe did not perish when its tribe lost the sole right to use it. It went with their carpets to the victors. The Salor gul, which is to be understood neither as a 'gül' = flower, 'gülcha' = little flower, nor as a 'Salor rose', was knotted with variations of its centre into innumerable torba and choval even by the women of other tribes, egged on by Russian demand for this pattern. In contrast to the 'living gul' the Salor gul had become a 'dead gul'. One step further leads to the 'gül — a flower understood purely ornamentally'. The Yomud whose tribal signs the 'kespe gul' and the 'dyrnak gul' were reserved for the large carpets, reproduced on their bags for tent utensils an old Yomud gul which was no longer recognised as a tribal pattern and was called a gül. Possibly we have here the one-time gul of a tribe like the Ikdyr who early lost their independence. Apart from the use in recent decades of the 'living guls' hitherto reserved for large carpets, it would seem that many emblems belonging to tribes that have become extinct or have dissolved survive on the smaller knotted pieces of western Turkestan.

The older women have bird names for certain elements of the geometricised floral-looking gul, such as the 'pecker' or the 'biter'. These ideas are now mostly just technical terms established by generations of use, and with a little imagination a bird's head can be made out in nearly every living or dead gul — as in the 'tauk nuska' of the Arabatch with its 'kushly', i. e. bird. But in fact on some chalyks which are 150 years old the 'ashik' ornament that covers the osmulduks in alternating rows (fig. 113) forms a lozenge frame for what are undoubtedly birds. The relationship of these bird drawings with those of the Anatolian animal carpets of the fourteenth century is a possibility worth investigating.

Turcoman carpets of the nineteenth and twentieth centuries

Turcoman carpets are for the most part worked in Persian knots; the Ghiordes or Turkish knot considered typical of the Turkish peoples plays only a subordinate part in the work of the Turcoman women. The warp is a right-hand twisted two-ply of undyed wool or goat hair; silk is only used in the very rare silk carpets. The same is true of the two-ply weft which is only lightly twisted or left untwisted; in the rare extremely fine pieces it may be single. Red-brown dyeing of the weft yarn is rare. For the pile fine wool is used, and for the smaller parts of the patterns silk sometimes; cotton is more frequent for white knots, since this is less affected by the smoke of the kibitka than wool, which takes on a sand or cream colour. Other co-lours too darken in the smoke. Bogolubow says that the Turcomans possessed a 'steppe breed *par excellence*' in their kharchi sheep who provided them with fine lustrous wool. The disadvantage of the lower durability of softer wool is compen-sated for in Turcoman work by an average high density of knotting unusual for nomads. Extremely high counts — sometimes over 7,000 knots per square dm. — are reached in the smaller objects of the bride's trousseau and the extremely rare carpets knotted entirely in silk will have up to 10,000 knots per square dm. The pile is short, only medium long in the mountainous regions. The kilim of the older carpets, which are more often very fine than fine, are often unusually long (kilimlik); their bands of pattern may be knotted. The end of the knotting or the beginning of the kilim is often formed by a narrow band on which are rows of güleidi or dagdan amulets. Since older carpets were made for use in the tent the largest only rarely exceed a format of about 350 × 230 cm., or they are of the same area and almost square. Older examples of much larger dimensions (see Beshir and Afghan) will have been commissioned for rich burghers and dignitaries of the towns.
Unlike all other carpet-makers the Turcomans keep the same ground colour for the border as for the central field. The basis of the design is an endless repeat of guls, güls, stars, or stylised floral motifs in vertical, diagonal or half-drop rows, and also on a quartered ground. Specifically Turcoman is an additional broad band on the border of the lower end or on both ends of many carpets. The carpets for closing the tent entrance, engsi (p. 231 and fig. 119) have the hatchlu (Haj = cross) sign. The ornamented fields separated by the arms of the cross are said to symbolise the old dream of the nomads of a firm house with wooden doors, whose panels divided by the rails and muntin are carved or inlaid.
Turcoman carpets are unfortunately known in the trade under the names of Bok-

112. Kisil-Ayak, Ersari Turcoman, 19th century. Engsi-tent entrance curtain. Hachlu. 169 × 136
(133—139) cm.

Warp: W. S-plied, 2 strands, twisted, undyed light.

Weft: W. Z-spun, 2 strands, untwisted, undyed brownish. 2 shoots alternating sinuous.

Pile: W. Z-spun, 2 or 3 strands, untwisted, and C. (white) Z-spun, 2 strands untwisted. Knots T. I: h. 58,
w. 34 = 1,972 per sq. dm. Upper end: —. Lower end: —. Selvedges: W. shirazi blue not original.
Quality: soft, now almost thin, smooth.

Colours: 7, *mahogany, gold-brown, surmey,* white, orange-brown, dark brown, yellow-brown.

Pattern: this standard pattern of the Kisil Ayak engsi is described on p. 250.

hara, Khiva, Pendeh and Beshir, the chief assemblage places. It would be more vivid, more reasonable and more just to divide them according to tribes into Tekke, Yomud, Ersari, Saryk and Chaudor. In cases of doubt the terms 'Turcoman' or 'Kirghiz' carpet (the Kirghiz are said to have learnt hand-knotting relatively late from the Turcomans) are more appropriate and just to the nomads than the names of towns where carpets are only traded. Mutual influences between the tribes do not allow of a perfect classification in the present state of our knowledge, and with the commercialisation of carpet production and the change of conditions in Turkmenia over the last decades it is questionable whether the lacunae in this knowledge will ever be filled in.

The finest Turcoman carpets are those of the TEKKE (fig. 110), Russian 'Tekinski', from the oases of Merv (Marv) and Akhal Tekke. The ground colour varies from mahogany and ox blood to a purplish dark red. In the central field are rows of Tekke guls joined by thin dark vertical and horizontal lines.

In the spaces, alternating with the guls, are smaller horizontally spread stars with beam-like rays in the centre of the quadrilateral fields created by the thin lines joining the guls. This additional gentle quartering of the central field seems to be a very ancient feature of certain Turkish tribes, for we meet it in a type of Anatolian carpet of the fifteenth century.

The border has many stripes, all of small-scale geometric patterns except for the main band, which is usually divided into larger motifs, stars with many stick-like rays, octagons and small stars, or a toothed band of lozenges. On the norrow ends there is usually an additional broad band with stylised or geometric floral designs. The pattern colours are white or ivory, dark blue, red, some yellow and, very rarely, green.

All the work is very fine or extremely fine and in Persian knots. Sizes range between 120 × 100 cm. and c. 350 × 230 cm.

The carpets of the Tekke appear on the market as BOKHARA (Bukhara). For the best pieces the term 'Royal Bokhara' has been invented, and for hatchlu (hatchly, katchly) the fancy name 'Princess Bokhara'.

The deceptive term 'Yomud Bokhara' refers to the most beautiful carpets of the Yomud. The ground colour of the YOMUD (Yamut) carpets is chestnut brown to

XXI. Turcoman, 19th century. Tainakcha=horse rug. c. 133 × 120 cm.
Warp: W. S-plied, 2 strands, twisted, undyed light.
Weft: W. Z-spun, 2 strands, untwisted, undyed brownish. 1 shoot sinuous.
Pile: W. Z-spun, 2 strands, untwisted. Knots P. I: h. 118, w. 47 = 5,546 per sq.dm. Upper end: 2 cm. kilim W. red turned back and sewn.
Lower end: as upper end, but kilim light.
Selvedges: shirazi W. blue and goat hair, brown 2 cord.
Quality: velvet fine, leather hard, thin, smooth.
Colours: 7, *morello red, vermilion, surmey,* brown-black, dark brown, white, some olive-yellow.
Pattern: vermilion and indigo striping. Miniature geometric floral design in the stripes. In the second vermilion band a minute (family) sign. This rug contains about 700,000 knots, an illustration of the saying 'the greater the love, the finer the saddle cloth'.

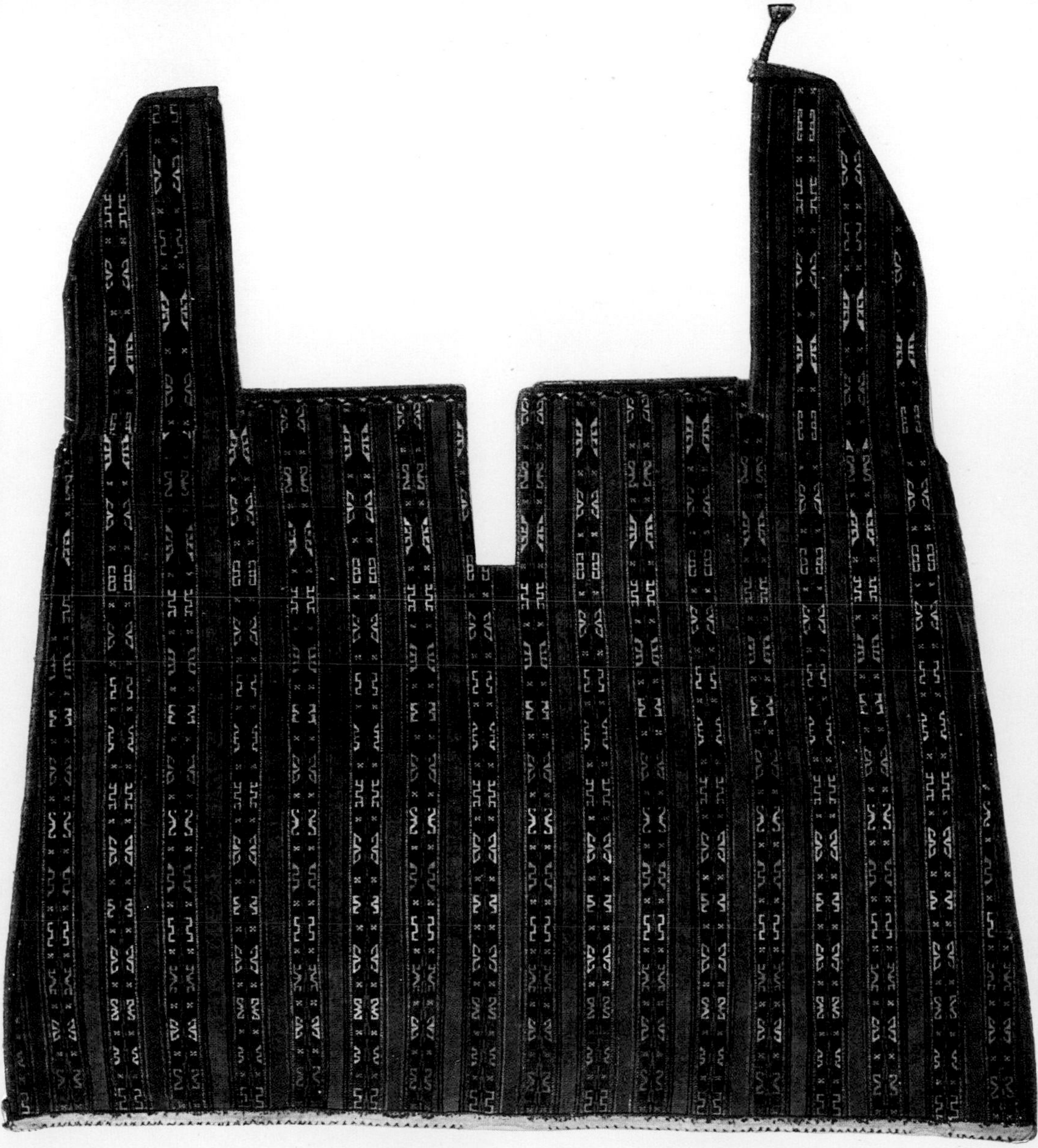

purple. They are not as lustrous as the Tekke carpets and on average not so densely knotted. A characteristic of many of the pieces, all in Persian knots, is a final row of Turkish knots.

The main motifs are the Dyrnak or Kepse gul (fig. 123) in half-drop rows. The border is narrower and usually has three stripes. The light main border is patterned with relatively simple large-scale geometric stems. In the broad additional border stripes on the narrow ends there is often a row of a motif peculiar to the Yomud, resembling a weeping willow or flying bird (eagle), besides the little ornament similar to the fir tree used also by the Tekke. The largest formats are about 3—400 × 200 cm.

BESHIR carpets may rightfully be called Bokharan, for the village of Beshir on the Amu Darya and the settlement area of a large part of the Bashyrs lie in the territory of the former khanate. The Turkish knot is often used in the medium to very fine Beshyr carpets. Goat hair is frequently used in the ground-weave and makes it very hard. The formats are generally twice as long as they are wide and can range from 200 × 100 cm. to 700 × 300 cm.

The designs are the most varied of all carpets knotted in western Turkestan. Both Persian and Chinese influence is apparent. The brick red or blue central field is closely covered with worm-like cloud bands ('Cloud band Beshir') or stylised floral motifs, over which may lie single octagons or rows of light arabesque stems taken from the Herati border, with the Herati motif or with vertical rows of hexagons. Although the characteristic Turcoman gul or gül does not appear, except occasionally as medallion-like octagons, the Beshir carpets are immediately recognisable as Turcoman. In the main bands of the multiple borders there are rows of zig-zag lozenges or soft light volute arabesque stem scrolls. Division into geometric trapeze-shapes, as shown in fig. 118, is also usual. This early Beshir with a goat hair ground-weave, is a child's practice piece: after a clumsy beginning and some improvements the pattern finally becomes clear in the middle of the carpet. The widespread anchor-like motif must have developed by geometricising the small oblique stylised flowerheads. Practice pieces like these, betraying all the pains of learning the art, were of course never intended for sale or export; it is all the more a cause for delight to the collector when he can acquire one of them.

The colour scheme of Beshir carpets is predominantly bluish red. Either the ground is blue and the close pattern red, or vice versa. Gold and white give a vivid sheen. The cucumber green of the Prophet (dark green mixed with orange) is sometimes used in the larger parts of the pattern. In the small prayer rugs white dominates the mihrab, and the long axis is stressed by a red stripe. The arch is often widened into a head shape.

Good old Beshir carpets are a rarity in Europe. The pieces which do occasionally appear are unfortunately almost always dyed with anilines.

PENDEH (Pandyih, Panjdih, Pendik), the name of the oasis lying south of Merv and inhabited mainly by Saryk, is applied to several different kinds of Turcoman carpets. First there is a type which is worked in very fine Persian knots. Its main ornament is the Salor gul or a gül with stepped outlines. The main colours are a rich red and quiet blue. White, ivory, other blue tones and a ruby or purple mostly of

113. Yomud, Turcoman, 19th century. Osmulduk = ornamental rug for the flanks of a camel.
65 × 124 cm. (above).
Warp: goat hair, S-plied, 2 strands, twisted, undyed light.
Weft: W. S-plied, 2 strands, slightly twisted, undyed brown. 2 shoots alternating sinuous.
Pile: W. Z-spun, 2 strands, untwisted. Knots P. Ib: h. 76, w. 34 = 2,584 per sq. dm. Upper end: 3 cm.
W. kilim red, turned back and sewn down behind, oblique stitch and sewn-on tassels. Lower end:
as upper end, but thick plaited cords with three-tiered tassels sewn on. Quality: soft, heavy, firm, hard.
Colours: 9, *chestnut-brown, ivory, surmey,* medium blue, dark green, red, vermilion, yellow-brown, brown-
black.
Pattern: lozenge lattice formed by the Ashik ornament with inscribed indented lozenge. Stepped polygons
in the stripes of the 7-fold border, running dog and (outside) the Dagdan amulet in rows.

114. Saryk, Turcoman, 19th—20th century. Kapunnuk = decoration for tent entrance. 69 × 146 cm.
(without tassels). (p. 245, above).
Warp: W. S-plied, 2 strands, twisted, undyed brownish.
Weft: W. Z-spun, single, undyed brown. 2 shoots: 1. straight, 2. sinuous. Pile: W. Z-spun, 2 strands,
untwisted, and silk (green and dughi) Z-spun, 2 strands. Knots P. II 25°: h. 54, w. 31 = 1,674 per sq. dm.
Upper end: W. kilim red, blue, cream turned back and sewn down, blue-red oblique stitch. Lower end:
Middle: W. kilim red, cream turned back and sewn down. Long fringe put in. Side flaps: blue-red oblique
stitching then warp threads bunched in 8s and firmly wrapped with brown-blue; tassels added of looped
and twisted wool.
Quality: rather hard, thick, coarse granular.
Colours: 9, *mahogany, surmey, cream, dark blue-green,* dark red, some yellow, green and dughi.

115. Afghan, 19th century. Namazlik = prayer rug. 89 × 72 cm.

Warp: goat hair S-plied, 2 strands, twisted, undyed light and brown.

Weft: W. Z-spun, single, undyed brown. 2 shoots alternating sinuous.

Pile: W. Z-spun, 2 strands, untwisted. Knots P. Ib: h. 40, w. 28 = 1,120 per sq.dm. Upper end: —.
   Lower end: —. Selvedges: W. hirazi dark brown, on the left 2 cord, on the right 3 cord.

Quality: dry, very firm, thick, slightly granular.

Colours: 7, *dark red, sand,* morello-red, rust-red, black-brown, brown, dark brown-red.

Pattern: so-called childrens' prayer rug with two light niches one above the other. Within them the heavy
   motifs exclusive to Afghan prayer rugs, surrounded by soft, stiff stems.

246

116. Yomud, 19th century. Namazlik, prayer rug. 107×83 (81—85) cm.
Warp: W. S-plied, 2 strands, twisted, undyed light.
Weft: W. Z-spun, 2 strands, untwisted, undyed brown. 2 shoots alternating sinuous. Pile: W. Z-spun,
    2 strands, untwisted. Knots P. Ia: h. 74, w. 32 = 2,368 per sq. dm.
Colours: 7, *cherry-red, ivory, surmey,* dark green, red-orange, dark brown, medium blue.

117. Turcoman, 19th century. Choval, large tent bag. 47 × 128 cm.
Warp: W. S-plied, 2 strands, twisted, undyed light.
Weft: W. Z-spun, single, undyed brownish, one shoot sinuous.
Pile: W. Z-spun, 2 strands, untwisted. Knots P. Ib: h. 128, w. 56 = 7,168 per sq. dm. Upper end: W. kilim
    (double shoots) blue, red, light turned back and sewn down. Lower end: 1 cm. remains of the palas
    for the back, now removed, long fringes introduced. Quality: velvety, thin, smooth. Colours: 6, *red,
    white* smoked to cream, *surmey,* rust-red, dark brown, some medium blue.

118. Beshir, early 19th century. (149—166) 157×138 (134—142) cm.
Warp: goat hair, S-plied, 2 strands, twisted, undyed dark brown.
Weft: goat hair, Z-spun, 2 strands, untwisted, undyed dark brown. 2 shoots alternating sinuous.
Pile: W. Z-spun, 2 or 3 strands untwisted. Knots P. Ib: h. 30, w. 29 = 870 per sq. dm. Upper end: —.
    Lower end: —. Selvedges: goat hair shirazi black brown 4 cord round 3 warp threads.
Quality: soft, now thin, coarse granular.
Colours: 7, *white, red, green,* yellow, surmey, black-brown, light blue.
Pattern: the pattern of this 'practice piece' only finds its ultimate form in the middle of the carpet.

119. **Beshir, Turcoman, 19th century. Engsi, hachlu pattern.** 156 × 142 (138—146) cm.

Warp: W. with goat hair S-plied, 2 strands, twisted, undyed brown.

Weft: W. Z-spun, 2 strands, untwisted, undyed brownish. 2 shoots alternating sinuous.

Pile: W. Z-spun, 3 strands, untwisted. Knots P. Ia: h. 43, w. 31 = 1,333 per sq. dm. Upper end: —. Lower end: a few shoots remaining of a W. kilim red. White/dark brown oblique stitching.

Selvedges: goat hair shirazi, black-brown 3 cord round 3 threads.

Quality: soft, thick, smooth.

Colours: 7, *cherry-red, white, dark blue,* medium blue, blue-green, black-brown, brown-orange.

Pattern: the four fields created by the hachlu are divided into rectangles bearing W-shaped geometric stems flanked by stars. In the two upper quarters camels instead of the stars, and comb-like and geometric floral motifs. The design on the cross beams in the typical Beshir colour combination of blue-green and brown-orange. The motifs of the broad horizontal border resemble those in the kasakh (fig. 36). To finish off, the trefoil motif from the Ersari gul in rows.

248

silk complete the range. The formats are namaseh and carpets of about 300 × 200 cm. P. 257 shows a choval of this type with more than 5,000 knots to the square dm. Secondly, there are harsher coloured carpets made in the last four decades which go under the name of Pendeh. They are always ornamented with a stepped gül. They are not as densely knotted as the older pendeh. The pile is longer and brown-red dominates the colour. The formats go from namaseh to room size.

Thirdly fine to very fine KISIL-AYAK (= red-footed) carpets made in the region are known as Pendeh. Their ground colour is a slightly sombre brownish red which makes a strong contrast with the white cotton knots. The larger formats of 350 to 400 × 200 cm. have patterns of güls, while the hatchlu design is the norm (fig. 112) for the sejadeh sizes. The ornamentation of the hachlu surpasses in complexity that of all other engsi: the many-striped border, to which a particularly broad brown-gold band is attached at the bottom, only leaves a relatively narrow field free for the cross. The vertical arms, like the main bands of the side borders, are patterned with a thin straight stalk with pairs of flower tassels attached. The horizontal arms have a multiple repeat of the motif which Turcoman women call 'kuchuk isi' (track of the young dog). Below the hatchlu design runs a horizontal panel divided into seven fields. Across the upper end is a row of seven (in more recent hatchlu sometimes only five) mihrab motifs side by side. Whereas all other engsi have vertical rows of W- or Y-shaped stems in the four hatchlu fields, this stem in the Kisil Ayak is in the shape of a thick stumpy pole, from which two small sprays branch out to one side.

KHIVA (KHARESM, KHORAZM, KHWAREZM) is illogically the term for yet more different types of carpet: first all Turcoman carpets with angular guls tending to a square shape; this ornamentation is reminiscent on a smaller scale of a type of Afghan or Tekke carpet — the latter with the Tekke gul inside the octagon — but it is not as fine either in gauge or in colour scheme. Secondly it means carpets with the classical patterns of the Yomud who live in the region of Khiva. Thirdly, the carpets of the Arabatch and Choudor with an H-shaped sign in the gul. Fourthly the Chaudor carpets with a lozenge-patterned central field; every lozenge is filled with a polygon reminiscent of the shape of the 'ertmen'.

According to their provenance the ground colour of the 'Khiva' carpets ranges from lustrous red to brown-red. The patterns are coloured in dark blue, white, ivory, orange and the Prophet's green used by the Chaudor, no longer so rare as it was.

The formats range from larger namaseh and carpets of 300 × 200 cm. to 350 × 240 cm.

The Turcoman carpets of the present day are among the most attractive examples of Soviet carpet production. Technically they are excellent. The traditional patterns are carried on with scarcely any alterations in form, though without reference to their original tribal allegiances. Even so the connoisseur finds the manufactory carpets wanting in warmth and originality. The largest formats exceed what was formerly usual. The centre of their production is Ashkabad. Between the two wars Bokhara were also produced in sedjadeh format with a blue ground and recently smaller hatchlu are produced in larger namaseh formats.

It is doing no injury to the beauty of the older Turcoman carpets to dwell on the greater charm of the smaller pieces knotted for daily use. The engsi (hatchlu, enessy, kachli), all kinds of bags (khurdjin, torba, choval), kibitka strips, decorative braids, cushions, kapunnuks, osmolduks, saddle covers and prayer rugs represent virtually the only artistic outlet of the Turcomans and reflect in a particular way their zest, industry, skill, colour sense and devotion.

The hatchlu design of the engsi differs from tribe to tribe. Being intended to hang over the tent entrance, the upper end is usually not sewn down but embroidered and provided with braided tapes to make it firm. These tapes are also attached to the bags hung inside the tent, the smaller torba and larger choval. In one corner of the knotting or in the weaving at the back there is always a family emblem to be found; it is also put on the extremely fine saddle cloths. There is a saying, 'The more the man is loved, the finer his saddle cloth'. Of all the kibitka strips the Tekke ones (fig. 120a) are probably the most handsome that could be devised to decorate the dark interior of the tent. A motif is never repeated throughout the length, which may be anything from ten to twelve metres. They are perhaps the women's substitute for literary expression.

The knotted pattern is all the more effective on the strips for being economical. The ground is light coloured and extraordinarily closely woven. The panama-like ground-weave only allows of one knot over three warp threads, and only the Turkish knot is suitable for this.

Their plain palas weaving also shows the great skill of the Turcoman women.

AFGHAN CARPETS

Afghan carpets used to be made by tribes related to the Ersari, both in the mountains of north Afghanistan and in the Russian district further north beyond the frontier. The new mass-produced wares come from Afghan manufactories.

XXII. **Beshir, Turkmenia 19th century. 'Namazlik' = Prayer rug.** 165 × 80 cm. (p. 251).
Material and structure as in fig. 118, but warp dark brown with white, occasionally grey.
Knots: P. Ib: h. 36, w. 26 = 936 per dm².
Upper end: 1 cm. remaining of a W. kilim red.
Lower end: 1 cm. remaining of a W. kilim brown.
Sides: Shirazi not original.
Touch: rather dry, almost light, coarse granular.
Colours: 7, *ivory, brick-red, blue,* olive-yellow, dark brown, red (faded to pink in the bottom third), dark blue.
Pattern: The dark brown central field is almost entirely filled by the thick light mihrab frame ending in a double hook, leaving only a relatively small niche. It is filled with two geometric flower stems. The light frame has a row of large flowers with a pair of leaves attached to the stalk that rises from a horizontal bar. Between them small geometric floral scatter. A similar close scatter on either side of the gable. Narrow border with two guard stripes. The two innermost stripes have a small wave band with hammer-shaped geometric flowers or red spandrel filling. The outer stripe has a triangular band with small geometric flowers.

Though the Afghans all look uniform at first sight there are notable differences in colour and design. The ground is brown- or yellow-red and the design has close rows of squarish octagons which may be up to half a metre in size. In the spaces — depending on the number of octagons — are small güls, hooked stepped polygons and stars, or larger finely articulated lozenge lattices. The surface of the octagons, which have sometimes the curved outline of the Tekke gul, is quartered diagonally by two contrasting colours. Their design is often very similar to the gülli gul or the temirjin gul (see p. 237) of the Ersari; but there can be other patterns inside the octagons. It is by no means compulsory for an Afghan carpet to have the clover-leaf element of the gülli gul inside the octagon. The borders of older pieces are either broad and made up of a number of bands, or may equally well be narrow with only two guard stripes to the main border with its geometric pattern.

More than five colours is rare. Combined with the red ground tone are dark blue, some ivory and green and — sometimes in large quantities — orange.

The pile is long, appropriate to life in the mountains, and made of Persian knots in lustrous wool; the count is medium fine. Carpets with a fine count and a short-cut pile are not uncommon among older pieces.

The ground-weave shows the structure usual in Turcoman carpets and consists mostly of goat hair. The two-plied warp is almost always grey-brown or brown, more rarely light. The red kilim at the ends are sometimes unusually long (kilimlik) and striped with the other colours appearing in the carpet.

The sizes are namaseh (Afghan-charpai), larger sejadeh, especially for the hachlu and carpets of 300 × 200 to 550 × 350 cm., rarely larger. The best Afghans were formerly sold under the name of kerki (Russian frontier village on the Amu Darya, and an assemblage place for carpets). Surprisingly, several thousand square metres of older Afghan carpets still appear annually on the world market.

The bulk of modern coarse to medium-fine long-pile Afghan carpets give the effect of being made in two colours. Either synthetic brown or cherry-red with blue-black or old gold (chemically bleached and redyed to 'Afghan gold' with blue-black). Recently produced carpets come on the market under more than half a dozen names. Qarquin are the cheapest, Davlatobod ones of good quality; the underside has a red sheen instead of the usual dirty grey-black. Pendiq are the very good ones, which may also have a brown or blue ground; the octagons resemble the Salor gul in outline.

The light Mauri lies outside this category of Afghans. It is finely knotted on a thin warp in the best Turcoman tradition and there is no parallel in the ordinary Afghan designs for its light geometric pattern.

The Afghan hatchlu are rather larger, thicker and simpler in design than the entrance curtains of the other Turcoman regions.

Afghan prayer carpets have the small namaseh format which here is called charpay = four foot. The niche ranges from a simple arch of two beams ending in a hook via the complicated pattern illustrated in fig. 115 to the bird's-eye townscape of Mecca with the Ka'ba in the centre.

Afghan torbas and chovals are also coarser than is usual in Turkmenia. The smallest pattern elements are generally green and are knotted separately in silk. On the woven underside the güleidi amulet is often embroidered in multiple repeat. The hand-knotted work of the nomad Baluchi tribes who also live in western Afghanistan is discussed in the following section.

BALUCHI CARPETS

The carpets of the nomad Baluchi tribes of Khorassan, west Afghanistan and the Irano-Turkestan border belong among the Turcomans. Their work is more varied in pattern, less conservative, and darker in colour than the rest, but they have many features of structure and details of pattern in common.

There are several conflicting accounts of the movement of the Baluchi into Khorassan. Their carpets are made neither in the east Iranian province of Baluchistan nor in that part of former Baluchistan which now belongs to Pakistan. The most probable story claims Nadir Shah as the originator of the migration of the 'ancient' Baluchi from Baluchistan and follows this first migration with a second, of the 'modern' Baluchi towards the end of the nineteenth century. Besides the Baluchi majority

120. Turcoman, 19th century. 3 decorative bands. (a) Large kibitka (tent) band, Tekke. 1100 × 26 cm. (b) Ditto, smaller, 435 × 16 cm. (c) Camel ornament, 530 × 9 cm.
(a) Warp: C. S-plied, 2 strands, twisted, undyed cream. Weft: W. S-plied, lightly twisted, extremely thin. 1 shoot straight and tight, producing panama weave. For pattern weft W. Z-spun, 2 strands, untwisted. Pile: W. Z-spun, 2 strands, untwisted. Turkish knots over 3 warp threads (see drawing p. 30). 25 knots per sq. dm. The patterns are knotted into the light woven band and stand out in relief. Only the small subsidiary pattern of the horizontal divisions are woven. Upper end: —: Lower end: —. Colours: 7, *dark brown-red, rust-red, surmey,* dark green, black-brown, brick-red, white smoked to dark grey.
(b) Warp and weft: as in (a) but ground weft W. and pattern weft W. 3 or 4 strands untwisted. Pile: as in (a) but 24 Turkish knots per sq. dm. The knotting is only done on the upper warp threads and like the woven parts of the pattern is invisible on the back.
Ends: every 10 warp threads are threaded through a white or blue glass bead, then firmly wrapped into a string, ending with a bead in a tassle. Each field with 3 knotted pattern stripes is followed by a field with woven zig-zag pattern: the borders and edgings are marked by coloured (therefore pattern-forming) woollen warp threads.
(c) Material and structure as (b). But no knotting and no beads. Embroidered stripes in the field divisions. Especial pattern in the two (larger) fields fourth from the ends. Tassles along both sides.

121. Turcoman, 19th century. Kibitka (tent) band, woven. (p. 255 centre) 1400 × 29 cm. (detail).
Warp: W. S-plied, 2 strands, twisted, dyed since pattern forming *rust-red, navy blue,* light blue, brown-black, brown-red, dark brown, some white. 88 warp threads per dm.
Weft: W. S-plied, 2 strands, slightly twisted, undyed black-brown. 60 shoots per dm.

122. Turcoman, 19th century. Small tent bag, dis-torba. 46 × 57 cm. (p. 255 below).
Warp: W. S-plied, 2 strands, twisted, undyed light.
Weft: W. Z-spun, 2 strands, untwisted, brownish. 2 shoots alternating sinuous.
Pile: W. Z-spun 2 strands, untwisted. Knots P. Ib: h. 79, w. 47 = 3,713 per sq. dm.
Upper end: W. kilim, vermilion turned back and sewn down. Lower end: as upper end, but wine.
Selvedges: now, after removal of back, W. shirazi red 2 cord.
Quality: dry, thin hard, fine granular.
Colours: 7, *morello, surmey, coral,* ivory, olive-yellow, black-brown, medium blue.

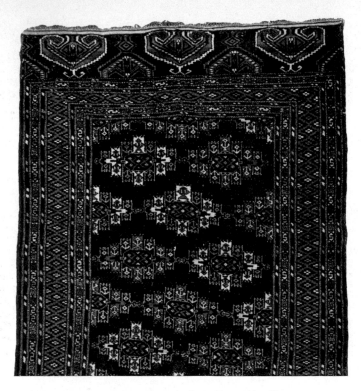

123. Yomud, Turcoman, 20th century. 212 × 122 (116—128) cm. (detail).
Warp: W. S-plied, 2 strands, twisted, undyed grey-brown.
Weft: W. S-plied, 2 strands, lightly twisted, dyed brown-red. 2 shoots alternating sinuous.
Pile: W. Z-spun, 2 strands, untwisted. Knots T. I: h. 66, w. 34 = 2,244 per sq. dm. Upper end: 2 cm. W.
  kilim with narrow red-black band, then warp threads knotted off in fives.
Lower end: as upper end. Selvedges: W. shirazi surmey 2 cord.
Quality: soft, fleshy, granular. Colours: 6, *morello-red, dark green,* red, white, brown-orange, black.
Pattern: morello-red central field filled with fragment of continuous half-drop repeat of rows of Yomud
  Kepse gul, in same colour diagonally. Main border has stepped lozenge band. 6 guard stripes. The broad
  additional borders at the ends have geometric trees or stems, typical of Turcoman designs, reminiscent of
  weeping willows or flying birds.

there are a small Mongolian tribe and several Arab tribes in different villages of
Khorassan all of whom knot Baluchi carpets. 'Arab' has become the name for the
most primitive kind. 'Meshed Baluchi' are the finest, 'Kuduani' a medium-fine sort,
distinguished by the smooth feel of the underside.
The warp as in all Turcoman carpets is of two-strand right-plied brown, grey-brown
or more rarely light wool, or of goat hair. This latter is almost always used for the
shirazi, usually untwisted. The end kilims are often woven in very handsome patterns which may even be completed by embroidery. The lustrous soft pile is in Persian knots at a density of between 800 to 1500 per square dm. Special pieces, such as
the small one on p. 261, may have a considerably higher count. The most usual measurements are 120 × 70 cm. to 220 × 110 cm. Carpets in formats of 300 × 180 cm.
to about 400 × 230 cm. are rare. Recently small pieces have come onto the market
with a cotton warp, occasionally even with artificial silk pile, and lacking the origin-

124. Turcoman, 19th century. Choval, large tent bag.
75 × 117 (115—119) cm.

Warp: goat hair, S-spun, 2 strands, untwisted, undyed light.

Weft: W. Z-spun, 2 strands, undyed brown. 2 shoots:
1. straight, 2. sinuous.

Pile: W., C. (white) and silk (red-purple) Z-spun, 2 strands,
untwisted. Knots P. III, 20°: h. 92, w. 56 = 5,152 per
dm². Direction of work contrary to direction of the
flowers in the borders.

Upper end: —. Lower end: —. Selvedges: —. Quality: velvety, thin, smooth.

Colours: 9, *red, surmey, dark blue, white,* purple, light blue,
medium blue, brown, some olive-yellow.

Pattern: red ground with rows of Salor guls, the central
motif somewhat altered, and repeated in the stepped polygons lying between the guls. A band of rectangular zig-
zag rosettes in the main border. Additional borders
anchor-shaped shrubs, in half-drop rows, 3 above and
9 below.

125. Turcoman. 'Guraband' (= against death) 70 × 63 cm.
According to two old men in Bokhara, who before the Revolution
were carpet merchants, it was worn by the best camel of the herd
to keep all evil influences away from the herd.

126. Baluchi, 19th—20th century. Khurjin, bag.
Knotted area, 68 × 74 cm.
Warp: W. S-plied, 2 strands, twisted, undyed light.
Weft: W. Z-spun, 2 strands, untwisted, undyed brown.
2 shoots alternating sinuous.
Pile: W. Z-spun, 2 strands, untwisted. Knots P. Ia: h. 40,
w. 24 = 960 per sq. dm.
Colours: 8, *medium blue, brown-black, purple-brown,* white,
medium brown, some yellow, orange and wine.
Pattern: a blue ground with 3 rows of 3 birds (cocks?).
The central one stands out, being white.

127. Baluchi, 19th—20th century. Namazlik, prayer rug. (145—151) = 148 × 90 (87—93) cm. (p. 259 left).
Warp: W. S-plied, 2 strands, twisted, undyed light and light with dark brown.
Weft: W. Z-spun, 2 strands, untwisted, undyed brown. 2 shoots: 1. straight, 2 sinuous.
Pile: W. Z-spun, 3 strands, untwisted. Knots P. II 30°: h. 36, w. 36 = 1,296 per sq. dm. Upper end: 5 cm.
kilim, W. 7 stripes, then warp threads knotted. Lower end: as upper end, but warp threads looped and
twisted.
Selvedges: goat hair shirazi, black-brown 4 cord round 3 warp threads.
Quality: soft, medium thick, firm, granular.
Colours: 10, *camel colours, red, dark blue,* dark brown, black-brown, green (only above the niche), white,
some orange-brown, yellow-green and faded purple.
Pattern: the typical Baluchi geometric tree inside the camel-coloured mihrab. The date in the arch is
back to front, because the carpet was knotted in imitation of another and to see the pattern more easily
the model was laid face down. The knotter, not being literate, knotted the inscription as she saw it.

ality of nomad work. The main colours are dark blue or blue-black and a browny
red or bluish lilac that gives the pile a purple sheen. If the ground of the central
field is not camel colour the general impression is pleasantly and quietly dark with
the sparsely used white standing out. Frankly bright-coloured Baluchi carpets also
exist.

The patterns are simple: lozenging, quartering, vertical stripes, half-drop or diagonal
rows of octagons, stars, hooked or zig-zigged lozenges (fig. 128), geometric floral
motifs and sometimes cocks as well (p. 261/271).

Inside the camel-coloured mihrab of many namazliks (fig. 127) a large angular tree
characteristic of Baluchi carpets grows up into the quadrangular arch; or large boteh
fill the mihrab on either side of a narrow tree represented in linear drawing. In the
small light rectangular fields beside the arch stand small trees or hands. The motifs
for the main border are stems with the Turcoman line, rows of lozenges, stars and
rosettes. Fig. 130 shows a 'Verneh Baluchi' with a woven and embroidered pattern.

128. Baluchi, 19th—20th century. Namaseh. (125—129) 127 × 86 cm. (without kilimlik), (right).
Warp: W. S-plied, 2 strands, twisted, undyed light and light with dark brown.
Weft: W. Z-spun, 2 strands, untwisted, undyed brown. 2 shoots alternating sinuous.
Pile: W. Z-spun, 3 strands, untwisted. Knots T. I: h. 40, w. 32 = 1,280 per sq.dm. Upper end: 15 cm.
  W. kilimlik, 14 stripes, then warp threads knotted. Lower end: as upper end, but 15 stripes and warp
  threads looped and twisted.
Selvedges: goat hair shirazi undyed, black brown 2 cord round 3 threads.
Quality: soft, medium thick, slightly granular.
Colours: 11, *camel colours, black-brown, red* faded to brick-red, medium blue, light blue, dark blue, green-
  blue, dark red-brown, white, faded purple, some green.
Pattern: central field relatively narrow, widening slightly after the first third, contains continuous half-drop
  rows of serrated diamonds on a camel ground. The excessively wide border is divided into fields containing
  groups of four geometric flowers, creating a tile effect. Running dog in the inner guard stripe.

KIRGHIZ CARPETS

The carpets knotted by the Kirghiz in the north and east of Turkmenia, in Kirghiz-istan and Tajikistan are primitive in pattern and technique in comparison with the work of the Turcomans. They have hardly reached Europe. According to Bogolubow the design, of which a detail is given on this page, is Kipshak, while the 'Jagal Baïli' (flying falcon) gül is used by Shodiri, Tuyayu and Kipchaks alike. Carpets with the 'kerech-kus' (lattice of the Kirghiz Yurte) motif and the 'alma' (apple) gül were

  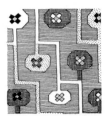

| Chagal Baili gül | Kereche Kus gül | Alma gül | Kipchak ornament |

knotted by the Shydirma, Tyuyasha and Kipchaks. Soviet-produced Kirghiz carpets with their stiff patterns are reminiscent rather of modern Caucasian than of Central Asian carpets.

XXIII. Baluchi, 19th—20th century. 94 × 48 cm.

Warp: W. S-plied, 2 strands, twisted, undyed light.

Weft: W. S-plied, 2 strands, lightly twisted, undyed dark brown. 2 shoots alternating sinuous.

Pile: W. Z-spun, 2 or 3 strands, untwisted, and silk, Z-spun, 4 strands, untwisted. Knots P. II 30°: h. 60, w. 46 = 2,760 per sq. dm.

Upper end: 8 cm. W. kilim red-brown, of which 2/3 in finest soumak technique (Dyeddyim) in wool and silk.

Lower end: as upper end. Selvedges: goat hair shirazi, left 5 cord, right 2 cord round 5 warp threads.

Quality: silky, firm, medium heavy, granular.

Colours: 9, *dark blue, brown-red, white,* vermilion, purple-brown, some light blue-green, yellow, purple and olive-yellow.

Pattern: 85 cocks in diagonal rows of the same colour on the dark blue central field; between them miniature flower stars. On the brown-red main border an angular stem forming the Turcoman line.

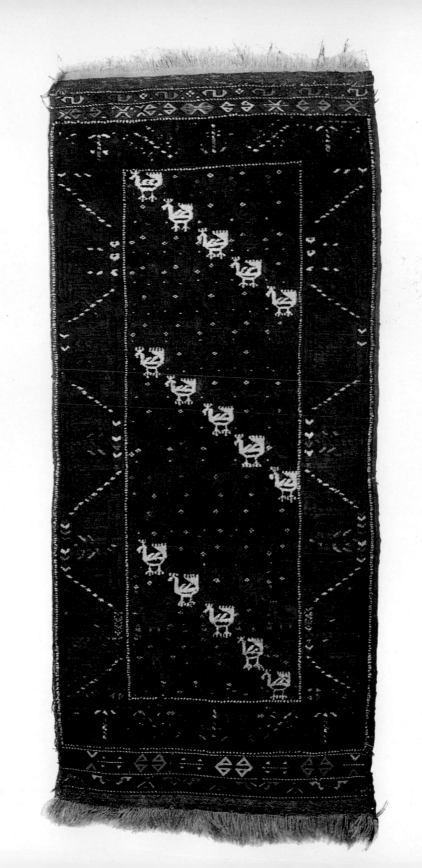

129. Afghan, 20th century. 177 × 114 cm. (detail).
Warp: goat hair, S-plied, 2 strands, twisted, undyed
  black-grey.
Weft: goat hait, Z-spun, single, 2 shoots alternating
  sinuous.
Pile: W. Z-spun, 2 strands, untwisted. Knots P. Ib:
  h. 30, w. 28 = 840 per sq. dm. Upper end: —.
  Lower end: 3 cm. remaining of a kilim dark
  red/black-grey.
Selvedges: goat hair shirazi black-brown 3 cord.
  Quality: silky, almost thin, coarse granular.
Colours: 5, *dark chestnut-brown, dark blue,* blue-
  green, dark brown, some yellow.
Pattern: a chestnut-brown ground with 3 close
  vertical rows of large octagons, their inner fields
  quartered. Characteristic Afghan trefoils in the
  quarters, corresponding diagonally in colour. In
  half drop between the octagons rows of lattice
  diamonds ending in little stars. A chequered band
  of diamonds in the main border.

**130. Baluchi, 19th century. Verneh Baluchi,
  woven and embroidered.** 151 × 80 (78—82) cm.
Warp: W. S-plied, 2 strands, twisted, undyed
  brownish. 64 warps per dm.
Weft: ground-weave: W. Z-spun, 2 strands, untwisted, 144 shoots per dm.
Pattern: W. Z-spun, 2 strands, untwisted. Combination of palas, kelim and verneh techniques.
Upper end: every 6 or so warp threads knotted
  together.
Lower end: warp threads looped and twisted.
Selvedges: W. shirazi brown 7 cord round 3 warp
  threads.
Colours: 7, *camel, black-brown,* brown-red, wine,
  dark blue, black, white. (cont. over)

Pattern: the side edges of the camel-coloured central field are formed by a reciprocal pattern of hooked half diamonds woven in kelim technique; the pattern was begun larger than it continued. Three geometric trees rise from a small panel—the narrow one in the centre only has pairs of leaves and separated flowers—to seven square octagons on the upper edge (verneh technique). At the ends are woven stripes, 17 above and 15 below, with every second stripe embroidered.

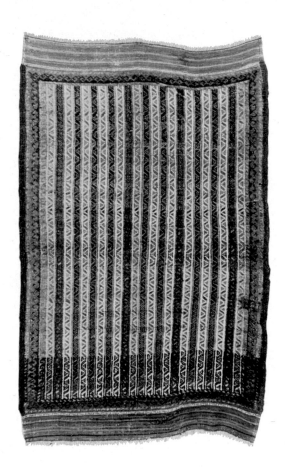

131. **Baluchi, 19th—20th century. Namaseh.** c. 111 × 81 cm.
Warp: W. S-plied, 2 strands, twisted, undyed light.
Weft: W. Z-spun, 2 strands, untwisted, brownish. 2 shoots alternating sinuous.
Pile: W. Z-spun, 2 strands, untwisted. Knots P. Ia: h. 42, w. 30 = 1,260 per sq.dm. Upper end: 9 cm. W. kilim, 14 stripes, patterned with bands of lozenges.
Lower end: as upper end, but 17 stripes.
Selvedges: goat hair shirazi 4 cord round 3 warp threads.
Quality: soft, rather thin, coarse granular.
Colours: 7, *navy blue, terracotta, white,* olive-brown, black-brown, fawn, some purple.
Pattern: the central field is divided into 24 vertical stripes. They all contain an angular wave stem, except the outer left-hand one, which has a running dog decoration. The border with 3 stripes was continued on the left with only two. In the bottom sixth of the carpet better quality wool and dye were used than in the remainder.

The carpets of East Turkestan

Geography and history

East or Chinese Turkestan lies in the heart of Central Asia. Almost the whole region, stretching 1,000 km. north to south and over 1,800 from east to west and with only three million inhabitants, is included in the Tarim basin, so called after its chief river. It lies half way between the Mediterranean and the Pacific Ocean, and half way between the frozen northern sea and the southern tip of India. This high desert plain crossed by shifting sands (700—1,500 m. above O. D.) is surrounded on the north (Tien Shan), west (Pamir) and south (Kunlun and Astingagh) by steep mountain chains with peaks of 7,000 to 8,500 metres. All the streams rising in these mountains dry up in the sand of the great desert of Takla Makan; the Tarim after a course of 2,000 km. is lost in the marshes of the land-locked Lop Nor. The extremely dry climate with violent changes of temperature only permits of settlement in oases at the sides of the streams on the edge of the uninhabitable desert. There irrigation brings good yields of cereals, fruit, vegetables and cotton. A narrow belt of grass along the foot of the mountains provides an environment for nomad economy, mostly Kirghiz. The excellent wool from their flocks is the basis of the carpet production carried on by men in the workshops of the oases.

The old caravan trails of the 'silk route' which divide west Turfan into two, one skirting the desert basin to the north and the other to the south, link the distant oases with each other and join again in Kashghar on the western edge of the basin. Topography and climate have been unfavourable to all efforts towards national unity during the two thousand years and more of this land's history. The isolation of these remote and small oasis settlements prevented any common resistance to conquest.

At an early date the Indo-European Turanians pressed into the area then already inhabited by Turkish nomads. These agriculturalists gradually pushed forward their settlement area eastwards from oasis to oasis along the base of the mountains, while the Turkish tribes continued their nomadic life in the grass belt. The Turanians spoke Indo-European dialects and had various manners of writing, mostly derived from Indian. Their European features are still characteristic of the majority of the population in the southern oases. Other population groups are Chinese in the towns and Kirghiz, east Turkish, Kasakh and Mongol nomadic tribes.

The Turkish nomads left the Turanian oasis areas alone, apart from raising tribute, even in the periods of the greatest Turkish expansion and power. Tribute also had to be paid to the Chinese, who dominated the region, with occasional interruptions, from the second century BC to the fourth century AD, and again from the seventh to the tenth, to the Hephtalite and west Turkish tribes (late fifth to mid-seventh century) and later to the Mongol conquerors. China, concerned only with securing her trade routes to the West, confined herself to establishing garrisons and left the oases independent in religious, cultural and economic matters. But Chinese domination was often interrupted for long periods, particularly by the Tibetans.

Khotan was the most important Buddhist centre in the land during the first millenium. In the wake of the monks foreign craftsmen disseminated the rich art of Ghandara, its roots fed from Greek, Indian and Persian sources, through monastic and sacred buildings which fell into ruin after the dwindling of Buddhist influence. From sources of the second century BC and accounts written in the fifth, sixth and seventh centuries AD it would seem that life in the oases then was little different from what it was in the first decades of the twentieth. Trade in gold and jade to China brought considerable wealth. At the end of the ninth century east Turkish tribes conquered the land and forced on it their language (Jagatai or east Turkish) and Islam. The whole great region became 'Turkestan'. Apart from the practice of the new religion life in the oases continued much as before, as it must under the dictates of nature. Khotan, Kashghar and Yarkand, near which cities the painful caravan route branches off over the Karakorum passes to India, became depots for the trade between East and West. Economic relations between the oases have remained unimportant to the present day, since their production is so similar. Even the conquest of east Turkestan by the Mongols in 1218 brought no profound change. Islam was deeply rooted in the population after two hundred years, and the Buddhist Genghis Khan showed himself tolerant in matters of religion. The period following Genghis Khan, when Jagatai princes ruled east and west Turkestan, was a sequence of family feuds and uprisings. Abu Bekr in the second half of the fifteenth century attempted to shake off the rule of the khans, but although his national government had initial success the geographical divisions of the land were stronger than the unity of language and religion, and it ended in failure.

In Kashghar and Khotan a lively economic and cultural life developed under virtually independent princes. The court art of Herat under Timur radiated to Turkestan through Samarkand. The lists of embassies drawn up by the Chinese court include under the gifts from Khotan jade, thoroughbred horses, hunting falcons, leopards, arms and armour, swords and daggers of steel (*The Ming History*, ch. 332). The physical isolation of the oases nonetheless encouraged intellectual isolation and fanatical Islamic sects made great headway, with the inevitable concomitants of rival demagogues and wonder-working saints. In the late seventeenth century the Mongols were called on for help by the banished leader of a sect and invaded the country from Tzungaria. Their khans maintained suzerainty for many years over a land torn by the religious conflicts of the hodyas. In the intellectual field the kadis and mullas, the Muslim judges and sages, maintained their control. Bokhara, centre of fanatical Islam in Central Asia, also controlled the intellectual and spiritual life of east Turkestan. Its influence even penetrated the craft work of the Tarim oases.

At the beginning of the second half of the eighteenth century the whole of east Turkestan fell with the conquest of Tzungaria to China under the Manchu dynasty. The Chinese again did not behave as colonisers. They were interested solely in the security of east Turkestan as an outpost to protect the inner provinces, and in matters of tribute and of trade. East Turkestan was now cut off from her western neighbours with whom she felt related in culture and religion.

The last attempt at national unity, made by Yaqub Beg in the second half of the nineteenth century, had no success. Today east Turkestan belongs to the autonomous region of Sinkiang in the Peoples' Republic of China.

The carpets of East Turkestan before the nineteenth century

The knotting craft of east Turkestan is certainly born of a long tradition. The carpets came late to Europe, and under the names of the west Turkestanian towns through which the trade was carried, like 'Samarkand', 'Kokand' or 'Margelan'; more rarely they were known by the places of their origin: Khotan, Yarkand and Kashgar. In China they were called 'Kansu' because they entered Chinese trade through this western Chinese city and province. H. Bidder, diplomat and collector, the sinologue who unfortunately died before the type was set for his book on the carpets of east Turkestan, recounts that in 1925 not a single Chinese in Pekin, art collector, antique dealer, carpet producer or caravan leader, could give him any information about the origin and ornament of 'Kansu' carpets. For China, whose population early went over to the use of chairs and tables, the floor carpet could never have the same importance as for people whose way of living kept them on the floor. Furthermore for many regions of eastern and southern China it is the mat rather than the carpet that is more suited to the climate as a floor covering. Carpet export from east Turkestan was therefore always directed primarily westwards and to a lesser extent southwards. In old Chinese documents there is scarcely a mention of the carpets of east Turkestan. For China jade and gold remained the most important imports from these lands. Yuan Chuang, a Chinese who went on a pilgrimage to India in 629, says of the inhabitants of the land of Chieh Sha (Kashgar): 'they make fine felts and weave fine felt and pile carpets', and of the land of Chü-so-ta-na (Khotan): 'they produce pile carpets and fine felt carpets and weave coarse silk fabrics'. For pile carpets the same word, ch'ü yü, is used as for the carpets of Iran.

The small fragments of hand-knotted carpet that owe their preservation to the extremely dry climate, found by Sir Aurel Stein in Niya and Lolan on the Lob Nur, are at latest of the fifth or sixth century, possibly of the third century AD. The finds throw little light on the apparent connection of their ornamentation with that of Turcoman carpets. F. H. Andrews, an authority on the technique, defines their material, composition and structure as follows: warp: thin, brown woollen yarn, some loosely twisted; sometimes double and of goat hair. Weft: four loosely twisted strands of wool or finer yellow-brown wool yarn, sometimes only twisted from two strands. The four wefts are well beaten down and sometimes cross four warp threads at a time. Pile: always of fine soft wool, four-ply. The knotting yarn is passed twice round each of the two warp threads and thus forms a firm knot. Length of pile 2.5 to 1.25 cm. (1 inch to $^1/_2$ inch). Density: 8 knots to 1 in. across by 4 knots to 1 in. in length (32 to the dm. $\times$ 16). A further technical characteristic of the several frag-

132. East Turkestan, 19th century. Khotan.
(229—334) 231 × 119 (115—123) cm. (268 above).
Warp: C. S-plied, 4 strands, twisted, undyed.
Weft: C. S-plied, 4 strands, twisted, undyed.
3 shoots: 1. and 3. straight, 2. sinuous.
Pile: W. Z-spun, 2 strands, untwisted. Knots
P. II 45°: h. 24, w. 34 = 816 per dm.
Upper end: 1 cm. C. kilim, undyed, with a few
final double shoots.
Lower end: 2 cm. C. kilim, undyed. Warp threads
looped and twisted.
Selvedges: W. shirazi wine-red round 4—6 warp
threads.
Quality: soft, fleshy, thick, coarse, rather hairy.
Colours: 5, *wine, pale blue, golden yellow,* black-
brown, light red.
Pattern: the 3 stripes of the border divide the
central field from the continuous wine-red

ground. Three pale blue disc medallions with flower crosses. *Yün-tsai-t'ou* in the corners, chequered half
lozenges down the sides. T-border, meander and oblique swastika band in the borders.

133, 134, 135. West China, 19th century. Kansu cushion, pillow or cart covers. 88 × 55, 91 × 57, 66 × 72 cm.
Warp: C. S-plied, 4 strands, twisted, undyed.
Weft: W.C. or W. with C. 2—4 strands, untwisted, undyed. 2 shoots alternating sinuous. Pile: W. Z-spun,
4 strands, untwisted. Knots P. I: 432—480 per sq. dm.
Upper end: a few shoots or double shoots alternating sinuous.
Lower end: —. Upper end. 131: warp threads looped and twisted.
Quality: soft, thick, coarse horizontal ribbing.

133. Selvedges: no strengthening. (268 below, left).
Colours: 5, *olive-yellow, medium blue,* faded rust-red, brown-black, ivory.
Pattern: tile pattern from half-drop rows of olive-yellow octagons with inscribed (faded) rosette. The
interstices are filled with small quartered squares. The narrow border has alternating semicircles.

134. Selvedges: W. shirazi 2 cord. (268 below, right).
Colours: 4, *golden yellow, medium blue,* rust-red, ivory.
Pattern: half-drop rows of golden-yellow cloud swirls make a diamond diaper of the rust-red ground
emerge. Swastika meander on ivory ground in the border.

135. Selvedges: C. shirazi 2 cord. (above).
Colours: 7, *dark blue, olive-yellow, flesh-pink,* faded rust-red, yellow-green, black-brown, ivory.
Pattern: half-drop rows of octagons with incribed rosettes produce a tile pattern. Small quartered squares
fill the interstices. Swastika meander in the border. This tile pattern appears on the main border of east
Turkestan carpets in earlier centuries.

ments is the introduction of loops without knotting on the underside under every
tenth weft thread in roughly every fifth row. These loops, whose ends stand out free
on the underside, are done in the same V or single-loop technique which was used for
the pile of early Egyptian carpets (see fig. 145—147 b). Furthermore the remark on
the wefts, '. . . and sometimes cross four warp threads', seems to indicate a technical
similarity with the non-Egyptian fragment from Fostat mentioned on p. 23, in which
of five single weft threads only the middle one runs through normally, while the
others each cross three warp threads from behind.

Chinese sources of the eighteenth and nineteenth centuries refer to carpet production in east Turkestan with centres at Khotan, Yü Tien, Lo-p'u and Pi-shan, with an annual capacity of about 5,000 carpets for export to Andiyan/Kokand (about eighty per cent), British India and Afghanistan (H. Bidder: *Teppiche aus Ost-Turkestan*). The oases on the southern border of the Tarim basin — less subject to unrest through political events and migrations — were able to lead a relatively undisturbed and independent life and formed a focus round which the development of art and craft could crystallise.

China, unaccustomed to their use, was no equivalent client for the carpets of east Turkestan, nor could she become the successor of the hodja and princes of nomadic origin as patron of the native craft. The periodic closing of the frontiers also stopped the supply of dyes from India, which were essential in spite of the numerous native natural dyes.

A more detailed description of the craft is contained in the Forsyth Report (1873) of a commission sent to east Turkestan by the British government to the government of Yaqub Beg, which they later recognised. The commission was instructed to study the conditions relative to the security of the country lying to the north of the Indian border in relation to the penetration of Russia into Turkmenia. The report stressed the independence in ornamentation and colouring and also the good quality of the wool of the carpets. The most common breed of sheep was the 'dumba' fat-tailed sheep. The wool obtained from the soft down under the long-haired winter coat (also procured by combing) was sent by the Kirghiz to Ladhak and sold there into Kashmir as 'Tibetan wool'. The more important breed for the production of finer carpets from the region of Khotan and Turkan was smaller. Its long-fibred, mostly white wool is considered the finest in Asia. Colours show more brilliantly on it. The natural colours indigo, madder and cochineal were imported. The photographs accompanying the report show both three-medallion (fig. 132) patterns and patterns influenced from Herat. Carpets with gold and silver brocading (fig. 139) were still obtainable, but were no longer being made. The 'Polish Carpets' of Isfahan had indubitably stood godfather to the brocaded carpets which were highly popular as presents not only in the courts of the Orient and in Europe, but all over Asia. A Chinese travel report of the end of the eighteenth century remarks of Kashgar, after

XXIV. **Baluchi, 19th/20th century. Khurjin.** 108 × 42 cm. (p. 271).
Material and structure as in fig. 126, but Weft: hair, grey. 2000 Pla per dm².
Colours: 7, *red*, *surmey*, *blue*, dark brown, ivory, dark violet, some red-orange.
Pattern: In both dark red central fields the sun rises over two lions and other quadrupeds standing in rows.
   Between them rosettes and two amphorae. In the main border which is accompanied by two guard stripes
   of 'running dog', a stem dissolved into a row of geometric motifs. The same motif in two of the seven
   stripes of the knotted middle section.

mentioning the luxurious life of the numerous courtesans: 'there are as well solid people who are very clever at knotting gold and silver brocaded silk carpets and five-coloured pile carpets'. On p. 33 the east Turkestanian manner of brocading with silver threads is illustrated. The thin gold threads were worked in in the same way, but four-fold instead of two-fold.

The older east Turkestanian carpets are unmistakable in their ornamentation, colour range and structure. The pile is worked in Persian knots at a density of from 800 to 1,200 knots per square dm., with two to four strands of untwisted wool on a cotton warp. The pile is medium high. In silk carpets with a count of between about 1,300 and 2,500 knots to the square dm. the silk thread for the knots is often used untwisted. The two- to four-ply weft consists of cotton, wool or both. The ends are done in kilim, in which the last rows of weft are woven double. The warp ends are left at one end as twisted loops, at the other they are frayed into a fringe or knotted together about ten at a time. The selvedge is formed by a wool shirazi, usually single cord. The carpets are almost all keley or keleyghi in format, and thus about twice as long as they are wide. There are also almost square examples. The underside as a rule feels slightly hairy, like all new carpets, because the finest little hairs come out of the pile, even after decades of use.

The colour-scale is limited, there are no half tones, the dominant colours are red, wine-red, light and dark blue, light and dark yellow, various tones of brown, natural ivory and brown-black. Outlining emphasises the clarity of the design. The colour of the ground is red, more rarely blue, yellow or ivory.

Contrary to the first impression Chinese influence is not dominant in the ornamentation of the old east Turkestan carpets. East Turkestan felt more closely linked with its western neighbours than with the far-off cultural and economic centres of China. The distance from Khotan to Pekin, either by the old caravan route or from Turfan with the railway, is almost 5,000 km.

The best-known patterns can be classified conveniently into five basic motifs: the almost circular disc medallion (fig. 132), the rosette gül, the pomegranate branch

Rosette gül

and vase motif (p. 271), the endless repeat of floral motifs, such as the Persian (Herat?)-influenced pattern in fig. 139, and the geometric arabesque partitioning of the ground with floral filling which probably came into the country with Islam.

136. N. W. China, 19th century. Ninghsia. Chair seat. 65 × 60 cm. (above, left)
Warp: C. S-plied, 3 strands, twisted, undyed.
Weft: C. Z-spun, 3—4 strands, untwisted, undyed light. 2 shoots alternating sinuous.
Pile: W. Z-spun, 3 strands, untwisted. Knots P. Ia: h. 18, w. 26 = 486 per sq.dm. Slight relief shearing.
  Upper end: —. Lower end: —.
Selvedges: C. shirazi undyed 2 cord.
Quality: soft, thick, coarse horizontal ribbing.
Colours: 8, *rust-red, surmey, olive-yellow,* olive-green, ivory, light blue, yellow, flesh pink.
Pattern: the ground was originally madder but has faded to red-brown. A *fo* (Buddhist) lion with a wild
  yellow mane floats on two cloud-shaped lotus stems over the 'sea waves and river foam' (*hai-shui chiang-
  ya*) or four-elements motif, probably signifying 'he guards against all evil' (border scroll, eternity).

137. N. W. China, 19th century. Ninghsia or Suiyuan. Chair seat. 71 × 71 cm. (above, right)
Warp: C. S-plied, twisted, undyed light.
Weft: C. Z-spun, 2 strands, untwisted, undyed light. 2 shoots alternating sinuous. Pile: W. Z-spun, 3—4
  strands, untwisted. Knots P. Ia: h. 30, w. 26 = 720 per sq.dm. Slight relief shearing.
Upper end: 2 shoots with a few rows of knotting turned back and sewn down. Lower end: —. Sel-
  vedges: C. shirazi undyed single cord round 3 warp threads and a few rows of knotting treated as upper end.
Quality: soft, thick, slightly coarse granular.
Colours: 9, *surmey, flesh-pink, ivory, yellow,* yellow-olive, olive, light blue, rust-red, dark brown.
Pattern: one large and two smaller dragons float above the four-elements motif, against a dark blue ground.
  The two young ones make bizarre movements as they play with the wishing pearl (*erh-lung hi chu* = 2
  dragons play with the pearl). The old one, guarding a jewel, watches them. The light blue outlines of the
  yellow scaley bodies refer to the saying *tsang-lung chiau tzu,* the blue dragon teaches his sons (wishes for
  progeny). The border has the same meaning as in fig. 136.

138. N. W. China, 19th century. Ninghsia. Chair seat. 72 × 71 cm. (below, left)
Warp: C. S-plied, 2 strands, twisted, undyed.
Weft: C. Z-spun, 2—3 strands, untwisted, undyed. 2 shoots alternating sinuous.
Pile: W. Z-spun, 3 strands, untwisted. Knots P. Ia: h. 20, w. 28 = 560 per sq.dm. Slight relief shearing.
Upper end: —. Lower end: —. Selvedges: C. shirazi undyed with 2 warp threads.
Quality: soft, thick, coarse horizontal rib.
Colours: 9, *brown-red, olive-yellow, dark blue,* flesh-pink, light blue, ivory, light brown, yellow-brown,
  yellow-olive.
Pattern: the centre of the brown-red ground is filled by two diagonally crossed lotus stems (one in the
  lucky colour red) with four bizarre butterflies, *tieh* (70 or 80 years old, long lived) attached to the lucky
  sign, *shou.* The meaning of the lotus thicket is *pen gu chi yung,* may the roots be fast and the branches
  luxuriant; a frequently-heard wish for the security and prosperity of the family. The unsymmetrical scatter
  pattern contains the sunflower-like mushroom *ling chi* and the plum blossom branch without leaves.
  The plum blossom is the queen of flowers; her noble posture raises her above the common things of
  every day. A play of words on *mei,* plum and *mei,* often, repeatedly.

139. East Turkestan, 19th century. Khotan. Gold and silver brocade. 403 × 251 cm. (detail). (below, right)
Warp: C. S-plied, 4 strands, twisted, undyed.
Weft: C. S-plied, 2—4 strands, twisted, undyed. 2—3 shoots: 1. and 3. straight, 2. sinuous. Pile: silk,
  Z-spun, multiple, untwisted. Knots P. II 50°: h. 34, w. 38 = 1,292 per sq.dm.
Brocading: copper (formerly silvered) round cotton. 2 strands dyed as in drawing p. 33. Gold round silk
  thinner, hence double the number of threads. Upper end: 1—2 cm. remaining of a C. kilim with thick
  shoots of 6-strand plied cotton. Lower end: —. Selvedges: knotting to the furthest warp threads. No
  special strengthening of the sides.
Quality: silky, thin, slightly wavy.
Colours: 4, old gold, dark blue, olive-green, dark brown.
Pattern: two cross-shaped stem motifs over the brocaded ground of the central field arranged in half-drop
  rows so that it looks like a rising pattern. In the main border, which has 6 guard stripes, a star-shaped stem
  set with flowers on a brocaded ground.

140. East Turkestan, 19th century. Khotan. Saph, communal prayer rug. (72—78) 75 × 286 cm. (above)
Warp: C. S-plied 6 strands, twisted, undyed.
Weft: C. Z-spun, 6 strands, untwisted, undyed. 3 shoots: 1 and 3. straight, 2. sinuous.
Pile: W. Z-spun, 2 strands, untwisted. Knots P. II, 40°: h. 42, w. 42 = 1,864 per sq. dm. Direction of work
    from left to right.
Upper end: —. Lower end: 1 cm. C. kilim with 10-strand untwisted shoots.
Selvedges: W. shirazi pale blue single cord. Quality: dry, medium thick, coarse ribbing.
Colours: 7, *brown-red, brick-red, yellow-green, pale blue,* some white and purple.
Pattern: the brown-red central field is divided into ten niches. In each niche a stiff bar ending in a lotus
    flower rises from a vase; it has attached pairs of leaves, flowers or pomegranate branches. In the spandrels a
    geometric scroll resembling the *yün-tsai-t'ou.* The main band of the border is yellow-green with angular
    wave band with a side view of flowers.

141. N. W. China, 19th century. Ninghsia or Suiyuan. Pillared carpet. 162 × 67 (63—71) cm. (above, left)
Warp: C. S-plied, 3 strands, twisted, undyed.
Weft: C. Z-spun, 3—4 strands, untwisted, undyed. 2 shoots alternating sinuous.
Pile: W. Z-spun, 2 strands, untwisted. Knots P. Ib: h. 20, w. 26 = 520 per sq. dm. Slight relief shearing.
Upper end: —. Lower end: —. Selvedges: no strengthening. Quality: soft, thick, coarse horizontal rib.
Colours: 7, *navy blue, olive-yellow,* light blue, madder faded to old gold, flesh-pink, dark olive, ivory.
Pattern: above the spray of the spurting *hai-shui chiang-ya* float 17 luck symbols, i. a. books, lucky mushroom,
    cloud, chrysanthemum, peony, plum blossom, cornucopia and gold or silver bars. Being a pillar carpet
    it has no side borders. From the garlands or upper border hang single word characters.

142. North China, 19th century. Suiyuan Paotu. Wall hanging 189 × 99 cm. (above, right)
Warp: C. S-plied, 3 strands, twisted, undyed, very thin.
Weft: as warp. 2 double shoots alternating sinuous.
Pile: W. Z-spun, 3 strands, untwisted. In places two different colours in one knot to make graded tones.
    Knots P. I over 4 warps: h. 33, w. 30 = 990 per sq. dm.
Upper end: 0.5 remains of a C. kilim undyed with double shoots. Lower end: —. Selvedges: C.
    shirazi round 4 warp threads, undyed.
Quality: soft, very thick, smooth. Colours: 11, *dark blue, brown, light brown, sand,* medium blue, light blue,
    light green, white, a little red, flesh-pink and orange-red.
Pattern: representation of the deer *lu* = lu = rich revenues, promotion in appointment (here the white
    speckled stag *gin tsien lu* or plum blossom stag *mei-hua-lu*) with the crane *ho* or *hou* (mount of the Gods,
    symbol of long life) and the fir tree *sung* (ever green, ever flourishing), which multiplies the wish under the
    large old *wu tung* tree. This is the tree of the fabulous *feng huang* and grows (as the lighting shows) on the
    south side of the great hill. It is also the year tree, which bears 12 leaves on each side for the 12 months
    (and, on the trunk, a leaf for the years with the leap month). On the bank above the agitated and (on the
    right) peaceful water the day lily *huan tsao.* It brings forgetfulness of trouble and is carried by pregnant
    women because it favours the birth of sons.

143. N. W. China, 19th century. Ninghsia or Suiyuan. 139 × 74 cm. (below)
Structure as fig. 142, but shoot untwisted. Colours: 4, *ivory, dark blue,* bright blue, some fawn.

The medallion is usually triple, sometimes alone or double, against the quiet, generally frugally patterned, ground of the central field (figs. 132 and p. 281), in the corners of which stand the yün-tsai-t'ou, rosettes or small rectangles with the rosette gül. Coffered frames round the medallion (cf. fig. 154, Spain, sixteenth, seventeenth century) and its repeat up to ten times are rare. The free interior design of the medallion consists of cruciform flowers, cloud scrolls or rosettes. The pomegranate-vase or a single large cruciform flower are not so frequent as filling for the medallions (p. 281).

As a ground pattern the pomegranate branch-vase motif is sometimes on one side, usually on both. The branching trees then rise from two vases or from two or three pairs of vases, which stand opposite each other at the narrow ends (p. 291). The pomegranate with its innumerable seeds symbolised fertility to many Asian peoples. This motif found its way in several variants into the mediaeval textiles of the West.

The rosette gül appears both alone in the coffers of the carpets with quartered ground and in endless repeat in simple, half-drop or diagonal rows. Single, as a medallion or corner filling, it is not quite so frequent. The old carpets with coffered güls are mostly knotted in undyed black, ivory, light and dark brown wool.

Cloud latticee

Cloud scroll,
or eddy volute

As against these three types of pattern those with stylised flower or arabesque stem patterns play a subordinate part in the carpets that have been preserved.

Almost every east Turkestanian carpet bears the old Turkish motif of the 'cloud head', Chinese 'yün-ts'ai-t'ou', whether as a cloud scroll broken up into a corner filling (i.e. in the carpet on p. 311), resembling the heraldic lily as on the border of the same carpet, as a 'cloud lattice' covering the whole central field (geometric scrolling perhaps?) or in one of many other forms; it scarcely ever appears however in the naturalistic Chinese form that was adopted in the Near East. The borders have other main motifs: rows of rosettes, a simply stylised wave scroll — set with rosettes or soft and bent as in the guard stripe of the carpet on p. 311, triple flowers with their

144. Damascus? 16th century. 168 × 123 (121—125) cm.

Warp: W. S-plied, 2 strands, slightly twisted, undyed light.

Weft: W. Z-spun, single, dyed red, in places undyed light or dark brown for the straight shoots. 2 shoots: 1. straight, 2. sinuous.

Pile: W. Z-spun, 2 strands, untwisted. Knots T. II up to 60°: h. 40, w. 28 = 1,120 per sq.dm.

Upper end, lower end and selvedges: no original strengthening.

Quality: now dry, thin ribbed.

Colours: 8, *geranium, pale green, blue-green,* light blue, ivory black-brown, light olive-yellow, medium brown.

Pattern: the red central field has two vertical rows of 2 ½ overlapping octagons. The vertical axis combined with the quartering of the interstices gives the impression of a square lattice. In each octagon are dagger-shaped leaves (little trees) separated by small floral motifs arranged radially round a 16-lobed central star. The main border is pale green-blue and broad (central field borders = 73 : 50) and has an alternation of a cartouche with a cartouche rosette, both accompanied by heavy stem scrolls.

stalks forming a right angle and transformed in colour and direction to a tile effect, the 'T' or key border common over the whole of Asia (fig. 132), close half-drop rows of small octagons like the pattern forming the central field of the small piece in fig. 135, and sometimes the swastika (hooked cross) familiar in every repertoire, in the typically Chinese arrangement of the swastika meander (fig. 132).

Prayer rugs once more form a special group. The form best known in east Turkestan is the saph, or family prayer rug (see fig. 140). Its mihrabs usually contain vases with rigid little trees ending in a blossom, with branches bearing flowers, leaves or pomegranates.

Carpets of east Turkestan in the nineteenth and twentieth centuries

In the nineteenth century the motifs that were chiefly continued from the old designs, apart from the family prayer rugs, were the disc medallion and the pomegranate branch and vase. In the borders the swastika meander becomes more prominent, either straight or diagonal, and the 'water mountains and clouds' motif in five colours, similar to the Chinese 'hai-shui chiang-ya' (sea waves and river bank) with the lily-shaped 'yün-ts'ai-t'ou' (p. 291). The rows of rosettes become less in evidence.

After the end of Yaqub Beg's secession in 1875 Chinese influence becomes more apparent in the borders: the lily-shaped yün-ts'ai-t'ou appears on diagonal rows of geometric waves and often disappears completely; the border then consists solely of a diagonally striped band. This development coincides with the use of the first aniline dyes, promoted by the closing of the frontiers. Right at the beginning of the 'nineties the dyers of Khotan declared that they used no more natural dyes. Following the inevitable failures — the violet of this period is particularly repulsive — they quickly began to think again about the old dyeing methods. Gradually, though it did not dominate, Chinese symbolism found an entry into the decoration of the central field (e.g. the geometric motif in the two upper medallions and at both ends of the carpet on p. 291 is the Chinese symbol 'shou' — long life). The outlining of the ornament gives way largely to the Chinese method of setting one colour within another ('tone

XXV. **East Turkestan, 19th century. Khotan.** (206—210) 208 × 116 (114—118) cm.
Warp: C. S-plied, 5 strands, twisted, undyed.
Weft: C. S-plied, 5 strands, lightly twisted, undyed. 2—4 shoots: 1. and 3. straight, 2. and 4. sinuous.
Pile: W. Z-spun, 2—3 strands, untwisted. Knots P. II, 20°: h. 31, w. 32 = 992 per sq. dm. Upper end: 2 cm. C. kilim, undyed light. First single, then a few double shoots. Warp threads knotted together in 10s.
Lower end: as upper end, but only single shoots. Warp threads looped and twisted. Selvedges: —.
Quality: soft, now thin, rather coarse, slightly hairy.
Colours: 7, *rust-red, navy blue,* light blue, blue-green, black-brown, ivory, olive-yellow.
Pattern: the five bands of the border divide the central field from the red ground. In the central field 3 disc medallions of typical Khotan form and several plum blossom and chrysanthemum branches. In the corners linear *yün-tsai-t'ou*. In the central medallion a pomegranate branch with 5 fruits in a vase. The main borders have a swastika meander and oblique swastikas.

in tone'). In recent decades only a very few carpets from east Turkestan have reached the western market. In Tashkent and Samarkand, that once lent them their names, these carpets are scarcely remembered at all.

Khotan, with about 166 square kilometres of oasis and 5,000 inhabitants, is situated at a height of 1,400 metres on the Yurung Darya. It was apparently the centre for most of the native crafts. Crafts and carpet production flourished in the residence of Kashgar as well, however, in Yarkand and in other oases. It is thus questionable to ascribe the finer carpets of east Turkestan to Khotan and the coarser ones to Kashgar and Yarkand. Present knowledge does not permit any definite conclusions from the pattern and structure, and coarsely knotted pieces with a density of from 450 to 750 knots per square dm. were, like cart blankets, used in all these centres. On the other hand the name 'aksu' to denote coarsely knotted pieces with a close pattern of coarsened east Turkestanian motifs — among them the tree from the saph mihrab — has more justification, because Aksu on the northern arm of the silk road was the chief collecting point for this kind of nomad work for many leagues around.

Examples of knotted carpet production from TIBET are lacking. What knotted carpets have come out of Tibet were all made in Khotan and the provinces of Kansu, Ninghsia and Suiyuan, which belonged to the Tibetan empire from the sixth to the ninth century. At present Tibetan refugees in Europe have taken up carpet knotting. Their patterns are coarsened versions of west Chinese motifs.

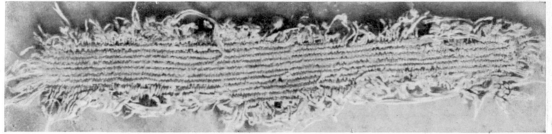

145. Egypt, 3rd—4th century. Fragment (detail). c. 20 × 25 cm. Towel or looped technique. (p. 284, above, left)

Warp: linen, S-spun, single, undyed, up to 80 threads per dm.

Weft: linen, S-spun, single, undyed. 3 shoots alternating straight, and so tight that they produce panama weave.

Pile loops: W. S-spun, 2 strands, untwisted, and linen (white) S-spun, untwisted. C. 10 loop rows to the dm. The technique is described on p. 30. It has its precursor in the loops cut down to a pile of about 5 cm. in the 2000-year-older carpets of the priests of Amun. In those, 6 strands of linen S-spun untwisted or Z-plied slightly twisted were used for the loops.

146. Egypt, 9th century (?). Fragment from Fostat (Old Cairo). c. 11 × 22 cm. Single loop technique. (p. 284, above, right)

Warp: linen, Z-plied, 2 strands, twisted, undyed light.

Weft: linen, Z-plied, 2 strands, slightly twisted, undyed light. One shoot straight.

Pile loops: W. S-spun, single. h. 36, w. 44 = 1,584 per sq. dm. (technique p. oo).

Upper end: —. Lower end: —. Selvedge, no special strengthening.

Colours: 5, *rust-red, light green, surmey,* cream, dark green.

Pattern: this is the fragment of the corner of a border. The main border has a half-drop row of hexagons. Smaller hexagons are inscribed concentrically.

147a and b. Egypt, probably 9th century. Fragment from Fostat (Old Cairo). c. 14 × 38 cm. Single loop technique. (p. 284, middle and below)

Warp: linen, Z-plied, 2 strands, twisted, undyed brownish.

Weft: linen, S-spun, 5 strands, untwisted, undyed brownish. One shoot straight. The thick bunched shoots make a coarse ribbing on the back.

Pile loops: W. S-spun, single. h. 27, w. 40 = 1,080 loops per sq. dm.

Selvedges: linen shirazi round 3 warp threads. Colours: 3, fawn, dark green, rust-red.

Pattern: fawn central field with large stylised dark green flowers. On the dark green ground of the border the beginning of a surah from the Holy Koran in Kufic script: 'In the name of Allah...'. (Prayer rug?)

148a and b. Egypt, probably 9th century. Fragment from Fostat (Old Cairo) 5 × 25 cm. Single loop technique. (above)

Warp: linen, Z-plied, 2 strands, twisted, undyed light.

Weft: linen, S-spun, 5 strands, untwisted, undyed light. 1 shoot straight. The thick bunched shoot makes the back coarse-ribbed.

Pile loops: W. S-spun single and C. (white). h. 40, w. 68 = 2,720 per sq. dm.

Colours: 2 remaining in this fragment-wine, white. Pattern: white inscription on a red ground: 'Son of Abssy appointed to the Caliph' (as head of finance or police).

285

149. Egypt, 15th—16th century. Mamluk carpet. 207 × 141 cm. (detail).

Warp: W. Z-plied, 4 strands, twisted, undyed light.

Weft: W. S-spun, 3 strands, untwisted, brownish. 2 shoots: 1. straight, 2. sinuous.

Pile: W. S-spun, 3 strands, untwisted. Knots P. II 85°: h. 40, w. 45 = 1,800 per sq. dm. Upper end: —.
  Lower end: —. Selvedges: W. shirazi wine-red round 2 warp threads strengthened by twisting 4
  normal warp threads together in S-ply.

Quality: silky, medium heavy, finely ribbed.

Colours: 3, wine-red, light blue, light green.

Pattern: kaleidoscopic arrangement of star-like geometric forms round the central octagon. Geometric
  motifs all from plant elements. Inclusion of the border into the pattern of the central field, with no change
  of colour scheme. The five-stemmed papyrus motif in the cartouches and the papyrus wave stem in the
  guard stripes appear in Ancient Egyptian art 3,000 years earlier.

150. Cairo, 16th century. 230 × 194 cm.

Warp: W. Z-plied, 4 strands, twisted, undyed. Weft: S-spun, 4 strands, dyed orange-brown; some shoots undyed. 3 shoots: 1. and 3. straight, 2. sinuous.

Pile: W. S-spun, 2—3 strands untwisted. Knots P. II, 60°: h. 36, w. 40 = 1,440 per sq. dm. Upper end: —. Lower end: —.

Selvedges: remains of a W. shirazi red 2 cord, warps twisted.

Quality: soft, thin, smooth. Colours: 5, *wine, pale green-blue, olive-yellow,* light blue, light olive-green.

Pattern: a small-scale lozenge diaper is created over the wine-red central field by thin angular olive-yellow stems combined with the green-blue arabesque leaves overlapping them. The stiff stem crosses ending in palmettes stress the vertical and horizontal orientations and give an additional impression of quartering and, by the arrangement of the arabesque leaves, also of half-drop rows of two equally important motifs (cf. the 'Lotto' carpets of Ushak, fig. 9). In the wine-red main border a regular alternation of a W-shaped flower scroll almost closed into a circle and a tree-like tulip. Papyrus wave stem in the guard stripes.

151. Cairo, 16th century. 192 × 132 cm.

Warp: W. Z-plied, twisted, dyed old gold.

Weft: W. S-spun, 4 strands, untwisted, dyed orange-red. 2. shoots: 1. straight, 2. sinuous.

Pile: W. S-spun, 2 strands, untwisted. Knots P. II 40°: h. 32, w. 44 = 1,408 per sq. dm. Upper end: 1.5 cm. W. kilim, then warp threads twisted in 10s. Lower end: as upper end.

Selvedges: W. shirazi red 2 cord round 3 warp threads twisted together.

Quality: silky, thin, flabby, ribbed.

Colours: 7, *wine, pistachio, old gold, dark blue,* pale blue, dark green, some white.

Pattern: in the wine-red central field a fragment of the continuous repetition of a motif characteristic of the Ottoman court manufactory: from a central diamond scroll, palmettes and ronded acanthus leaves grow symmetrically into a medallion-like motif of which a quarter is repeated in each corner. In the broad main border a delicate curving scroll with large fronded leaves, palmettes and composite flowers.

152. Cairo, mid-16th century. Prayer rug. 190 × 140 cm. From the tomb of Ṣultan Selim, said to have served Sultan Ahmed I as a namazlik.

Warp: W. Z-plied, 4 strands, twisted, dyed orange.

Weft: silk, S-spun, 2 strands, untwisted, dyed wine red. 2 shoots: 1. straight, 2. sinuous.

Pile: silk, W. S-spun, 3 strands, untwisted. Knots P. II, 45°: h. 74, w. 64 = 4,736 per sq. dm. Upper end: —.
　Lower end: —. Selvedges: —.

Quality: silky, thin, firm. Colours: 7, *olive, wine, light blue,* ivory, medium blue, green, light olive.

Pattern: in the olive central field an ivory-coloured band with light blue arabesques forms the curved arch
　of the niche. Similarly patterned corner pieces at the bottom. In the centre of the niche a pointed oval
　medallion with rising floral pattern of fronded leaves with rosettes; composite flowers in the centre. In
　the wide main border a complex fronded leaf scroll with composite flowers and palmettes on a wine ground.
　6 guard stripes.

Chinese carpets

The great empire of the Chinese peasant people derives its name from the state of Ch'in in the Wei valley, which was the starting point of the unification of the eighteen provinces. Its king assumed the title of Ch'in Shih huang-ti (First Emperor of the House of Ch'in) in 221 BC, and reigning despotically, set aside the old feudal system. Four years after he had gone mad his dynasty was overthrown by the Han, which took power after some internal dissensions in 202 BC and adopted ready-made the foundations for a centralised state system which has survived to the present day, despite all uprisings, revolutions, wars and attacks by foreign conquerors. Shih huang-ti had created a disciplined administration conducted by civil servants, standardised the gauge of track for carriages and built the road network. The forts on the military road along the northern frontier were linked by walls; this frontier wall was replaced in the fifteenth century by the 'Great Wall'. The script was standardised, and the Emperor assembled a group of learned men at the court to compose an encyclopaedia which should confirm the unity of Chinese culture. Unsatisfactory texts were confiscated and 460 recalcitrant sages were executed.

Art as a whole developed rapidly during the feudal period after the safeguarding of the northern frontiers (sixth century BC) and, protected from the south and east geographically and from the north politically, it rose to unbelievable heights during the next two millenia under the Han, Sui, T'ang, Ming and Manchu dynasties and ripened to a splendid and elegant maturity. Invading conquerors, one after the other, be it Liao in the nineteenth century, Chin in the twelfth or the Mongols of Genghiz Khan in the thirteenth, all were caught with the fascination of Chinese culture and soon laid their weapons aside. From early times Chinese culture fused into its own the cultures of the more primitive peoples who became absorbed by the state. Cloud, dragon, deer and many other Chinese symbols have their origin here. The most important external influences came from India with Buddhism and from Persia in the Sasanid period. Chinese art reached the climax of its effect on the West at the time of the Mongol domination of Persia in the fourteenth century.

XXVI. **East Turkestan, 19th century. Khotan.** c. 168 × 119 cm. So-called Samarkand.
Warp: C. S-plied, 6 strands, twisted, undyed.
Weft: C. Z-spun, 3 strands, untwisted, undyed. 3. shoots: 1. and 3. straight, 2. sinuous. Hamail.
Pile: W. Z-spun, 2 strands untwisted. Knots P. II to 90°: h. 34, w. 33 = 1,122 per sq.dm. Upper end: —.
    Lower end: —.
Selvedges: W. shirazi purple, single cord.
Quality: silky, fleshy, rather thick, coarse granular, slightly hairy.
Colours: 7, *light mauve blue, brick-red, olive-yellow,* purple, brown-black, light blue-green, pale green.
Pattern: the mauve-blue central field is covered over with two widely branching pomegranate trees. They
    rise from a vase at each end. Main border has *hai shui chiang ya,* T swastika band in the inner of the two
    guard stripes.

It would seem that no knotted carpets were made in China until very late. It is not known when production started. In any case it met a highly developed art. The official annals after the tenth century note the import of felt carpets from the empire of the Tanguts, to which the Ordos region and parts of Kansu belonged. Its capital was present-day Ninghsia. During the Mongol period (1260—1341) the felt carpet grew to be a luxury article. The beauty of its colours and appliqué patterns and the perfection of the silver-brocaded felt gauze were prized and the large quantities of carpets delivered to the court were noted. There is no mention of knotted pieces. Even Marco Polo, who lived at the court of Kublai Khan from 1271 to 1294 and travelled about in China, makes no reference to them. The first real interest taken by the court in knotted carpets seems to have been by the Emperor Kao Tsu, called Ch'ien Lung (1736—96), the great and cultivated Manchu emperor whose forebears came from the steppes. In the following of his concubine Hsiang Fei, the daughter of a prince from Kashgar, came scribes, mullas and a Turkish bodyguard of 500 men. The pains-takingly detailed annals make no mention of carpet manufactories, and Bidder, who hoped to settle the origin of the 'Chinese Ninghsia carpet' 'on the spot', found not the slightest hint of a state manufactory either in the chronicles nor in the memory of the inhabitants of the oases. There is a report of a journey by the first Manchu Emperor, K'ang Hsi, to the eastern provinces, given by the Jesuit priest Gerbillon who was present on the journey at the order of the emperor (Du Halde, *Description de la Chine*, The Hague 1736: *le Sixième voyage du Père Gerbillon en Tartarie, fait à la suite de l'empereur de la Chine 1696*). Of the emperor's stay in Ning Hia (Ninghsia) from the 26th April 1696 onwards he writes that the emperor was pre-sented with silks — the most beautiful from Uzbekistan — and carpets — apparently similar to Turkish ones — that were made in Ning Hia. The emperor inspected the manufacture of such carpets.

The craft of hand-knotting probably found an entry from east Turkestan into the provinces of Ninghsia and Kansu, which over long stretches of their history have not belonged to China. The carpets are loosely worked in Persian knots on a cotton under-weave, and the tradition of the felt carpet is still very much in evidence in the patterns. They give the impression (figs. 136, 138, 141, 142) of felt appliqués. The wool is less resilient than that of the Tarim basin and hardly stands up at all. The warp and weft threads are usually equally thick, and the Persian knot occasionally takes in two pairs of warp threads. The colours are set in without any outlines and some patterns are only helped to some clarity by the slight embossing at the trans-itions, a process that must derive from the quilting of felt. Among the colours flesh pink and grass green are in evidence (entered in the annals as typical of the felt carpets). The madder red has faded to old gold. In old examples the main motifs are crude east Turkestanian designs and an endless repeat of small geometric elements for Kansu, and horses and stags for Ninghsia and Suiyuan (Paotao). Horse and stag were common motifs in the bronze animal style prevalent in the Ordos region, the Altai, south-west Russia, Luristan and even the countries of the Danube, and the chief ornament of the Pazyryk carpet. Later dragons, fo (lion) and many Chinese symbols are added. Most of these ornamentations taken over from other branches of art are not really suited to the floor carpet. But in no other people has the sense of the symbol remained so alive right up to the present day as in the Chinese (p. 295).

The use of chairs and other furniture in China made the carpet less important there than in other parts of Asia. Knotted pieces were used mainly for draping pillars (p. 277 and fig. 141), covering chair seats (figs. 136—138), and as wall hangings (fig. 143) and cushions for chests and carts. All China's needs in this direction were met by the western provinces.

The age and origin are unknown of some relatively thin carpets knotted in a wool which has the lustre of silk, wholly Chinese in pattern and aesthetic arrangement, of which all too small a number has been preserved. In them the border serves primarily as the frame for the picture in a self-contained central field; it does not enter into the original oriental conception of cutting off a fragment of eternal flow. The feeling of the Chinese artist for avoiding symmetry and giving rein to the free sweep of the brush is revealed here in the asymmetrical arrangement of a number of naturalistic small-scale filling patterns round the solitary medallion. The colour scale is small. The designer likes to vary the tones of a single colour before going on to another. Often three colours suffice.

The annals and an encyclopaedia of 1725 give no information on hand-knotted carpets. Reliable dating is not possible on the basis of material, because of its poor durability — every Chinese carpet looks 'antique' after a decade of ordinary careless wear — nor on the basis of its patterns because of the conservative character of late Chinese art. The repeated mention of hand-knotted carpets in the later lists of gifts from western diplomats is an indication of the non-existence of manufactories or even of court manufactories in central China. If these had existed the presentation of foreign carpets would have been looked upon as the grossest discourtesy. It can thus only be assumed that this group was knotted in north-east China in the second half of the eighteenth and in the nineteenth century.

The West only began to pay some attention to the Chinese carpet at the beginning of the twentieth century, after the Boxer Rising. Demand arose, primarily in America, so spontaneously that even the copies by Smyrna ('Japonais', 'Chinois') did a roaring trade, as well as the products of the old manufactories and those quickly founded in Pekin, Tientsin and other Chinese towns. Besides the quiet Chinese floral patterns

153. Spain, 16th—17th century. Fragment. c. 163 × 185 cm. (detail) (p. 295, above).
Warp: W. S-plied, 2 strands, twisted, undyed light.
Weft: W. Z-spun, 3 strands, untwisted, dyed red. 1 shoot straight.
Pile: W. Z-spun, 2 strands, untwisted. Knots Spanish: h. 38, w. 48 = 1,824 per sq. dm. Upper end: —.
   Lower end: —. Selvedges: —.
Quality: smooth, firm, almost thin.
Colours: 4, *rust-red, dark green,* green-blue, olive-yellow.
Pattern: in the rust-red central field two vertical rows of dark green garland medallions with geometric stem design inside. In the interstices quartered lozenges with hooks and stylised flower heads. The border is very discreet in colour. On the dark green-blue ground of the main border is a dark green Renaissance scroll.

294

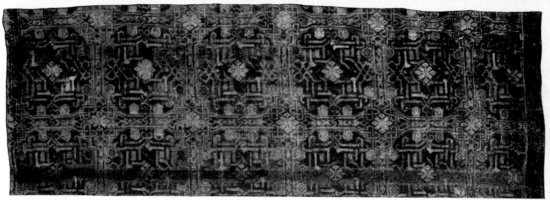

154. Spain, 16th—17th century. Fragment. 297×186 cm. (detail). (below)

Warp: W. S-plied, 2 strands, twisted, undyed light.

Weft: W. Z-spun, 3 strands, untwisted, undyed light. 1 shoot sinuous.

Pile: W. Z-spun, single. Knots Spanish: h. 44, w. 44 = 1,936 per sq. dm.

Upper end: —. Lower end: —. Selvedges: —.

Quality: dry, thin, granular.

Colours: 5, *blue, yellow, red,* moss green, dark brown.

Pattern: the blue central field quartered by coffers. In each coffer an arabesque braid pattern in red, yellow and brown round a yellow central rosette. These yellow rosettes come also at the crossings of the green coffer frames formed by interlaced ribbons.

and designs using symbols, the westerner was offered whole townscapes and similar 'Chinese art'. Latterly a new type of very thick carpet in sugary pastel shades has grown increasingly popular, especially for ladies' bedrooms. Its exaggerated concave embossed relief is appropriate neither to textile nor carpet. The Persian knot in five or six strands of wool on a cotton under-weave with a very thin weft shows a peculiarity in the latest pieces: so as to make the Persian knot more quickly it is done the opposite way from the normal (see drawing P. II, P. III on p. 29). It goes right round the hinder thread of the strongly depressed warp while it only surrounds the fore-

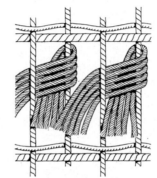

Persian knots in modern Chinese carpets

most warps on three sides. Thus the foremost threads show along their whole length when the pile is folded lengthwise, and even the weft threads crossing them are revealed. Only the very long pile prevents their wearing out at once. On the underside, the second, thinner thread of the two wefts (the first is straight and not seen), in contrast to the multiple wefts of the old Chinese carpets, is hardly visible.

Symbols in Chinese carpets

No other people can have such a pronounced leaning for the language of symbolism. This predilection for expressing themselves in symbols, for grasping abstract ideas through concrete images, coincides with the poverty of sounds in the Chinese language. The Chinese script, which has grown up as the abstraction of a pictorial script, has a character for every idea of course, but the language often has only one sound for a large number of characters. Yü = fish sounds like yü = excess. The abstract concept of excess can be understood by every Chinese in the representation of a fish. Chu = bamboo sounds like chu = to pray, to wish someone something; mei = plum = spring; lu = stag = riches; ch'ing = sounding stone = blessing; p'ing = vase = peace; fu = bat = happiness; butterfly = hu tieh, tieh = long life. Fo-shou, the finger citrus, became the lucky symbol of the 'Buddha's fingers' because fo = Buddha in some dialects is the same as fu = good luck.

These sound rebuses are numerous in Chinese symbolism. Other images are drawn from nature both animate (animals of all kinds, plants, trees, flowers) and inanimate (water, mountains, clouds, rocks, thunder, fire), from mythology (fabulous beasts) and religious teachings (spirits and their attributes). The teachings of Confucius (b. 551 BC) is a compendium of older teachings to which Chinese symbolism owes the most varied motifs. One of the aims of Taoism, the teaching of the fourth century BC philosopher Lao Tzǔ concerning the Way as the origin and goal of all existence, is the lengthening of life. Thus most of the images derived from Taoism are symbols of long life. Buddhism, adopted from India in the last centuries BC, had important influence on Chinese art. The fo = Buddist lion shih-tzu (fig. 136) — often represented by a sphere for the male and a puppy for the female — and the 'eight auspicious objects' (pa-chi-hsiang) originate here. The images derived from the religions have taken on for the Chinese a symbolic character regardless of belief, and lost their religious meaning. Other symbols are in the form of the products of human activity and written characters.

The number, form and colour of the objects, their combinations and positions in relation to each other enlarge further the symbolic content: single representation — for example the crane as the first of the birds — may mean the only or the first (at court), in pairs they mean happiness and long life. Five bats symbolise the five great blessings: long life, riches, health, virtue and an easy, happy end. A long-necked vase = long peace, round = t'uan = completeness. The lotus in bud, in flower and withered represents the past, present and future, the stalk means continuity, eternal duration or perpetual return, a clump of lotus, pen ku chih jung = 'may the roots be fast and the branches flourish', an often-heard wish for the security and prosperity of the family; flowers and sprouting buds from a root = harmony, agreement. The red bat — red is the colour of happiness and a defence against demons — always stands for great happiness. Stag and crane are both symbols for old age; 'mayest thou grow as old as stag and crane'; their representation in the landscape (fig. 142) increases it a hundred fold, the combination with the swastika pattern a thousand fold. A grasshopper (civil servant) on the top of a chrysanthemum (duration) expresses wishes for permanent high rank.

Real or attributed qualities decide the symbolic content: the dragon = lung, the first of the pachyderms, stands for the light, the male, creative cosmological principle (yang); the female phoenix, fang and huang the royal bird, for the female, nurturing and dark (yin). A pair of mandarin ducks is a symbol of marital fidelity; plum blossom of detachment (from the common things of everyday life also), because its blossoms come before the leaves.

Symbolic meaning may come from usage and custom: fresh bamboo, chu, used to be thrown into the fire in ancient times, particularly at the New Year, so that the crackling should scare away evil spirits, and it can stand for perpetual return. It may also stand for modesty and humility, because its leaves hang down and its heart (hsin) is hollow, empty (hsü) — or for fame: 'May his name be handed down on bamboo (brownish paper) and silk (forerunner of rag paper).'

Sometimes the meaning is derived from an ambiguity: the well-known fat-bellied monk Putai can hold much inside him. Jung = it contains, and the same word and character also means forgiveness, overlooking. Therefore the figure can imply being 'smilingly above things'.

Only the consummate formal gift of the Chinese artist could unite so many heterogeneous elements into a harmonious composition. The patterns of most old Chinese carpets are composed entirely of symbols. While only a few of them were used in isolation and purely decoratively when they were adopted in west Asian carpets, they were combined in China in great numbers and as expressions of wishes for good luck through their symbolism. This is relatively easy to achieve by transforming a symbol through repetition into a linear or surface ornament. The swastika (Sanskrit: svāstika, Chinese: wan tzǔ), a symbol for happiness when standing alone, acquires the meaning of ten thousand-fold when in an involuted line (hui wên) (i.e. p. 281) or in rows as a surface ornament. The 'Chinese pattern' (han wên) usually has the form of the 'T frieze' (fig. 132) or the angular 'key frieze' similar to the 'running dog' pattern. The perforated coin-cash = yen-ch'ien = 'before the eyes', worn as an amulet against illness and other visitations of demons, usually appears as a border (p. 301) or surface pattern. This pattern is thus also called the 'golden money pattern'.

Water in movement is represented in zig-zags or waves, when still, in the form of segments of circles (fig. 142). The motif of the life-giving 'sea water and river bank' (hai-shui chiang-ya) is repeated along the border (fig. p. 275). The cloud pattern (yün-wên) serves as a border (cloud-trefoil border) or in the form of separate luck-clouds scattered throughout the main pattern as a surface filling (p. 277) — at the same time emphasising the representation of the earthly spheres. Cloud bands surround separate symbols. The wish-granting pearl (Sanskrit: ratna or cintamani, Chinese: chu) also returns as a beading.

The dragon lung (fig. 137 and p. 301), first of the four fabulous monsters and leader of the 360 pachyderms, symbol of yang, as a blue-green dragon (ch'ing lung) is Lord of the East, the sunrise, spring and rain. Originally he was a composite beast, with antlers on a camel's head, demon's (hare's) eyes, snake neck, frog's belly, carp's scales and eagle's or falcon's claws. No other of China's fabulous beasts is so laden with mythological and cosmological notions as he. Cosmological speculation distinguishes t'ien-lung = sky dragon, ti-lung = earth dragon, shên-lung = spirit dragon and fu-ts'ang-lung = treasure-guarding dragon. With five toes he was reserved for the imperial court and the emblem of the emperor.

The phoenix fêng-huang (fêng = little man, huang = little woman), symbol of the yin and yang, expresses the concept of the dual powers of the cosmos, whose alternating influences sway the universe. It is in addition a symbol of sexual union and was the emblem of the empress. Originally it had a pheasant's head, a swallow's beak, tortoise neck, dragon body and fish tail. Its dwelling is the Wu t'ung = tree (fig. 142). In association with the dragon it brings blessing.

The fabulous ch'i-lin, also a zoomorph, has the body of a stag, the tail of an ox, fish scales, cloven hoofs and a horn covered in fur (like the sword in the sheaf a symbol of an armed peace). It brings good luck and progeny.

Cloud pattern
yun wen

Fabulous beast
feng-huang

Thunder pattern
lei wen

Wheel with fire
(thunder)
lun

Eight
trigrammes
tai chi t'u

Fu sign
(good luck)

Long life
shou

Luck knot
p'an ch'ang

sceptre
ju-i

The 14 treasures
ssu shih pao

The thunder is represented in the continuous thunder pattern and in the form of a fiery (lightning) wheel. Fire or lightning are portrayed by flickering flames.

Mountains and rocks appear rising from the water, with dragons or among the 'nine insignia or emblems'. The relationship between the female and male principles yin and yang is symbolised by the t'ai-chi-t'u. It is usually surrounded by the Eight Trigrammes (pa kua). These signs composed of whole (male potency) and interrupted (female potency) lines (cf. p. 297) signify with the three whole lines = ch'ien = NW, beginning the sky (clockwise): tui = W, water, steam, seas; k'un = SW, earth; kên = NE, mountains; k'an = N, water; li = S, fire, heat, light; ch'en = E, thunder; sun = SE, wind. The sequence is voluntary and not laid down.

The character shou, symbol for long life, is found in carpets nearly always in the reduced forms, either circular, long or fragmented to fill a corner, similarly the character for happiness.

The sceptre, ju-i, ending in a cloud trefoil, was attributed to the gods of the sky. Its symbolic meaning is 'May all be successful'.

The 'Eight Genii' or blessed (protective) spirits or Immortals, pa-hsien, are represented on carpets by their attributes, being themselves invisible spirits. These are symbols from the legends which have been woven round each of these followers of Lao-tzû: the fan which revives the dead; the bottle-gourd-shaped calabash that contains the drink of immortality; the demon-slaying sword with a horse's tail as a cloud broom; a flower or fruit basket, the magic lotus flower or the peach which feeds the immortals; bamboo clapper, 'fish drum' and flute.

The 'eight Buddhist treasures' (pa chi hsiang) are: the *shell* that calls to prayer, the wheel that symbolises them, the *baldaquin* that shields living creatures, the *umbrella* that shades the healing herbs, the *vase* that is a symbol of perfect wisdom, *goldfish* that signify salvation, the *infinite luck knot* (Sanskrit: sriwatsa; Chinese: p'an-ch'ang) which is never-ending happiness, the *lotus* which is the symbol of purity. Lotus and peony (dignity, riches, distinction) have the same dominant place among the numerous symbols from the plant world that is held by the dragon and the fêng-huang among the other images. Floral symbols are combined, like all others, together with fruits, trees or other symbols or among themselves. Among trees the wu tung and the fir tree as symbols of permanency, of the eternal changeless green, and also of hundred-fold increase are widespread.

Combinations of four or eight treasures are also much liked: of the literati (harp, chess, books, paintings) or of the learned; or the 'fourteen treasures' (cf. p. 303): the wishing pearl, coin or lozenge, silver or gold bars, rhinoceros cup (shows up poison in drinks), picture rolls, books, (jade) sounding stone, acorn, banana and mugwort (wormwood) leaf, luck clouds, tripod, gold or silver shoe, and the spirit-, god-, miracle-, magic-, wonder- or luck-bringing mushroom of long life ling-chih (after F. Lessing, *Über die Symbolsprache in der chinesischen Kunst).*

XXVII. N. W. China, 19th century. Paotou. Pillar carpet. 247×138 (136—142) cm.
Warp: C. S-plied, 4 strands, twisted, undyed.
Weft: C. Z-spun, 2—3 strands, untwisted, undyed.
Pile: W. Z-spun, 4 strands, untwisted. Knots P. I: h. 24, w. 27 = 648 per sq. dm. Slight relief shearing.
  Upper end: —. Lower end: —. Selvedges: C. shirazi single cord undyed.
Quality: soft, heavy, coarse. Colours: 11, *rust-red, dark blue, yellow,* olive-yellow, ivory, olive, flesh pink, light blue, light brown, pale blue, light brown-red.
Pattern: on the rust-red ground a large blue-scaled dragon surges wildly upwards. His mouth is wide open, and the gigantic feelers below the round eyes, the horns in the mane, the fire playing round his body and his sharp claws all give him a frightening aspect. He is surrounded by clouds and above on the right is the wish pearl. Symmetrical waves rise from the lower edge of the carpet, and break with spray on the rocks. On the large central rock to the left is a small wish pearl, on the right an abacus. On the rust-red main band of the upper border is a cash frieze. Being a pillar carpet it has no side borders. The slight relief shearing allows every detail of the pattern to stand out clear in spite of the coarse knotting.
Significance of the symbolism: the dragon (*lung*), the 'first of the 360 scaley dragons', first of the *ssu-ling* (four magic beasts), is the symbol of the male, light, striving force of nature, the *yang*. This is probably *ch'ing lung*, lord of the East, of the sunrise and of rain. He is playing with the wishing pearl *jui-chu*. This corresponds to the chintamani of the Buddha, who according to legend wished in one of his previous existences to steal the wish-granting treasure from the dragon king in his great desire to help the poor. But the dragon remembered his own previous existence and, recognising the Buddha as his son, gave him the jewel.
The soaring rocks splashed with spray and the clouds lift the scene from the earthly sphere. While the meaning of the picture implies strength, high repute, power and fulfillment of all wishes there can be another interpretation whereby the pearl = chu stands for the spider = chu, in a play on words typical in Chinese symbolism. This would then be a fight between a gigantic poisonous reptile and the poisonous spider following the Chinese popular belief in the fight between poisons and their mutual destruction. The meaning then would be protection from all evil. The abacus on the right of the main rock refers to the legend of the three old men who each enquired the age of the other. One of them answered that he no longer counted in years, but each time the sea changed into a mulberry plantation he moved a bead and when the plantation was flooded again he moved another (thus reckoning in geological time). Together with the small wishing pearl on the left it means 'a sea of fulfilled wishes and a very long life'. The cash (coin with a square hole, carried as an amulet) frieze in the upper border gives a multiple repetition of the wish for the power of the coin to ban all evil influences. Because of its square hole the cash is also called hole cash = yen-ch'ien = 'before the eyes'. Here in the sense 'what is wished in the main motifs to be always before the eyes'.

Carpets from other countries

The first evidence of Egyptian hand-knotted work probably dates from the ninth century, in the form of the fragments found in Fostat (Old Cairo) (fig. 145—147b). On them is employed the most primitive manner of knotting imaginable: the single- or double-stranded pattern threads are brought under each second warp thread to make a V-shaped loop (p. 30). It used to be thought that these V loops, which are displaced along one warp thread at every row, were loops in the weft thread that had been taken round rods laid over the warps and subsequently cut, but this thesis is untenable. For one thing it is contradicted by the manner in which the separate loops are bedded in the thick, straight, four to seven stranded wefts, and for another, a different weft would have had to be introduced for each colour in the pattern on each row, and colours are often numerous and change frequently. Such weft threads, less exposed to wear in the ground-weave than in the pile, would of necessity still be present in the weave; but there is not a trace of them in any of the fragments investigated. The Egyptian pieces among the Fostat fragments are easily distinguishable from the structure of the material, because the Egyptian women-folk still spin clockwise today. The plying is consequently in the opposite direction. The material of the fragments is entirely of linen for the under-weave including the selvedge (shirazi), and for white pattern loops, and wool for all the coloured elements of the pattern. By strong beating the weft threads have been pressed into thick straight bundles, which result in the strongly ribbed structure of the underside. The patterns are geometric and seem related to those of the Seljuks and Turcomans: lozenging by finely stepped diamonds, close-packed eight-trayed stars etc.; inscriptions stand out clearly on a monochrome ground. The palette is limited. The chief colours are rust to wine-red, green, white, surmey, light blue and various olive and brown tones. The brown-black parts of the pattern are completely decayed.

The next examples are the Mamluk carpets, preserved in greater quantity and dating from the fifteenth and sixteenth centuries (fig. 148). They are worked in Persian knots with wool or silk on a woollen or sometimes a silk warp. The characteristic colours of the early pieces — warm red, light green and pale blue — are later joined by a radiant yellow. The colour range sometimes comprises twelve different tones. The name 'tapedi damaschini' in the old Venetian inventories most likely refers to Mamluk carpets.

After the occupation of Cairo by the Ottomans in 1517 the Mamluk patterns were gradually displaced by the designs of the Ottoman court manufactory (see p. 58). These 'Cairenes' all (fig. 150, 151) have naturalistic floral patterns, except for the chintamani used as a background for one type. As a rule they are dominated by curved feathery lanceolate leaves (fig. 150, 151). Medallions, often very narrow, are usually used in rows and in isolation over the dominant ground pattern; this contrasts with the original Persian use of them to emphasise the centre. The Egyptian carpet illustrated in fig. 149 represents the transition from the Mamluk to Ottoman patterns. The ornamentation of the subsidiary border is an original adaptation of Mamluk designs. The scheme of the design of the central field is more complicated than it seems at first sight: thin bent stems combined with the arabesque leaves cutting across them evoke the impression of a small-scale lozenge system; the stiff stem crosses ending in palmettes which emphasise the verticals and horizontals, produce quartering. These palmette crosses combined with the arabesque leaves are, however, closely related to the 'Lotto' carpets of Ushak (cf. fig. 9), while the large arabesque leaves are already foreshadowed on a very small scale in Mamluk carpets.

The large manufactories in Cairo must have ceased production in the eighteenth century at the latest. Cairo was second only to Istanbul as a trading centre for oriental carpets. It only lost this position in the late nineteenth century. Today carpets are knotted in Heluan near Cairo, mainly copying Persian patterns in rather unattractive colours. On the other hand the Egyptian kelims of handspun and mostly natural-coloured wool have found a wide market in recent years.

Uncertainty still exists over the origin of a type which must be of the sixteenth and seventeenth century, an example of which is illustrated in fig. 152. It is similar to another type with small-scale quartering and finely radiating rosettes enclosing a Maltese cross at the intersections and both types are strongly Mamluk in character. The knotting however is Turkish and the material neither Turkish nor Egyptian. Until this is elucidated we have to abide by the old name of 'Damascus' which was also used for the Mamluk carpets until their Egyptian origin was established.

North Africa
(Libya, Tunisia, Algeria, Morocco)

Hand-knotting probably started early in the regions of North Africa conquered by the Arabs, but no evidence is forthcoming. Of the carpets termed 'Mahgreb' those from Qairawan are better known because they are less coarsely knotted than the products of Gabes and other towns.

These Tunisian carpets have played no more role on the world market however than those of Algeria and Tripoli. In present production Persian patterns dominate, mostly in the natural colours of ivory, light to dark brown and grey wool. The most important manufactories of Morocco were at first those of Marrakesh and Casablanca, later those of Rabat and Fez. Their carpets were not so well known as the Moroccan embroideries, leather, gold and silver work. Before the First World War France endeavoured to re-animate carpet production in Morocco. Old Moroccan carpets are more reminiscent of Mamluk than of Middle-Eastern patterns. For some time therefore some experts attributed the Mamluk carpets to Morocco. The colour scheme in the small-scale geometric patterns of the older Moroccan carpets is dominated by bright red, blue and yellow. Of all North African carpets only the

'Berber' carpets have had any success in Europe in the last decade. Their simple patterns, suited to the coarse knotting and long pile, often the colours of natural undyed wool, are appropriate to many modern furnishing styles.

India

The tropical climate of India did not give any incentive to the development of the hand-knotted carpet. Mats and simple deri weaves have remained the most appropriate floor coverings. There is no knotting done in peasant home industry.

The luxury-loving Mughal emperors introduced Persian carpets for their palaces and craftsmen from Persia to set up manufactories. During the reigns of Shah Akbar (1556—1605) and Jehangir (1605—27) — admiring everything Persian, the Great Mughals had adopted the Persian title and introduced the Persian court language — carpets were produced as good as the Persian. About 1600 manufactories were flourishing not only in the residence of Lahore but in Fathepur, Agra and many other towns. Jean Baptiste Tavernier (*Les six Voyages ... en Turquie, en Perse & aux Indes...*, Paris 1692) reports that in India carpets were produced in wool (in the neighbourhood of Agra), silk, silk with gold and with gold and silver brocading (in Amadabad and Surate). He notes however that the colours of these well-made carpets are not as fast as the Persian. Tavernier had visited the court manufactory in the south-west corner of the meidan when he was staying at the Persian court in Isfahan in 1664 ... 'dans laquelle on travaille de beaux tapis d'or & d'argent, de soye & de laine'. His asseveration that these splendid carpets of gold and silver did not darken, and lost nothing of their lustre with the passage of time has been disproved by the years. He does not omit to report that the Shah himself has his shoes removed before he treads on the carpet when he receives the ambassador in the great audience hall. Early Indian carpets are extremely fine, worked in Persian knots with a soft silky wool, sometimes on a silk warp. At first the patterns are entirely under the influence of Herat and Kirman. The Herati pattern with bent acanthus leaves is still enclosed by a cartouche border at the beginning of the seventeenth century. A few decades later an independent style becomes equally noticeable on many borders and in the central field in the floral filling of the curved stem lozenging characteristic of Kirman. The figured carpets, hunting, animal and paradise, like the prayer rugs are all unmistakably Indian: the plants and animals are drawn naturalistically. The branches of the trees bend under the weight of the blossoms. The whole wealth of Indian vegetation appears in the carpets. F. R. Martin writes: 'The plants look as though they had come from a herbarium.' Single flowering shrubs are executed with every detail of the leaves, flowers, buds and sometimes even the roots, or hundreds of minutely drawn blossoms flower on a single spray. The animals could serve as zoological demonstration specimens, they are so life-like and three dimensional. Symmetry is avoided as far as possible. The ground is usually monochrome so as to bring out the patterns to the full. Flowers and trees dominate the main borders in the same naturalistic and plastic manner, or finely articulated flowered stems with contorted palmettes and birds. Yet admirable as these efforts of designers and knotters may be, the subject destroys the composition. The modelling of the separate elements makes them seem to fall out of the pattern. The intrinsic Indian character of the decoration is unsuited to the character of the carpet and it had no future.

The carpets of the Indian manufactories in the mid-nineteenth century were equal in quality to the Persian carpets that they imitated — one kind was a close and detailed copy of the Isfahans, called 'Indo-Isfahan' — but in the 'eighties and 'nineties quality rapidly declined. Most of the manufactories in Multan, Srinagar, Amritsar, Lahore, Agra, Sind, Jaipur, Mirzapur, Madras, Vellur Patna and other towns in North India, which relied on exporting, were forced to produce more cheaply by the cut prices of the workshops set up in the prisons. Patterns, colours, knotting and material all deteriorated. Plant fibres and European patterns crept in. The name of the Indian carpet was ruined. Present production, improved to some extent, has some sale because of preferential customs treatment inside the Commonwealth.

Pakistan

Pakistan, the second largest successor state to the British Empire in India, has managed to find an entry on the world market for the knotted goods from its manufactories. The patterns are imitations of the Tekke and other Turcoman designs, mainly on a cream coloured ground. Density and quality vary considerably. There are 'Pakistan Bokharas' both medium fine on a cotton warp and extremely fine on a woollen warp. But even with the finest count and the best soft Kashmir wool they remain imitations. This is true also of the 'Ghiordes' prayer rugs and 'Persian' patterns which have been knotted in Pakistan for the last two years or so.

Spain

Between the eighth and the fifteenth century the Iberian peninsula was at first entirely and later partly under Arab rule, and was the first European region to take up carpet knotting. Spanish carpets were known in Cairo at the court of the Caliph in 1124. The Spanish knot and the earliest patterns both indicate that the technique found its way to Spain through Egypt. The Spanish knot which goes round only one warp thread one and a half times (see drawing p. 30) is an improvement on the Egyptian V-loop. If the analysis of the material of some of the Fostat fragments justifies their attribution to Spain (in Spain they practise Z-spinning and S-plying) it would be a Spanish invention. Like the Egyptian V-loop (see drawing p. 30) the Spanish knot is done from row to row, moving along one warp thread each time, between four or five thick straight wefts. The wefts often contain linen (flax) as well as wool. This technique and structure is still seen in the carpets from Cuenca of recent centuries.

The date of the beginning of hand-knotting in Spain is unknown. The most important centres of production developed in Almeria, Cuenca and Alcaraz. In the region of Valencia the Turkish knot later prevailed. The earliest intact examples are from the fifteenth century. They show either connections with Egyptian work, with small-scale geometric arrangements of diagonal rows of octagons, stars etc., or they are imitations of Anatolian carpets, particularly the 'Holbeins' (fig. 6). The cursive Kufic script on the borders of these imitations is softer and more adorned with flourishes. In the sixteenth and seventeenth centuries European renaissance and baroque patterns were prevalent (figs. 153, 154), in the eighteenth century the style of contemporary French and English work. Red, green and blue set the tone. As in the fifteenth century the crests of Spanish families often appear in the patterns. Christian influence is visible in religious symbols and emblems. At the same time there were imitations of Ushak (Lotto, fig. 9), Herat and Cairo carpets. In the eighteenth century production declined. Today a state manufactory is endeavouring to export its wares.

A few (especially Cuenca) antique Spanish carpets are still to be found on the European market. The well-known Alpujaras are not hand-knotted carpets but looped weaves and folk craft.

Portugal

In Portugal too hand-knotting has continued since the Arab domination up to the present day. Saracenic ornamentation was followed by patterns of various styles from baroque to Bauhaus. Export at present is very modest. The 'Portuguese' or 'Goa' carpets, which have their corners of the central field decorated with European sailing ships, with dark-skinned men and Europeans in Spanish costume sitting in them, are neither Portuguese nor Goan, but were made in Persia.

Greece

Only Greek carpets among all those produced in the borderlands can be considered as oriental carpets. After the first Balkan war (1912—13) many Greeks who had been settled in Turkey returned to Greece. Greeks had been living in Asia Minor for centuries, even millenia, but they were expelled in 1922 after the unsuccessful military attack on Anatolia, and thousands of skilful knotters were among them. Greece was anxious to solve the refugee problem as quickly as possible and pressed on with carpet production. Instead of working in Turkey the knotters now made their good Turkish carpets in Greece. French and east Turkestanian patterns were added. As the refugees were integrated into other branches of production, carpet production declined. It has however retained a certain importance for the economy of this small country.

Yugoslavia, Bulgaria, Rumania, Hungary

During the centuries of Turkish occupation in the Balkans carpet knotting seems to have been started in various regions. Although most of the 'Siebenbürgen' carpets must be importations from Anatolia — the city accounts of Kronstadt note the import of more than 500 carpets for the period from 7th January to 6th November 1503 alone — the custom of the dealers of Istanbul to name certain types of carpet after places in the Balkans implies considerable production in south-east Europe. In the last decade Yugoslavia, Bulgaria and Romania have been trying hard and successfully to obtain a footing in the European market for the products of their state manufactories. The carpets are for the most part only coarse to medium fine, but the knotting and finishing are as accurate as mechanically produced carpets. In Yugoslavia the manufactories are concentrated in Macedonia and produce carpets in matt but good wool, mainly in Tabriz and Afghan patterns. Rumania has thousands of looms. The knotting in matt wool is coarse and at most reaches medium-fine density. Everything is copied, Persian, Anatolian, Caucasian, east Turkestan and Chinese patterns. Bulgaria has the largest production of all the Balkan countries. One of the largest manufactories was founded by Ochanes Bochosjan from Istanbul in 1892. The wool is finer than that used in Rumania and Macedonia. The gauge is usually from 400 to 500 knots per square dm., the main patterns are Persian and Turcoman in style. More interesting than all these imitations are the colourful Balkan Kelims, especially the Yugoslavian, and the folk style carpets of Hungary. The Hungarian woollen carpets called 'Suba' and 'Racka', which are thick and like a shaggy pelt, mainly in natural wool colours, have also found friends outside Hungary.

France

Three types of carpet have French names: Gobelin, Aubusson and Savonnerie.
The Gobelin is very finely woven in Kelim technique. It is only suitable for wall hangings, covering chairs or as a coverlet, and is the most perfect of all wall tapestries. It is named after the house of the Paris family of dyers, in which Flemish weavers set up a manufactory.
The Aubusson is also a tapestry, but is thicker than the Gobelin. It can serve as a decorative floor carpet, but having no pile it is sensitive to wear and not very warm.
The Savonnerie carpet has a pile. The manufactory was founded in the Louvre, but is named after the children's home on the site of an earlier soap factory where it later was housed for a time, the Hospice de la Savonnerie.
To make the pile, the pattern thread is led round an iron rod laid horizontally in front of the warp threads each time it is woven round the warp threads. At the left-hand end of the rod is a little knife. By pulling the rod out to the right all the loops are cut. These knots, which resemble the Turkish knot, are firmly beaten down after the weft has been introduced and clipped to the desired height. The manufactory at

first worked exclusively for the court and later received many commissions from the nobility. A prohibition on the import of foreign carpets allowed it to develop freely without competition. The early floral designs were followed by the architectural patterns of baroque, roccoco, empire, neoclassical and second baroque styles. This continuation of ceiling and wall decoration to the floor covering is the first original European carpet style. In 1825 the manufactory moved into the Manufacture Nationale des Gobelins. There the visitor can watch the production both of Gobelins, some with the most modern designs, and of Savonnerie carpets. The well-dressed craftsmen, carrying out exclusively government commissions, sit in animated conversation in front of the looms. They knot at about a tenth of the rate of that usual in the Orient.

England

How highly the oriental carpet was prized in England is shown in the story of the bribing of Cardinal Wolsey by the Signoria of Venice. The cardinal dragged out negotiations with the Venetian emissaries about the import of Cretan wines for years, until in 1520 Venice at last dug deep into her pocket to present him with sixty of the hundred 'tapedi damaschini' demanded by him. The archives of Venice are full of details about the import and transmission of oriental carpets. The carpet is rarely mentioned in the inventories as for use on the floor. A precious oriental carpet was placed as a cover on tables and chests. When Leonora of Castille married Edward I in 1255 the carpets she brought to London, some of which had been used on the floor, excited attention and criticism. The Count of Leicester, favourite of Queen Elizabeth I, left a considerable collection of carpets.

At the end of the sixteenth century the English sent the dyer Morgan Hubblethorn as a 'work spy' to Persia to find out the secrets of their wool dyeing and carpet knotting. Like France, England was anxious to encourage home production and economise on the currency sacrificed on importing the oriental carpets so coveted as luxuries. But it was not until 150 years later that production was really started by two workers who came from the Savonnerie. Interrupted at times by financial difficulties and wage disputes production continued in England until 1835.

The technique of most seventeenth century carpets cannot yet be called true knotting. The ground-weave of an example in the Victoria and Albert Museum shows hamail. The patterns are at first small-scale geometric Turkish, including cursive kufi borders, later naturalistic florals. Noble crests and dates knotted into the designs make it possible to date them accurately. In the eighteenth and early nineteenth centuries the patterns, as in the Aubusson and Savonnerie carpets, are influenced by architecture.

Italy

Italian folk art adopted hand-knotting at an early period. In the surviving examples striped patterns with European motifs predominate. Oriental influences are rarer. A manufactory of knotted carpets initiated in the early eighteenth century by Pope Clement XI lasted only a short while.

Finland, Sweden, Norway

In the northern lands folk art discovered the knotting technique in the Middle Ages. Small shaggy 'Rya' rugs survive in hundreds from the eighteenth and nineteenth centuries. The patterns, with a few exceptions, are purely Scandinavian.

Poland

The Polish knotted carpets of the eighteenth century show oriental influence in the motifs or, if the patterns are European, in the dividing up of the ground. Among the examples surviving are a number with Polish armorial crests. Manufactories which employed Persians among their knotters are said to have been founded in several Polish towns. It is possible that carpets were made in the manufactory founded in Slucz at the end of the seventeenth century by Prince Radzivill to produce silk scarves and brocaded materials. The gold and silver brocaded 'Polish carpets' (see p. 163) were made in Kashan and Isfahan.

Germany

In Germany carpets are produced both as folk craft and in the manufactories. The primitive patterns of the coarse knotted 'Masuren' carpets of East Prussia are based on oriental and sometimes Scandinavian models. K. Erdmann reports that in Pomer-

XXVIII. **East Turkestan, 19th century. Khotan.** (249—255) 252 × 126 (120—132) cm. So-called Samarkand.
Warp: C. S-plied, 5 strands, twisted, undyed.
Weft: W. Z-spun, single, undyed brown in the 1st quarter, last part and in some isolated shoots. Otherwise C. S-plied, slightly twisted, undyed light. The back therefore is striped horizontally. Mostly 3 shoots: 1. and 3. straight, 2. sinuous; also 1. sinuous, 2. and 3. straight, or vice versa.
Pile: W. Z-spun, 3 strands, untwisted. Knots P. II 60°: h. 24, w. 28 = 672 per sq. dm. Upper end: —.
Lower end: C. kilim undyed: first single then double shoots. Warp threads looped and twisted.
Selvedges: W. shirazi old gold 2 cord. Quality: soft, fleshy, heavy, coarse granular.
Colours: 7, *old gold, medium blue, yellow,* light blue, brown-black, light blue-green, olive-green.
Pattern: the main border and guard stripe divide the central field from the old gold coloured ground. In the central field 3 large blue disc medallions. In the lower a pomegranate, in the two others a geometric form of the character 'shou' which is also repeated above and below. As corner filling a broken down, linear *yün-tsai-t'ou.* The *hai-shui-chiang-ya* border in its old form in the main border.

ania in the region of Prerow carpets were still being made between the two wars. At present there is still one hand-knotter working in West Germany; he only produces small pieces with armorial crests.

Knotted carpet manufactories were founded in the nineteenth century in Silesia and in the Spreewald. The illustrated memorandum issued by the German carpet manufacturers at the time of the exhibition of their wares in Berlin in 1911 gives much circumstantial information: the efforts of the Prussian government to provide remunerative work for the poor of Silesia stimulated Geheimrat Schmidt, owner of the cloth factory of Gevers and Schmidt in Görlitz, to send some of his weavers to the East to learn the technique of knotting. Production began in Lähne in 1854 and in 1857 in Schmiedeberg in the Riesengebirge. After initial difficulties the 'Schmiedeberger' carpet obtained a good reputation; it gave its name to a whole group of carpets. The illustrations show women of Spreewald knotting at modern looms in a spacious hall of the manufactory and place beside it for contrast a picture of oriental women at their work on primitive looms in a dark workshop (karhaneh). A sketch of the technique represents two Persian knots side by side, done at the same time and separated afterwards by a cut. The memorandum was published by the firms of Barmer Teppichfabrik Vorwerk & Co., Koch & te Kock Olsmitz i. V, Sächsische Kunstweberei Claviez AG Altdorf i. V, Gebrüder Schoeller Duren and Vereinigte Smyrna Teppichfabriken AG Berlin, and was aimed at persuading the government to establish protection against the import of inferior oriental commercial wares. Good quality oriental carpets are expressly excluded from the desired import restrictions. The import of oriental carpets had risen from 270,000 in 1906 to 608,000 in 1907 and to 912,000 in 1910. The section on knotted carpets ends: 'The fact that in spite of American protective tariffs the German knotted carpet today occupies an esteemed place in America serves to prove its worth and its competitive ability. It is recognised above all that it has a peculiar advantage in that because of the multiplicity of its designs it can always be brought into harmony with the character and colour scheme of any room.'

'It is understandable however that, in face of the mass import of oriental carpets, the constant rise in labour costs in comparison with the low wages of the orient are a serious problem, especially in the time-consuming production of very fine qualities. In the past year it has been possible to make considerable economies of time in the production of these densely knotted carpets with the help of a loom in which hand and mechanical work are combined, so that the great difference between European and oriental wages is more nearly balanced. These carpets appeared in the exhibition as Iran and Isfahan carpets.'

Attempts to get the knotting done by machine instead of by hand have not been wanting. Of the various systems that of the Austrian Dr M. Banyai is the best known. The complicated apparatus knots at a density of about 500 per square dm., seven times faster than a hand-knotter. But the Banyai carpets have none of the characteristics and worth of a work done by hand.

Age and authenticity

In many cases it is not easy to decide even the origin of a knotted piece, and its precise dating is nearly always a matter of even greater difficulty.

Carpets made 100 years ago are considered as antiques; those made between 70 and 100 years ago are called semi-antique and those made before the beginning of the First World War, old. According to customs regulations every carpet more than one hundred years old is an antique. If Empire and Early Victorian furniture is considered antique there is no reason why carpets of these periods should form an exception, unjustifiable on grounds of style. The following classification is to be preferred.

Antique carpets = all those knotted before the first use of aniline dyes in the Orient and the large-scale spread and imitation of patterns, that is to say, before 1860.

Semi-antique carpets = knotted carpets of the period from 1860 to 1914.

Old carpets = carpets at least twenty-five years old, made since 1914.

In order to find some point of reference for the dating of antique carpets W. v. Bode compared them with the representations of carpets in paintings. The patterns appearing must be at least as old as the paintings. A type of animal carpet (see p. 22), of which not even a fragment survives, has been preserved solely in its representation in paintings. For dating the Pazyryk carpet, which is evidently not Scythian work, it was possible to have recourse to stylistic comparison of the associated grave goods with other examples of Scythian art and also to radio-carbon analysis. For mediaeval carpets, apart from paintings and miniatures, the stylistic comparisons to be made with architecture, ceramics, metal work and other textiles can help with their chronological classification. Sometimes a date can be established from old invoices, or entries in inventories, annals and archives. Dates knotted into the pile as in the Ardebil carpet are exceptions in ancient examples, but more frequent in pieces of more recent centuries. Radio-carbon analysis is not yet sufficiently accurate to be used to advantage on textiles less than 1,000 years old.

Knotted dates give the year after the Hijra. The flight of Mohammed from Mecca took place in AD 622. Since Muslims reckon according to the lunar year and not the solar year of the Gregorian calendar which is eleven days longer, the determination of the date AD must take this three per cent difference into account. The simplest way of converting into years AD is to divide the Hijra number by thirty-three to one decimal place, rounding off the decimals, then to subtract the quotients from the Hijra number and add 622 to the remainder. Reference points are H 1318 = AD 1900 and H 1215 = AD 1800.

The knotted date must be carefully scrutinised. If the wool of the numbers or of parts of them is different from the rest of the carpet, it is a forgery. The second number is most often changed, so that the 3 or 2 becomes a 2 or 1, making the carpet appear to be 97 years earlier. On every Turcoman carpet we have examined with a 2 in the hundreds of the knotted date, it was forged; but in Caucasian and Persian carpets too — even on an oversize example intended for a world exhibition — there are liable to be subsequent alterations of the date. Knotted dates may not correspond to the age of the carpet even when a forgery is not intended, for sometimes earlier carpets have been copied in every detail. Mirror-image renderings of inscriptions and dates (see fig. 127) show that the knotter was using another carpet as a model. This would be reversed because it is easier to see the disposition of each knot on the back. The knotter, being illiterate, would then knot the date and inscription backwards into her carpet, not knowing its meaning. If the Hijra date on a piece of the last three centuries has only three numbers, the first has been left out. Knotted dates of the Christian era occur not only on European carpets, but on oriental ones too. They are a sign that the knotter or the client was a Christian.

The relatively safe criteria for judging age are not patterns and colours alone, but material, structure and condition of the whole piece. The design must be compared in the smallest details — especially the patterns on guard stripes — with the illustrations of similar pieces in carpet books, or with the originals in museums. Neglect of the ornamentation of the smaller guard stripes or a cruder rendering of the pattern are nearly always a proof of lesser age. In any case the designs deteriorated in many types that continued for long periods. Colours can only be compared with the help of originals; if chemical dyes have been used the piece can in no case be older than a hundred years. In comparing the structure the first thing is to see whether pile, warp, weft and — insofar as it occurs — the selvedge (shirazi) and the finishing off of the ends are appropriate to the provenance. Copies (e. g. 'Panderma') are often more densely and more carefully knotted than the originals, or done in a different type of knotting and wool. The material and shoot of the weft may also be different. If a knot is removed and the wool can be smoothed out straight without curling back at once into its previous shape, it cannot have been very long in the knot. The age of the wool cannot be determined by the feel alone. The fabric of ancient carpets has certainly deteriorated in hardness and resistance, but the dry feel at the fingertips due to gradual loss of wool fat can only result from washing wool with chemicals. Old warp wool tends to pulverise when twisted. If the material of the under-weave is unusual for the place of origin or is mechanically spun or twisted this also implies an imitation and consequently a lower age. Old cotton is always strongly felted. The silk of old carpets is of good quality. Jap silk is not known before the twentieth century in carpets.

The corrosion of brown-black areas of the pattern and the general wear of the carpet are no proof of great age. Dark brown and celadon green wool only corrodes when gall acid or metal salts have been used for the dye. The dyeing may have been done without these additions or naturally dark wool may have been left undyed. In Anatolian carpets the black parts are often corroded right back to the under-weave after a few decades, in other carpets again not until after centuries. In the matter of wear it should be remembered that a carpet that has hung for centuries on a wall has had no wear while another may have been trodden away in a few decades by careless use. Intentional ageing by rubbing away the pile or by burning can be recognised because the interior of the fabric is not aged thereby and the selvedge and plain unpatterned surfaces (especially the mihrab on prayer rugs) are usually left out of the treatment. It is harder to detect deliberate ageing when it has been brought about on a street in the East by the daily treadings of men and animals. The urine and droppings of animals alter the weave all the way through. If a slightly hairy feel on the underside is not typical of the provenance and if the piece has not been spared by use as a cushion cover, chair seat etc., then finely protruding fibres of wool on the underside of the carpet indicate recent fabrication even if the pile is worn. In new pieces these wool fibres can however be removed by singeing. The most successful forgeries are probably to be found among the innumerable 'Panderma' carpets. But here too the copy is betrayed by the hardness, resistance and roughness of the feel. Nonetheless, if a copy is from the hand of an experienced and skilful craftsman who is up to all the tricks, even the shrewdest expert can be taken in — as in all spheres of art (see p. 66). Such master forgers are not born in every decade, however. All hand-knotted copies, imitations and forgeries, are after all genuine knotted carpets, even though they are unauthentic as regards origin and age if these are concealed.

The dimensions of large-format carpets can give a limited indication of age. Having regard to the narrow ground-plan of oriental rooms and the custom of the oriental to lay a runner of equal length along either side of the main carpet (see p. 323) most of the old large-format carpets are roughly twice as long as they are wide. Carpets of room size with a length suited to European houses only 20 to 30 per cent larger than the width have been produced since about 1880. It is curious how widespread is the error that the breadth of the border is an indication of age. It is by no means true that antique carpets always have narrow borders. Some groups of design that have continued for centuries show a gradual increase of the borders, it is true, and most of the oldest surviving carpets from the Caucasus and Kirman region have a strikingly narrow border. On the other hand by far the majority of antique examples, beginning with the Seljuk carpets, have wide borders. The removal of the boundary between central field and border, as shown in fig. 95, is a phenomenon of the twentieth century. Without firms dates and proofs it is only possible to identify carpets of a few definite periods.

With nomad carpets in which the designs, colours, materials and technique are preserved unchanged for generations, the age is of minor importance. This unperturbed tradition-conscious holding to what has been handed on is not the same thing as imitation or copying. In the last resort it is not as a rule important whether a good Turcoman carpet was knotted in the nineteenth or the eighteenth century.

The oriental carpet is no longer a luxury object as it was at the beginning of our century. It is counted now among the higher needs.

The new style of furnishing has made possible this growth in the popularity of oriental carpets. The simple clear lines of modern furniture are a consequence of architecture. Concrete and steel buildings have given us light rooms with wide windows. At the turn of the century the mutely lighted rooms of the upper bourgeoisie were over-filled with furniture and pictures, then some purists fell into the opposite extreme. According to their dogmas the modern living room should remain empty but for furniture and curtains, and the heating and lighting equipment must all be constructed on lines and circles. Rooms like these are cold and heartless, and man desires warmth — he does not wish to live in an operating theatre. Surrounded by machines and using technique all the restless day, he wants peace, relaxation, creation when at home. His furnishings must be more than a minimum of maximally useful and practical objects, produced in series. He can only achieve a relationship with something that is well shaped, individually made by hand in the present or the past. There also arose the desire to enfold the past in the present. Modern, not just modish, furniture accommodates well with companions of earlier styles, if they are well made. Every good form is simultaneously timeless and contemporary. Whether it be a gothic chest, a baroque cupboard or an old peasant piece it can breathe more freely in clear, light surroundings and shows up to better advantage than in rooms overfilled with antiques. Good oriental carpets are timeless in the same way. From whatever provenance, they are made of thousands of individually hand-tied knots. The patterns and colours make free use of what the material provides; they are not hemmed in by the rational requirements of mechanical serial production. In time long past it was a sin to sell a carpet; presumably the exchange was done as it is now when acquiring a Holy Koran: the faithful 'gives' the bookseller the money, and the bookseller 'gives' him the Holy Koran. But now the carpet has become an object of trade and an important article of export. Saleability and buyers' tastes become considerations. Yet even the manufactory carpets, like all hand work, retain something incalculable and immeasurable. The knotted carpet diffuses peace and warmth in a literal sense as well: its good wool retains the highest measure of natural elasticity when knotted by hand; it deadens sound and repels the cold. It is hard to imagine a room which would not be improved by the right oriental carpet. It is true that the often-heard adage 'the oriental carpet is always right' is mistaken, but indeed *an* oriental carpet *is* always right, be it a primitive thick nomad piece on the stone floor of a country pub or a delicate Isfahan or Chinese carpet on the velvet of a boudoir, a Heris on the boards of a dining room or a medallion Kashan on the polished parquet of a drawing room, a Tekke on the haircord of the study or a keley with an endless repeat on the linoleum of the conference hall.

317

A thought before purchase: the oriental carpet must enhance the effect of the room and it must fit harmoniously. Thus format, pattern and colour are deciding factors. A large light-coloured carpet leaving a space of about eighteen inches all round the walls makes the room seem higher and larger, a darker carpet makes it smaller, one strongly coloured makes it seem lower. A large carpet in the old Persian narrow format increases the length of the room and so do runners, unless their pattern stresses the horizontal or diagonal and thus shortens it. Two correspondingly placed carpets can divide a room optically, a 'bridge' in the wider passage from one room to the other joins them. Carpets with medallion patterns should lie as free as possible; if table and chairs stand in the middle of the room an all-over pattern is preferable. In particular cases it may be desirable to arrange two or three carpets as is customary in the Orient. The prosperous oriental lays a kenareh (= river bank) at either side of a keley, all of the same length, and perpendicular to these three pieces a keleyghi as long as the three together are wide.

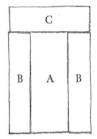

Carpet layout in the East: A main carpet 'keley', B kenareh (bank)
C 'keleyghi' (= small keley)

If there are several carpets in the room they must not clash or kill each other. Two identical carpets make a dull effect. On landings, passages and in front of often used doors to terraces and balconies, fine sensitive pieces are not in place; robust ones give better service. In the choice of colour the curtains and chair covers must be considered. Floor coverings today are usually neutral in tone. For wall hangings carpets with two-way patterns are not suitable. In every case it should be considered whether the carpet is to make the atmosphere of the room lively or more peaceful, ceremonious or intimate, rustic or elegant.

Time should be given for purchase. An oriental carpet is an acquisition for a lifetime and, carefully treated, for generations. Furthermore a good oriental carpet is never cheap, though considering the seemingly endless time taken to produce it — 90 per cent of production costs go in wages — and its durability, it is surprisingly good value. For purchasers who are thinking about capital outlay it should be mentioned that in the last fifty years the value of carpets of the usual formats in harmonious patterns and good quality material, colours and knotting, has risen by 600 per cent. Antique and old collector's pieces have risen much higher in price, for the supply is not unlimited. There are also 'cheap' hand-knotted carpets, but good mechanically knotted carpets give better service than this rubbish. Innumerable peddlars live by selling these inferior goods. One could fill several books with their tricks. Each one has his own brand of persuasion, and its success apparently has no limits. One thing they all have in common: they disappear as soon as they have done a deal, never to be seen again. The trusting buyer may consider himself lucky if he has got a cheap 'Persian' and not the most inferior sort of mechanically and 'oriental patterned' Tournay carpet. No one would think of buying a gemstone on the doorstep: why then an oriental carpet, whose purchase is equally a matter of trust? It is different when the representative of a respectable firm comes to the house to show carpets. These firms can always be got hold of. Even so, a purchase should never be concluded before the quality and price are compared with what is offered in the established shops. If the salesman presses for an immediate decision or only a few days to think it over, there is something suspicious in the whole affair.

Buying in shops entails no risk. The experienced carpet merchant is not interested in a single deal with exaggerated profit, he would rather win the purchaser as a permanent client. After hearing all the requirements he will willingly show all the pieces of his large selection that might answer them and offer to try them out in the room for which they are intended. He is always ready to give advice from the benefit of his long experience and shows understanding when it is not easy to decide. If the choice between several carpets is difficult, it is best to choose the simpler quieter pattern. The pattern must be balanced in composition and colour. Length of pile, material and density of knotting must suit the design. As well as density, the harmony of these five components decides the value of a carpet. Density of knots is a relative quality. A count of 2,500 knots per square dm. is exceptionally high for a Heris, and the minimum for a good Isfahan. The advantages of vegetable dyes are treated in detail in the section on Colours and dyeing. Vegetable dyes can only be required from those provenances where they are still in use. In Kashan, Kum and other knotting centres all dyeing is now done with good chemical dyes. The materials should be the best of the region of origin. Neither especial sheen in the wool nor in silk is an absolute criterion. Silk is unsuitable for floor carpets that are much trodden on and it never renders the design with the force of wool. The wool must be elastic and springy. If it does not straighten up or if flabby skin wool (tabachi) is used the pile will be trodden down prematurely.

Carpet names as indications of origin are only important for the purchaser, if he is not a collector, to protect him from buying imitations. The most important thing remains the effect of the carpet in the room; it can be influenced by the laying. The direction of the light makes the carpet look darker or lighter according to whether it goes with or against the pile. The carpet should be observed at different times of the day and in artificial light to see which is its best position.

Even the conscientious merchant may overlook little defects, and when they are brought to his attention he will do all he can to eliminate them. But one should not require that tedious perfection of machine-made goods from hand-knotted carpets. Small holes are easily seen if the carpet is held against a bright source of light and looked at from the underside. Most old carpets will show some small repairs. If these are carefully executed, with suitable materials and not too extensive, they no more reduce the value than corroded wool in small areas where the knots are black-brown. Large areas of restoration, worn-down pile and rotten places in the under-weave should only be tolerated on historically valuable antiques. To test the ground-weave the back is examined in suspiciously light places, which may indicate an early stage of mildew infection. In these, and in other places, the carpet should be bent first in the direction of the weft and then of the warp into a sharp fold, which you then try to break apart. If it makes a splitting noise the carpet is rotting and virtually useless. Carpets with a fine and delicate weft (e. g. Bidjar and Saruk) and old collector's pieces should naturally not be submitted to such a test.

Vegetable dyes are in no way better proof against light, air, washing, wear, acid or alkali than good chemical dyes. Natural dyes are only preferable on aesthetic grounds. Of course the low quality and colours of the early aniline dyes make a sorry chapter in the history of the subject, but it is precisely the not quite perfect fastness of natural dyes to light, air and wear which gives ancient carpets their much-prized patina. Too little resistance to wear shows if the pile is rubbed firmly with a dampened white cloth. If the cloth gets strongly coloured the dyes are either inferior or not sufficiently fixed. Purchase is emphatically not advised. In many nomad pieces however it may be a matter of excess dye. These pieces are an exception to the general rule that the first cleaning should be by washing: they should only be cleaned chemically. After this dry cleaning the colours are usually adequately fast against washing and wear. If light parts of the pattern have been stained by darker colours running during previous washes then the dyes were not fast to washing or alkalis or else the washing has not been properly done. The value of the carpet is prejudiced according to how far the pattern has been blurred. If the carpet is bent back where the pile is light coloured and shows strong colours at depth, the carpet has generally been subjected to a strong bleaching wash. This reduces the life-span of the material by 8 per cent to 12 per cent and anything up to double in the case of the 'gold Afghans' which have been given violent bleaching and then re-dyed.

Manufactory carpets should not show any great irregularities of length and width. Differences in both directions are the rule in nomad carpets. Even so they must lie well without creases or swellings, or the pile wears out prematurely on the parts that project. Up to a point these faults can be rectified by dampening and stretching the carpet; but this time-consuming operation should be left to the expert. Rolling up the edges of densely knotted carpets prevents having to iron liquid washing starch into the underside to keep them flat.

Special circumspection is needed when buying bargains from private sellers or at auctions, for it is rarely possible to return the goods afterwards if they are found to be faulty. A fee for expert advice should not be grudged if the piece is a valuable one. What has been said earlier about peddlars should be borne in mind when traveling in the East: good old carpets are dearer in the East than in Europe and new wares, both good ones and souvenir rubbish, are hardly any cheaper in the end after paying for customs and transport. If the collector is prepared to persist he may yet occasionally find small original nomad pieces at an interesting price in the bazaars. The great enemies of the carpet are moth, sand and continuous damp. Dirt brought in on shoes and walked into the fabric acts like emery paper. The best care is regular vacuum cleaning. It should first be done along the pile, so as not to press in the surface dirt. If the vacuum cleaner is then worked against the pile it must be run along the pile once again afterwards. Small bits of wool in the dust bag are no cause for concern; they are fibres which have been rubbed off in wear. If the carpet is vacuum-cleaned regularly there is no need to beat it. This should only be done on to the underside, and the best time to do it is in winter, on to clean dry snow. Stretching large carpets on a carpet frame cannot damage any but old and antique pieces whose under-weave has deteriorated in firmness with the years, but such forceful treatment is rarely necessary. Surface soiling from dust and soot can be removed with a foam wash. The foam should be put on as dry as possible and only removed with the vacuum cleaner when it has completely dried after several hours, otherwise it carries dirt into the depth of the pile. This brings us to the time-honoured process of rubbing with sauerkraut. It is in fact easier and safer to rub it over with a cloth moistened with water to which a dash of vinegar has been added, and it freshens the colours equally well. Rubbing with damp tea leaves to produce the opposite effect of a patina is no more than a uniform dirtying of the surface. Spots must be removed at once before the interior of the fibres is affected, if necessary with a chemical cleaner. If the carpet is regularly cared for in this way it will be many years before the carpet needs washing. When this happens it is best done by an oriental carpet laundry. There one is guaranteed that the carpet will be treated with the utmost care and given the mildest wash after testing the colours for fastness. Chemical cleaning takes the patina from the pattern and the natural fat content from the wool. It reduces, even if only by a small percentage, the firmness of the under-weave. If the carpet has been touched up with spirit dyes it may be essential to have it cleaned chemically. The obscure art of refreshing and restoring old patterns by touching up sometimes bears strange fruit both in East and West. The most unashamed cases I have met with were a Tekke of about five square metres in size and an Anatolian prayer rug. The finely knotted old Tekke stemmed from the aniline period about 1900. Its whole unlikely wine-red ground had been touched up so strongly round the guls, week after week, that the dye in some places had seeped right through to the underside. On the prayer rug the gay animals and vivid inscription with the date all proved to be freely invented, and under them there was an entirely different faded floral design. A comparison of the pattern on the upper and underside can guard against some unpleasant surprises.

Moisture in itself does not harm a carpet if it is carefully dried again within a reasonable time. As the air has little access to the underside it is easy for mould to develop there if it remains damp, and this rots it. Damp carpets must be turned upside down and dried, where possible hanging in a draught. If there are any patches of mildew they should be brushed out after the carpet has been intensively dried. If it is badly infected it can only be saved from serious damage by a fundamental wash. When the floor is washed the carpet should only be unrolled and spread again when the floor is completely dry.

The surest protection against moth is proofing. The experience of several decades now goes to prove that this damages neither the colours nor the durability of the material. It is important not to spoil the patina on those pieces that have it, during the necessary preparatory wash for this process.

The time when moths fly is June and July. They eat the wool and lay eggs. In August the worms hatch, and form pupas in a white web. The full measure of damage by moth is not seen until the pile is brushed out. The moth eggs need peace to develop. Regularly walked-over and vacuum-cleaned carpets are in no danger, it is the parts under furniture that suffer, and any wall hangings. They must be sprayed periodically in the summer months with one of the usual products, or strongly shaken every few days. Moths consider feathers a greater delicacy than camel-coloured or brown-red wool. A few bunches of feathers hung in the room draw moths away from the carpets. The carpet worm is as rare as the book worm. There are products in every chemist for destroying them. Felt underlay with a rubber base is the best way of preventing carpets with a soft underside from slipping and it repels moth at the same time. It lengthens the life of every carpet and makes it a better insulator against sound and cold. Every carpet-dealer sells this underlay with sewn edges in all sizes, which would be chosen 10 cm. smaller than the carpet. Dealers also sell semi-adhesive canvas which stops carpets slipping on smooth floors, but this is not advisable for the sensitive under-weave of very old and antique carpets. If it is impossible to avoid putting furniture on the carpet the constant pressure can be reduced by putting supports under the feet. The weight of heavy cupboards standing against the wall can be kept off the carpet by putting additional supports under then just before the edge of the carpet. If a piece of furniture has thin and sharp-edged feet and it is frequently moved about it should be provided with castors. Stiletto heels are less dangerous than wear from rubber soles and heels. If the carpet is already worn it should be put somewhere where it is not walked on. Under writing and dining tables especially the soles of shoes rub the carpet because people move their legs without knowing it. It is a good idea to change the position of the carpet after a few years so as to wear it equally. If the shirazi and kilims round the sides and ends begin to fray it is not difficult to mend them. If the carpet is left until knots begin to fall out it will have to go to a good carpet repairer. Good repairs are not cheap but inexpert botching is dearer in the end. An expert will show extraordinary feeling for the pattern, colour and material as well as for the structure in his repair, and help to add years to the life of even rotted carpets by putting in additional warp und weft threads. The simplest and safest way to hang a carpet on a wall is to sew a band right across the width below the upper end, leaving enough room between the upper and lower seams for a metal bar. There is no particular difficulty in storing carpets. A large carpet after thorough cleaning is folded down its length to about a metre in breadth and then rolled or folded for tying up. Smaller pieces can be folded or rolled against the direction of the pile. Bidjar and very rigid carpets should only be folded backwards and are better rolled. Silk carpets and antique pieces with cotton or silk warp are rolled round a bar or drum or another firm carpet. It is best to store them in plastic bags against moth, dust and damp in a cool dry place. The bags are only kept shut during the moth period; otherwise slightly open to let in the air.

On collecting oriental carpets

There is hardly another field at present where the collector with relatively small means has such great opportunities as in that of the oriental carpet, provided of course that he has sufficient knowledge. The collector changes without knowing it from being an admirer and lover to being an expert on the artistic expression of foreign peoples. The oriental carpet will never let him go, once he is under its spell. He is no longer content to furnish his house, he acquires carpets for other reasons. There is a more or less conscious idea behind this collecting. A collection is more than a number of separate pieces; it needs arranging, consistent thought and a structure.

Which kinds of knotted work are worth collecting? The man starting a collection is often inclined only to think of the carpets of earlier centuries. Apart from the few occasions when these can be obtained they require considerable financial means, even though the carpet has participated relatively little in the enormous increase in the price of antiquities. In the East the prices for old examples are much higher than those usual in the West. For the not very well-off the opportunity only arises in those places where value and charm are not recognised by others.

Of the products of our own century, unique in their quantity, the vast majority, commercial wares, are not for the collector. These carpets knotted in manufactories of varying size for export lack immediacy and originality even when material and fabrication are of the highest quality, and the same is true of most of those made at home for sale, and even of many, though to a less degree, of what the nomads make for barter or for sale. There remains for the present day the apparently inconceivable mass of work done by nomads, semi-nomads and peasants for their own use. In them the artistic feeling of the peoples is expressed most directly. Their designs are still a reflection of the soul, knotted folk songs of the tribes, many of whom still have no written language. Here vibrate those depths in which the subconscious and unconscious repose, which the intellect has long since left behind; those irrational realities which are for the oriental the ultimate truth.

Among all these powerful languages and dialects the collector is forced to limit and concentrate his interests. Whether he chooses the group of Bergamo, of Kasak, Anatolia or the Caucasus as a whole, Shiraz or western Turkestan, the Kurd or the Baluchi regions, is a matter of preference and inclination; and second in importance a matter of money, for the Caucasus will require the most. Valuable pieces of all these regions are still to be found. On the other hand to concentrate on east Turkestan would be disappointing, because the appearance of good examples in the last decades has become a rarity.

Even today carpets can appear from provenances unknown to the West. An example is the Kelardasht. Fundamental changes in their economic position in the last few years have made the inhabitants of this area willing to sell a few of the knotted pieces previously made exclusively for their own use, or jealously guarded as the bride's dowry. The carpet reproduced on the cover is an outstanding example of this type, closely related to the Kurd Kasakhs. It was finished in 1904. Even that region has now begun to produce directly for selling, but there is nothing comparable among the excellent pieces they have made in the past few years. This is not a case of carpets being previously produced under the name of another group, but the appearance of work from provenances until now unknown outside Iran. It is to be supposed that this situation will be repeated in the future as society gradually changes in the Orient.

It can be interesting to collect through all provenances in quest of the answer to specific questions, tracing back through generations to the archetype the history of the development of certain patterns and motifs through the alteration of their forms and the shifts of emphasis of various elements. All these relationships, influences, connections, similarities, are fragments in the mosaic of cultural and historical relationships. An example is to trace back the history of the Herati pattern through all its variants — in principle the endless repeat of the lozenge stem lattice with four curved leaves symmetrically attached to it — to its first emergence in a curved flower and leaf scroll system. Or there is the boteh in all its changes; or the development of the Herati or Ferahan border; the forms of the arabesque, that transformation of dynamic natural growth into an abstract static decorative motif and ornament; the wave scroll in the carpet, a decorative form, an ornament and symbol of the problem of space and time in one; the appearance of the various forms of mihrab etc. The oriental carpet offers a wealth of such unsolved questions.

By setting remote goals of this sort fragments and more or less badly preserved pieces are often needed as links in the collection. The decision to buy a piece which is no longer intact can only be seen in relation to its value for the collection as a whole, in the same way as the decision to embark on a costly restoration will be taken from the same point of view.

On this count it is easier to collect bags, saddle covers and the decorative strips of nomad peoples. The supply of delightful, well-preserved bags of the most varied sizes, forms and provenances is still relatively abundant. The necessary small repairs can be done well and quite cheaply.

The collector will always be wanting to go from the present into the past of his field. It is precisely in collecting the older knotted work of nomads, semi-nomads and peasants that money means little; intuition, knowledge, patience and a lucky hand are almost everything.

Sources for acquisition are carpet shops, sales from private possessions and auctions. Although shops today are numerous, the really good ones are very rare. In the 'expensive' houses the collector can sometimes find something going cheap that is not known or valued by other people, if he has enough time to look through the stock. The 'cheap' bazaar-like shops deserve no more than a quick look. It is very rare to find anything of worth hidden among their inferior commercial wares. Their stock is delivered in bales or lots with scarcely anything unusual in them. Until a few years ago it was nonetheless possible occasionally to come upon old pieces in need of repair for which expert dealers would be prepared to pay many times the price quoted. Another category of carpet shop is the small but genuine businesses whose expert owners have almost always something worth showing to the collector.

Purchase from a private seller is difficult if the seller does not ask a fixed price. In the majority of cases the owner first enquires of the collector what is the value of the pieces he wishes to part with. One should then give the price to the best of one's knowledge, but should not be inhibited about saying the amount one is prepared to spend.

Knotted goods come up periodically at auctions. Study of the catalogue — in addition this is a good indication of the development of prices — is in itself a pleasure. At the preview there must be leisure to examine everything carefully. The hunting fever sets in as soon as one has discovered an unusual or valuable example, the 'find'. It is a good plan to decide on a limit before the excitement of the auction begins. Otherwise a chance may be lost while one is deliberating, and the bids fly by with a nod of the head or a wink. Rare carpets are worth buying at advantageous prices even when they lie outside the domain of one's own collection, for they can later be used for exchanges.

Every new acquisition should be entered as soon as possible in an inventory with a description and a photograph. Descriptions and photographs are not only indispensible if one is doing any work, they are the surest way of retrieving stolen carpets.

Index

Gabeh (fringed or unclipped carpets. Tn Shiraz region of Persia) *27, 48, 224*

Gabes *304*

Gabystan (Shirivan province [Caucasian] attributed by L Kerimov) *133*

Gaichi = scissors (Tn Azerbaijan term for pile carpets) *27*

Gailanden = pipe bag *105*

Garden carpets *49, 210, 164*

Garga = raven (P Caucasian) *123*

Gashgai *50, 156, 220, 224, 102, 104—9, XVIII*

Gashya carpet *50*

Gasvin, *see* Kasvin

Gaychi = shears *150*

Gelim (textile) *33*

Gemsir = warm land plain *156*

Gendje (Gyanza, R Caucasian) *70, 99, 113, 120, 41, 42*

Gendje Kasak carpets *113*

Genghis Khan *54, 158, 266, 290*

Gentlemen's carpets *233*

Geok-tepe (village near Ashkabad, Turcoman) *229*

Geometric patterns *93*

Georgia (Soviet Republic. Capital at Tiflis) *99, 159*

Geravan, *see* Yoraghan

Gerbillon (a Jesuit priest) *293*

German Persian Carpet Co (Petag) *11, see also* Petag

Germany *310—13*

Germech (U Turcoman) *49, 234*

Gerus (R North West Persian) *183*

Ghain *214*

Ghali (F Persian, large knotted carpets) *24*

Ghalidshe, *see* Keleyghi

Ghanats (subterranean canals carrying water to the oases) *225*

Ghandara *266*

Ghiordes (V Anatolien) *64, 66, 73, 80, 83, 86, 16, 17*

Ghiordes knot *73, 238*

Ghiordes prayer rugs *63, 306*

Ghom *193, see also* Kum

Gilima (edge of weaving) *26*

Gilim Baf (woven edge or kilim at the edge of a carpet) *26*

Giotto (1267—1337, Italian painter) *21*

Glass beads *93*

Goa carpets *307*

Goat hair *35, 55, 73, 214, 243*

Gobelins (Tn French) *42, 308—9*

Goblet border *46*

Goklan (branch of the Yomud tribe, Turcoman) *229*

Golbaryasteh = rising flower (textile with patches of pile also called nimbaff = half knots) *32, 48*

Goldfish *300*

Goltuk, *see* Koltuk

Gombad-i-Rabus (assembly centre for the carpets of the Yomud and Tekke) *214*

Gonabad (V Persian Khorassan-Meshed region) *213*

Gordion (central Anatolia) *34, 53*

Gorgon (assembly centre for the carpets of the Yomud and Tekke, south of the Atrek) *214*

Graph paper, used in design *41*

Gras = pile (mispronunciation of migrasi = scissors, Arabic. In the Caucasus the usual word for knotted carpets) *150*

Graveyard carpets (CP U Turkish) *46, 49*

Greece *19, 54, 157, 307*

Greek carpets (Tr) *48*

Griffon *46*

Gul = flower (Octagonal pattern in Turcoman carpets but not a tribal pattern) *46, 236—7*

Gulaidi *236, 238*

Gulli gul *236, 253*

Gyanza *113, see also* Gendje

Hachlu *112, 119*

Hafez (1326—89, Persion poet)

Hafis, *see* Hafez

Hai-shui chiang-ya = sea waves and river foam (P) *280*

Haj = cross (P Turcoman) *46, 238*

Haji Yalil Marandaila (celebrated carpet knotter from Marand near Tabriz) *174*

Halil (knotted carpets) *24*

Hamadan weave *30, 176*

Hamadan (formerly Ektabana. R V West Persia) *12, 31, 156, 178, 183, 184, 186, 80, 81, 82*

Hamail *83*

Han dynasty (206 B.C.—A.D. 220) *290*

Hands in design *46, 110*

Hanging lamp design *46*

Hapsburg, house of *166*

Harun ar Rashid, Caliph of Baghdad (786—809) *12, 213*

Harun carpets *48, 196*

Hatchlu (U CP tent entrance curtain with cross pattern. Turcoman) *49, 238, 249, 253*

Haute Lisse *31*

Hebatlu (tribe in South Persia) *224*

Heluan (town with a carpet manufactory near Cairo) *304*

Hemp *35*

Hephtalite *265*

Herat (town in Afghanistan) *100, 159, 164, 168, 190, 210, 266, 270, 307*

Herati pattern (P Persian) *46, 123, 183, 186, 213, 243, 305, 324*

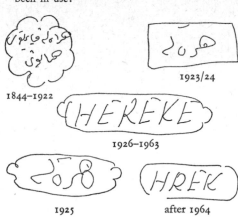

Persis 156
Petag (Persian Teppich Gesellschaft AG. Petag
produced carpets in the following qualities:
Cyrus 50 regh   Hamayan 35 regh
Rustan 45 regh   Pertov 30 regh
Tsimuri 40 regh
After the war oriental merchants tried to sell
inferior carpets under the designation of the
best quality Petag which were well known)
49, 123
Peshm-i-Meshed (wool from Meshed) 176
Phoenix (P) 47
Phoenix-dragon motif 21
Photographs, of your collection 325
Phrygians (Indo-European people in Central
Anatolia with their capital at Gordian, the
finding place of textile fragment in Soumak
technique, 8th—7th century B.C.) 53
Picture carpets 41, 49, 110
Pillar carpets 50, *141*, XXVII
Pi-shan 270
Poland 168, 310
Polish carpets (metal brocaded carpets made of
silk, of the 17th century, made in the Orient
usually with Polish emblams) 32, 38, 48, 66,
159, 163, 270, 310, 70
Pomegranate 47
Pomerania 310
Pontic Mountains 53
Portraits in carpets 41, 49, 110, 210
Portugal (R) 307
Portuguese carpets (Persian carpets made to order
from Portugal) 48, 307
Prayer mats, see Namazlik
Prayer niche 47
Prayer rugs 41, 49, 241, 280, see also Saph
Prayer stone 110
Prerow 313
Prussian government 313
Pud = weft 24, 29
Pushtis (U Persian for small rugs serving as
pillow covers) 49, 173, 220, *78*

Qairawan 304
Qarquin (Q cheapest Afghan quality) 253
Qayan (Mountains) 155
Qum, see Kum

Rabat (V Indian) 304
Racka carpets 308
Radde (anthropologist) 98
Radio-carbon analysis (determination of age
through the decomposition of the radio-active
carbon c 14 in organic materials) 314

Radzivill, Prince 310
Rafsanyan (place where carpets are produced in
the region of Kirman, South Persia) 210
Rages (Rayy, near Teheran, once capital of
Persia. Carpets for Teheran are washed here
because the spring water is especially suitable)
158
Rashid ad Din (historian) 22, 227
Ravar (V South East Persian Kirman type) 203
Realism 110
Reffahan carpets (R) 48
Religion in design 42
Renaissance 9
Reshd 34, 178
Reversible carpets 48, 176, see also Doruye
Reza Khan, Shah 159
Rhine 157
Rhodes carpets (designation of Megri carpets)
73, *15*
Riesengebirge 313
Rion 97
Rize district 53
Roman Empire, fall of 23
Romanian carpets (Tr) 48
Romans 19, 158
Rosette 47
Rot, in carpets 321
Rudenko, S. J. (Russian archaeologist) 14, 16
Rumania 308
Running dog motif 19, 47, 140
Rupalani carpet 50, *83*, XVII
Russia 11, 54, 98, 99, 159, 176, 214, 225, 270
Russian carpets (Tr) 35, 48
Rutakali (U horse rug or blanket) 50, *106*
Rya (Scandinavian knotted rugs) 310

S border 47
Saadi (1184—1282, Persian poet, born and buried
in Shiraz) 220
Sabzevar (V North East Persian) 210, 213
Saddle covers 250
Saffavid (Persian dynasty ruling from 1501—1721.
Golden age of the Persian carpet) 48, 159, 163,
166, 196, 200, 214, 228
Safishani 224
Saidabad 214, *101*
Sajada (U Arabia) 49, see also Sejadeh
Salachak (child's carpet U Turcoman. Also a
prayer rug) 234
Salian 133
Salor gul (P Turcoman) 236, 237, 243, 253

Carpets in Museums

Important collections are preserved in the following museums:

Berlin, Staatliche Museen, Islamic department.
Boston, Museum of Fine Arts.
Cairo, Museum of Islamic Art.
Hamburg, Museum für Kunst und Gewerbe.
Istanbul, Türk ve Islam Eserleri Müzesi.
Jaipur, The Maharaja's Carpet House.
Leningrad, Hermitage.
London, Victoria and Albert Museum.
Lyon, Musée historique des tissus.
Milan, Museo Poldi-Pazzoli.

Moscow, Museum of Oriental Culture.
Munich, Bayerisches Nationalmuseum.
Nara, Shōsōin (early felt carpets).
New York, Metropolitan Museum.
Paris, Musée des Arts Décoratifs.
Philadelphia, Museum of Art.
Washington, Textile Museum.
Vienna, Österreichisches Museum für angewandte Kunst.

Many museums contain carpets:

France: Paris — Musée du Louvre-Musée des Gobelins (Gobelins)
German Federal Republic: Dusseldorf; Essen; Frankfurt/M.; Hannover; Cologne; Munich — Völkerkundemuseum — Residenzmuseum (Gobelins)
Hungary: Budapest
Iran: Teheran — Archaeological Museum; Kum-Shrein; Meshed-Shrein
Netherlands: Amsterdam; The Hague

Sweden: Stockholm
Turkey: Istanbul — Top Kapu Sarayi Müzesi; Konya
USA: Cincinnati; Detroit; New York — Hispanic Society of America; Seattle; St Louis; Washington — Corcoran Art Gallery
USSR: Ashkabad; Baku, Erivan; Moscow-Kremlin; Tiflis

Bibliography

The most comprehensive bibliography on oriental carpets, containing about 600 titles is in K. Erdmann: Der orientalische Knüpfteppich, 3rd ed. Tübingen 1965.

General:

G. T. Pushman, Art panels from the handlooms of the far orient. Chicago 1902, spät. Aufl. 1905 u. 1911
H. Jacoby, Reisen um echte Teppiche. Wiesbaden 1952
A. U. Pope, Neue Studien über die künstlerische Bedeutung der Orientteppiche. Pazyryk, Nr. 1/1968
S. Azadi, Die Stellung der Farben bei den Orientteppichen. Heimtex, Nr. 8, 9, 10, 12/1967, 4, 6/1968
J. V. McMullan, Islamic Carpets. New York 1965
Ch. Grant Ellis, Some Compartment Designs for Carpets, and Herat. Textile Museum Journal Washington 1965
U. Schürmann, Orientteppiche. Wiesbaden o. J.
Stanley Reed, Orientteppiche. Frankfurt/M. 1967
R. de Calatchi, Orientteppiche. München 1968
Kybalova-Darbois, Orientteppiche. Hanau 1968
K. Erdmann, Siebenhundert Jahre Orientteppich. Herford 1966
M. S. Dimand, The Kervorkian Foundation, Collection of Rare and Magnificent Oriental Carpets. New York 1966
A. L. Kiss, Ismerjük Meg A Keleti Szönyegeket. 1963
J. M. Con, Carpets from the Orient. London 1966

Exhibitions:

Die Ausstellung Deutscher Teppiche im Hause der Abgeordneten, Berlin 1911
H. Trenkwald, Ausstellung orientalischer Teppiche in österreichischen Museen. Die bildenden Künste III 7/8, S. 122 ff.
H. Gerson, Ausstellung antiker Teppiche, Berlin 1928
The Metropolitan Museum of Art: Loan exhibition of oriental rugs from the collection of James F. Ballard of St. Louis, Mo., New York 1931
Villa Hügel, 7000 Jahre Kunst in Iran, Essen 1962
Mathildenhöhe Darmstadt, Türkische Kunst 1965
Kunsthalle Darmstadt, Orientteppiche aus vier Jahrhunderten. Sammlung R. G. Hubel 1965
The Textile Museum Washington, Near Eastern Kilims 1965
Fogg Art Museum: Turkoman Rugs. Cambridge, Massachusetts 1966
Karl-Ernst-Osthaus-Museum Hagen: Orientteppiche und Nomadenknüpfarbeiten vergangener Jahrhunderte, Sammlung R. G. Hubel, 1966
Nassauischer Kunstverein Wiesbaden: Meisterstücke Orientalischer Knüpfkunst, Sammlung Anton Danker, 1966
Kestner-Museum Hannover: Orientteppiche 16.—19. Jahrhundert, 1966
Abbot Hall Art Gallery: 1000 Years of Persian Art, 1967
The Textile Museum Washington: East of Turkestan, 1967
Staatl. Museum für Völkerkunde München: Orientteppiche und Nomadenknüpfarbeiten vergangener Jahrhunderte. Sammlung R. G. Hubel, 1967/68/69
The Textile Museum Washington: H. McCoy Jones und R. S. Yohe, Turkish Rugs, 1968
Museum für Kunsthandwerk Frankfurt/M., Islamische Teppiche, 1968
Staatl. Museen Preußischer Kulturbesitz Berlin: Islamische Kunst, 1967

Museums:

M. Mostafa, The Museum of Islamic Art, Cairo 1961
R. G. Hubel, Orientteppiche in den Museen von Leningrad, Moskau und Usbekistan.
Heimtex Nr. 8 und Nr. 9/1966
Ch. Grant Ellis, Vase Rugs in The Textile Museum. Textile Museum Journal Washington, 1968

On the beginnings of the carpet:
J. Wiesner, Eurasische Kunst in Steppenraum und Waldgebiet. Ullstein Kunstgeschichte 4. S. 91 ff.
Frankfurt/M. — Berlin 1963
K. Jettmar, Die frühen Steppenvölker. Baden-Baden 1964

On the Egyptian carpet:
A carpet from Cairo. Journal of the American Research Centre in Cairo I, 1962
Ch. Grant Ellis, Mysterys of the Misplaced Mamluks. Textile Museum Journal Washington, 1967

On the Turkish carpet:
N. N. Schawrow, Kowrowoe Proiswodstwo w Maloi Asii. Tiflis 1902
J. Zick-Nissen, Das Wolkenbandmotiv als Kompositionselement auf Osmanischen Teppichen. Berliner
Museen 1966, Heft 1
M. H. Beattie, Coupled-Column Prayer Rugs. Oriental Art, Vol. XIV, No. 4
A. L. Kiss, Gebetsteppiche. Heimtex Nr. 11/1967, 1 und 2/1968

On the Siebenbürger carpet:
A. Eichhorn, Kronstadt und der orientalische Teppich. Forschungen zur Volks- und Landeskunde,
Band 11, Nr. 1, Bukarest 1968

On the Caucasian carpet:
G. Sahakian, Kaukasische Teppiche. Heimtex Nr. 8/1963, Nr. 4, 5, 6, 7, 9/1964
H. Jacoby jun., Orientteppich und „Tierdarstellung". Heimtex Nr. 1 und 2/1965
U. Schürmann, Teppiche aus dem Kaukasus. Braunschweig o. J.

On the Turcoman carpet:
W. König, Die Achal-Teke. Berlin 1962
S. A. Milhofer, Die Teppiche Zentralasiens. Hannover 1968
D. H. G. Wegner, Nomaden- und Bauernteppiche in Afghanistan. Baessler-Archiv, Neue Folge,
Band XII, 1964

On the Persian carpet:
K. Otto-Dorn, Die Kunst des Islam. Baden-Baden 1964

On the Indian carpet:
U. Schürmann, Altindische Teppiche. Heimtex Nr. 2/1967

On the Portuguese carpet:
R. G. Hubel, Die Portugiesischen Arraiolos-Teppiche. Die Weltkunst, Nr. 20 a/1967

On the Chinese carpet:
Ch. Grant Ellis, Chinese Rugs. Textile Museum Journal 1968

On Chinese history:
W. Speiser, Die Kunst Ostasiens. Berlin 1946

On symbolism in Chinese art:
F. Lessing, Über die Symbolsprache in der chinesischen Kunst. Sinica IX und X (1934/1935), S. 121—288

On English, Irish and Flemish carpets:
M. Beattie, Britain and the Oriental Carpet. Leeds Art Calendar No. 55, 1964

On the Savonnerie carpet:
Duhamel de Monceau, Die Kunst Türkische Tapeten zu weben. Schauplatz der Künste und Hand-
werke VII Theil, Leipzig und Königsberg 1768

On calligraphy:
J. G. Lettenmair, „Kufische" Borte — ja oder nein? Heimtex Nr. 6, 7, 8, 9/1965
A. L. Kiss, Kufisch? — Nein hieroglyphisch. Heimtex Nr. 1/1967

On the restoration of Oriental carpets:
D. Lehmann, Restaurieren und Konservieren an Orientteppichen. Melliand Textilberichte Nr. 6 und
7/1965

List of Owners

The carpets illustrated belong to the following:

Bayer. Nationalmuseum, Munich: 6, 9, 70, 150, 153

Hermitage, Lenengrad: I

H. Jacoby jun., Frankfurt/M.: 7

I. Langlotz, Bad Wiessee: 111, 122

Museum für Kunsthandwerk, Frankfurt/M.: 139, 151, 154

Museum of Islamic Art, Cairo: 146, 147, 148

Österr. Museum f. angew. Kunst, Vienna: 67, 69

Petag (Pers. Teppich-Ges. KG), Frankfurt/M.: 8, 62, 72, 73, 75, 78, 84, 85, 86, 87, 88, 89, 91, 93, 94, 95, 97, 110, 123, 129

I. Schwind, Aschaffenburg: 37, 38

Staatl. Museen, Islamic Section, Berlin: 31, 32, 149

Top Kapu Sarayi Muzesi, Istanbul: 152

Turk ve Islam Eserleri Muzesi, Istanbul: 1, 2, 3, 4, 5, 10, 21

Victoria and Albert Museum, London: 68

H. Wald, Munich: 92

All the other carpets illustrated belong to the author's collection.

The photographs for plates 6, 9, 31, 69, 150 and 153 were taken by the respective museums.

Illustrations for plates 30, 65, 98, 99, 100, 140, 143, II, VII, XXII and XXIV have been provided by the Staatl. Museum für Völkerkunde, Munich.

All the remaining photographs and colour transparencies by Petag (Pers. Teppich-Ges. KG) Frankfurt/M.; the transparency for colour plate I was provided by the Holle Verlag GmbH, Baden-Baden.

Acknowledgements

I would like to thank all those who have contributed to the completion of this book.

My greatest debt is to Herr H. Jacoby, Director of the Petag (Persische Teppich-Gesellschaft KG), Frankfurt/M. The extensive photographic work for the numerous illustrations was carried out almost entirely under his direction, and he always managed to find time for the discussions so indispensible to the author.

I have been helped by the generous facilities for studying the carpets in their collections provided by the following:

Mrs. Waffiya Ezzi, Museum of Islamic Art, Cairo

Frau Dr. J. Zick-Nissen and Herr Enderlein, Staatl. Museen, Islam. Abt. Berlin

Herr Dir. Dr. V. Griessmaier, Österreichisches Museum für angew. Kunst, Vienna

Mr. Can Kerametli, Director, Türk ve Islam Eserleri Müzesi, Istanbul

Dr. P. W. Meister, Director, Museum f. Kunsthandwerk, Frankfurt/M. who very kindly undertook the transcription of the Chinese characters

Monsieur le directeur R. de Micheaux, Musée Hist. des Tissus, Lyon

Prof. Dr. T. Müller, Director, Bayer. Nationalmuseum, Munich and Mr. H. Ors, Director, Top Kapu Sarayi Muzesi, Istanbul

I received valuable help in collecting material from: Dr. R. Anhegger and Frau K. Heintzel, Deutsch-Türkisches Kulturzentrum, Istanbul

Mr. Vahac Yagubian, Istanbul
and Dr. Zahabi, President of the Iran Carpet Company, Teheran

This book was originated by Verlag Ullstein GmbH

The drawings are by Frau R. Görtz-Renzel

I have especially to thank Frau I. Langlotz for many years of indefatigable and patient collaboration, and for her innumerable stimulating suggestions.

Istanbul
Hereke
Çanakkale
Pandermo
Brussa
Ezine
Balikeshir
Eskishehir
Mihaliççik
Ankara
Kütahya
Soma
Demirçi
Bergamo
Simav
Turkey
Ghiordes
Çal
Kirshehir
Bünyan
Ushak
Muçur
Smyrna
LAKE TUZLA
Inçesu
Kayseri
Kula
Yürük
Ürgüp
Ladik
Aksaray
Obruk
Nigde
Isparta
Konya
Yahyali
Burdur
Bor
Karapinar
Milas
Karaova
Döçemealti
Karaman
Yürük
Adana
Megri

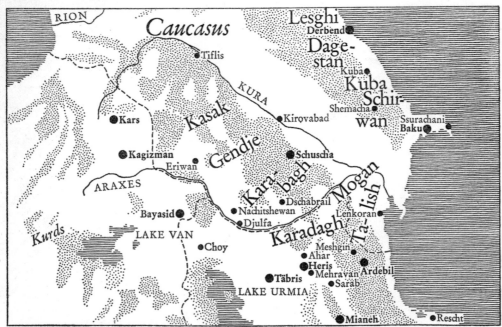

RION
Caucasus
Lesghi
Derbend
Dage-
stan
Tiflis
Kuba
KURA
Kuba
Schir-
wan
Kasak
Kirovabad
Shemacha
Ssurachani
Kars
Baku
Gendje
Kagizman
Schuscha
Eriwan
Kara-
bagh
Mogan
ARAXES
Nachitshewan
Lenkoran
Bayasid
Djulfa
Ta-
lish
Kurds
LAKE VAN
Karadagh
Choy
Meshgin
Ahar
Heris
Ardebil
Tábris
Mehravan
Sarab
LAKE URMIA
Mianeh
Rescht